MAO

Michael Lynch

Routledge
Taylor & Francis Group

LONDON AND NEW YORK

First published 2004
by Routledge
2 Park Square, Milton Park, Abingdon, Oxon, OX14 4RN

Simultaneously published in the USA and Canada
by Routledge
270 Madison Ave, New York, NY 10016

Reprinted 2005, 2006

Routledge is an imprint of the Taylor & Francis Group

© 2004 Michael Lynch

Typeset in Garamond by
Keystroke, Jacaranda Lodge, Wolverhampton
Printed and bound in Great Britain by
TJ International Ltd, Padstow, Cornwall

British Library Cataloguing in Publication Data
A catalogue record for this book is available from the British Library

Library of Congress Cataloging in Publication Data
Lynch, Michael J., 1938–
    Mao / Michael Lynch.
        p. cm. — (Routledge historical biographies)
    Simultaneously published in the USA and Canada by Routledge.
    Includes bibliographical references and index.
    1. Mao, Zedong, 1893–1976. 2. Heads of state—China—Biography.
    I. Title. II. Series.
    DS778.M3L93 2004
    951.05'092—dc22   2003025698

ISBN 0–415–21577–3 (hbk)
ISBN 0–415–21578–1 (pbk)

In loving memory of
Winifred and Patricia Lynch

CONTENTS

ILLUSTRATIONS

PLATES

(between pages 110 and 111)

MAPS

Chronology

Date	Personal	Political	General
1893	Born in Shaoshan		
1895			military defeat of China by Japan
1895–99			Western 'scramble for concessions' in China
1898		100 Days reform programme	Britain leases Hong Kong territories
1889–1910		China's industrial revolution	USA declares 'open door' policy
1898		Tan Sitong leads an anti-Qing reform movement	
1898–1901		Boxer rising	
1900	begins working on the family farm	flight of Qing	international army of 8 powers set up
1901–06	attends local primary school		
1902		Qing return to Beijing	Anglo-Japanese Alliance
1904–05			Russo-Japanese war
1905		Alliance League formed under Sun Yatsen	Russia recognises Japan's rights in Manchuria
1908	betrothed to Miss Luo	death of Dowager Empress Cixi and Emperor Guangxu	
1909	attends school in Xiangtan	Yuan Shikai dismissed from royal court	
1910	witnesses famine in Hunan		Korea annexed by Japan

Date	Personal	Political	General
1911	joins rebel army in Changsha	Double Tenth Rising	international banking commission established
1912	enters teacher-training school; writes essay on Yang Shang	Qings abdicate; Yuan Shikai installed as president of Republic of China; Gusmindang (GMD) formed	
1913		Yuan raises a £25 million foreign loan	
1913–16		'Reign of Terror' in Hunan	
1914			war in Europe; Japan joins the Allies
1915	joins protests against Yuan Shikai; meets Yang Kaihui		Japan's 21 Demands
1916	defends Tang Xiangming's terror tactics in Hunan	Yuan Shikai declares himself Emperor; renounces throne; dies	
1917	tours Hunan Province	China declares war on Germany	Bolshevik Revolution in Russia
1918	founds New Peoples Study Society; graduates from Changsha college as qualified teacher; active in Hunan independence drive	*The Victory of Bolshevism* by Li Dazhao	end of war in Europe; Russian civil war begins
1919	becomes a librarian in Beijing University; death of his mother; organises strike to challenge Zhang; Launches *The Xiang River Review*	4 May movement begins; Chen Duxiu arrested in Beijing; suicide of Zhao Wuzhen	Versailles settlement; Allies hand Qingdao to Japan; Comintern created

Date	Personal	Political	General
1920	visits shrine of Confucius; Marries Yang Kaihui; founds the Cultural Book Society; reads *Communist Manifesto*		
1921	founder member of the Chinese Communist Party (CCP)		
1923	joins GMD; organises workers' strikes	CCP joins with GMD; '7 February Massacre'; Third Congress of the CCP	Comintern agents sent to China; GMD friendship pact with Moscow
1924	attends first congress of the GMD	CCP-GMD united front formed; Beijing falls to Feng Yuxiang	Russia seizes Outer Mongolia
1925	helps organise Northern Expedition; organiser of the GMD's peasant training department; editor of *Political Weekly*	death of Sun Yatsen; 30 May Incident; Chiang Kaishek becomes leader of GMD	
1926–28		Northern Expedition	
1927	Produces *Report on the Peasant Movement in Hunan*; leads Autumn Harvest Rising; becomes involved with He Zichen; leads Red flight to Jiangxi	Chiang Kaishek's 'White Terror'	
1928	forms first Red Army; divorces Kaihui; marries He Zichen	Zhu De joins forces with Mao	
1929	suffers from malaria		Great Crash in USA

Date	Personal	Political	General
1930	opposes the Li Lisan Line; death of Yang Kaihui	Li Lisan becomes chairman of the Central Committee; '28 Bolsheviks' return to China under Wang Ming	
1930–31	crushes anti-Maoists	Futian Incident	
1931	declaration of '8 Conditions for a Great Victory'; son, Mao Anlong, dies	Li Lisan replaced by Wang Ming	Japanese occupy Manchuria
1931–34	involved in internal party struggle	Jiangxi Soviet	
1932	appeals for national resistance to Japan; withdraws from political battle	Red attack on Guangzhou; Ningdu conference	Manchuguo created
1933	returns to political scene	CCP Central Committee relocates to Ruijin; arrival of Otto Braun from USSR	Japan withdraws from the League of Nations
1934	joins Long March	Jiangxi abandoned; start of Long March	
1935	wins crucial vote at Zunyi; reaches Shaanxi; conflict with Zhang Guotao	Reds reach Yanan; Zhang Guotao sets up alternative Central Committee; '9 December movement'	Japanese intensify hold on northern China.
1935–36		30 million Chinese affected by famine	
1936	leads campaign into Hebei province	Xian Incident	Anti-Comintern pact formed
1937	meets Jiang Qing	Yanan Soviet established; Wang Ming arrives from Moscow; second CCP–GMD united front	Japanese invade China; Rape of Nanjing; fall of Beijing, Shanghai, and Nanqing

Date	Personal	Political	General
1938	divorces He Zichen, marries Jiang Qing; first house in Yanan bombed	GMD moves capital to Chongqing; Wuhan falls to Japanese; end of united front	
1939			war in Europe
1940	*On New Democracy* published; organises the '100 Regiments' campaign'	'New Government of China' at Nanjing	
1941	encourages stern measures against unco-operative peasant areas		Japanese attack on Pearl Harbor
1942	institutes 'Rectification of Conduct' campaign		Britain and USA abandon extra-territoriality in China
1943		Chiang Kai-shek's *China's Destiny* published	Comintern dissolved
1943–44	becomes chairman of Politburo and Secretariat	'self-criticism' by CCP leaders	
1944	makes token self-criticism	USA's Dixie mission to China	
1945	flies from Yanan to Chongqing for discussions with Chiang Kai-shek; CCP honour him as 'Great Leader'	seventh CCP Congress; General George Marshall sent to Chongqing	Yalta conference; atomic bombing of Japan; Japanese surrender; Sino-Soviet Treaty of Friendship
1946	announces renewal of war with GMD	Failure of Marshall mission	
1946–49	directs CCP war against GMD	CCP–GMD civil war in China	
1947	leaves Shaanxi	Wang Shiwei executed	

Date	Personal	Political	General
1948	moves to the Fragrant Hills	Red victories at Mukden and Xuzhou	
1949	declares creation of PRC; appointed chairman of the PRC; moves into Zhongnanhai	Reds take Nanjing, Shanghai, Canton and Beijing; GMD flight to Taiwan; PRC founded	Soviet Union develops the atomic bomb
1950	visits USSR; Mao Anying killed in Korea		Tibet invaded by PLA; new Sino-Soviet treaty
1950–53		Korean war	
1951	launches 'Anti-movements'		
1952	bans political parties other than CCP	Five-Year Plan started	
1953	tightens political controls over PRC	Third Line begun	death of Stalin; end of Korean war
1954	launches attack on Rao Shushi and Gao Gang		
1955	writes The Immortals	100,000 members of CCP arrested	Bandung Conference
1956	sends Jiang Qing to Moscow for cancer treatment; angered by Soviet weakness towards satellites	eighth CCP Congress	Khrushchev's 'Secret Speech': de-Stalinisation begun; Hungarian rising
1957	second visit to Moscow; calls for 'a hundred schools of thought to contend'	collectivisation of the peasantry; launch of 'Hundred Flowers' campaign; Great Leap Forward begins	Soviet Union launches two 'sputnik' satellites
1957–62		Great Leap Forward	
1958	gives up presidency of PRC		Khrushchev visits China
1958–62		famine in China	

Date	Personal	Political	General
1959	defeats Peng Dehuai at Lushan	Lushan conference	
1961	last meeting with He Zichen	Chinese walk out of Moscow Congress	
1962	attends the '7,000 Cadres' conference'; first meets Zhang Yufeng	Socialist Education Movement set up; Liu Shaoqi and Deng Xiaoping tackle food problem; Lin Biao begins organising cult of Mao	Sino-Indian war; USSR supply MiG fighters to India; PRC condemns USSR over Cuba
1962–66	makes partial withdrawal from front-line politics		
1963		'Little red book' becomes a standard text	
1964	acts vindictively against Liu Shaoqi	A-bomb exploded by Chinese	
1965	discussions with Kang Sheng and the Gang of Four in Shanghai	The Dismissal of Hai Rui from Office attacked by Maoists	
1966	returns to public by swimming in Yangxi River; launches Cultural Revolution	Tiananmen Square rallies	
1966–76	oversees Cultural Revolution	Cultural Revolution	
1967		H-bomb exploded by Chinese	
1967	introduces 'to the mountains' campaign	'to the mountains' campaign	
1968		Liu Shaoqi and Deng Xiaoping dismissed	

Date	Personal	Political	General
1969	condemns Brezhnev Doctrine	death of Liu Shaoqi	Sino-Soviet split
1970		Third Line completed	
1971		Lin Biao killed in plane crash	USA accepts PRC's right to represent China at UN
1972	meets US president	'criticise Lin Biao and Confucius' campaign started; President Nixon visits China	USA abandons Chiang Kai-shek
1973		Liu Shaoqi dies in prison; Deng Xiaoping returns	
1974	loses coherent speech	Politburo formally appoints Zhang Yufeng as Mao's private secretary	
1975	undergoes surgery	Deng regains his place as party secretary	death of Chiang Kai-shek
1976	death	death of Zhou Enlai; Tiananmen Incident in Beijing	

INTRODUCTION

China has stood up. No one will insult us again.

Mao Zedong, Oct 1949

On 1 October 1949, a fifty-six-year-old peasant stood on a balcony of the South Gate of the Forbidden City in Beijing. Tall for a Chinese, with sloping shoulders, a broad face, high forehead and puffy cheeks, he read from a flapping sheet of paper into a crackling microphone. In a high-pitched voice whose accent denoted his Hunanese origins, he proclaimed the creation of the People's Republic of China. His name was Mao Zedong and he was the ruler of the most populous nation on earth.

Mao had travelled a long road to be where he was on that day. In pursuit of his goals for China he had suffered and had made others suffer. He had had four wives and discarded three of them. He had sired ten legitimate children, seen two of them die and watched while two others were taken into slavery. As a young man in Changsha during the 1911 revolution, he had been an onlooker as soldiers methodically battered their prisoners to death. For two decades after 1927 he had been hunted across China by warlords and Nationalists, seeking to destroy him and the Chinese Communist Party he had helped to found in 1921. Surviving only by the most desperate means, he had become inured to privation. Even as he had struggled against his internal enemies, he had also led a committed resistance to the Japanese invaders who occupied China for fourteen years after 1931. Yet while fighting on all these fronts, he had been ruthlessly gaining mastery over his party. By the mid-1940s he had established an unchallenged authority that left him free, following the surrender of the Japanese in 1945, to lead the party to its final triumph over Chiang Kaishek's Nationalists in 1949.

Paradoxes are found in all great men. One need think only of the contradictory principles and impulses that motivated such twentieth-century figures as Stalin, Roosevelt, Churchill, de Gaulle and Mandela. The contradictions were even more marked in Mao. As a Chinese revolutionary, he rejected Western values but made it his mission to match Western achievements; he led a revolution against the world to join the world. His driving purpose was to liberate China from decades of foreign oppression, but to realise this aim he adopted a Western political theory – Marxism. He selected it because he saw it as an essentially destructive force, and he believed that in China destruction must necessarily precede construction. He sent his young Red Guards storming through the nation in the 1960s to destroy 'the four olds', his term for the remnants of China's past. Yet this was a man steeped in China's history, whose daily reading was the Chinese classics and who took as his political and military mentors not contemporary texts but the writings of the ancient Chinese masters.

Mao was a poet of genuine distinction and often showed great sensitivity of feeling, but he was ruthless with those who stood in his way. His path to the leadership of the Chinese Communist Party was littered with the dead or broken bodies of those comrades who had opposed him and whom he had ordered to be killed or tortured. In the process of consolidating his power as head of the People's Republic of China between 1949 and his death in 1976, he killed millions. At the height of his authority in communist China, he presided over the *laogai*, a vast system of prison-camps, which vied with Stalin's gulag in its denial of the human spirit. Yet he had a capacity for exciting the most intense loyalty and admiration among his people, who regarded him as little less than a god. No emperor had ever wielded such power as he or been so loved by his subjects.

No person can be understood except against his background. This truism has particular force in regard to Mao and China. It is impossible to make sense of the violence and suffering that accompanied him throughout his career unless the character of the China from which he sprang is grasped. China in the twentieth century was shaped by violent upheaval. Mao was both a product and a creator of this.

IMPERIAL CHINA

By the end of the nineteenth century, China was a nation in ferment. It was suffering from two profound shocks. One was the rise in its population, which doubled to half a billion between 1800 and 1900. This placed burdens on its political and social structure and its food supply system which proved unbearable. The other was the cultural trauma brought about by enforced contact with the West. Until the early nineteenth century China had regarded itself as a society supreme over all others. It was not that there had been no relations with the outside world. Indeed, modern scholarship has shown that at times China was more open to, and affected by, international currents of thought that the Chinese were prepared to admit.[1] Nevertheless, these contacts did not undermine China's sense of its own uniqueness. One particularly interesting result was that the Chinese were slow to develop a concept of historical change of the kind that had become basic to Western ways of thought. Without a refined notion of progress, China's rulers seldom felt the need to engage in reform. This was not indolence on their part. Disinclination to change was a product of Taoism and Confucianism, sophisticated patterns of thought which had prevailed in China since the fifth century BC.

The central concept in Taoism is that the whole of existence relates to the Tao. This is usually translated in English as 'the way' – the driving force which gives everything its purpose and proportion and creates the harmony of nature. The Tao is unknowable through the senses; it can be understood only through inner contemplation. Confucius, who lived from 551 to 479 BC, incorporated Taoism into his thinking. He was not a religious thinker in Western terms. While he did not deny the existence of gods or of an after-life, he felt that these were questions beyond the capacity of humans to determine. His concern was with how people behave in this life. His core principle was that happiness could be found only in the ordered life. Individuals were born into an existing world that contained other people. The individual's task was, therefore, to come to terms with the world as it was and to relate harmoniously to the people in it. But the individual needed guidance to enable him achieve this. Confucius and a later disciple, Mencius, sought to provide this guidance by constructing a code of social behaviour. In practical terms, the Confucian code amounted to a set of admonitions encouraging people to accept things as they were and make the best of them.

The emphasis in Confucianism on accepting the *status quo* led to the notion that obedience to authority was a binding obligation. The dutiful citizen could best preserve the natural harmony of things by conforming to prescribed laws and social conventions. This put an irresistible weapon into the hands of those in authority; they could denounce any challenge to their powers as an affront to the natural order. A notable feature of Chinese history is the severity of the punishment meted out to rebels. This was not gratuitous cruelty; its purpose was to convey the anger of righteous citizens towards wrongdoers who had tried to disturb the harmony of society.

Confucianism did not survive for two and a half millennia merely because it was a coherent theory. What gave it permanence was that it became part of the fabric of China. It pervaded public life and provided the political establishment with its right to hold power. Adherence to Confucian principles was a badge of public office. The civil service which ran China was drawn wholly from the mandarins – a scholar class trained in Confucianism. The mandarins went through a series of rigid examinations in the subtleties of Confucian thought which, once passed, gave them entrée into government and administration. An exclusive elite, the mandarins became the propagators of the concept of China as a unique culture whose unchanging character was the proof and guarantee of its worth.

Confucianism did not deny change in absolute terms. The seasons, birth and death, growth and decay, were obvious signs of mutability. But all these belonged to a larger cycle of nature. A Western scholar has suggested that Chinese thinkers were 'natural dialecticians and understood that everything contains within itself the seeds of its own opposite'.[2] Especially notable was the way Confucian principles were stretched to encompass political change. Even the greatest emperors and dynasties passed away, and these events had to be explained. The answer lay in a neat intellectual side-step known as 'the mandate of heaven'. This was a formula for accommodating change after it had occurred. 'Heaven' in its Chinese context meant the dynamic or force that preserved natural harmony. When a weak emperor was overthrown and replaced by another, the new ruler claimed that he had inherited the mandate of heaven; his elevation marked the restoration of the harmony that his predecessor had undermined. In effect, what the mandate of heaven did was to legitimise successful rebellion. Rebels who fought against the current regime and failed deserved the execution they then suffered. But rebels who fought against the existing system and defeated it were no longer rebels; they had transformed themselves into the legitimate heirs to 'the mandate of heaven'. What this amounted to was an argument for justification by success. It left a strong mark on Chinese attitudes. The traditional Chinese approach to politics was essentially utilitarian. Ideas had to be of practical value; purely abstract principles were of limited appeal. There was little sympathy for failed causes.

Until the twentieth century, Chinese history was measured by reference to the fifteen imperial houses which ruled from *c*.2200 BC until the last of them, the Qing (Manchu) dynasty, collapsed in 1912. Through military conquest, the earliest emperors had established themselves as the chief rulers and law-givers, entitled to rule over their subjects. In time the position became hereditary and acquired an absolute authority underpinned by Confucian principles. Such was the power invested in the emperor that only he could authorise reform in Chinese society. To attempt major adjustments that were not sanctioned by the emperor was to engage in treason. The implications of this were profound. In the time of a strong or enlightened emperor, China enjoyed confidence and guidance. When a weak or incompetent ruler occupied the imperial throne, China lacked leadership and direction. It so happened that at precisely the time when China faced its greatest external threat it was ruled by the Qing, a dynasty that had become effete and incapable of meeting the challenge.

THE IMPACT OF THE WEST

Centuries of belief among the Chinese that their country was culturally superior and materially self-sufficient encouraged the notion that China needed nothing from outside. This Sino-centric view sometimes created problems for China, for there were occasions when it did need materials from abroad. To square this circle, the Chinese referred to their foreign commerce as a system for accepting tribute from inferiors. The fiction was maintained even when China's exports were greater in value than its imports. An interesting example was its purchase of opium from India and Burma. Beginning in the 1750s, British merchants from those countries established a flourishing opium trade with China. This brought excellent returns for the traders but drained China of its silver reserves. It also greatly increased drug addiction, which had debilitating effects on large sections of the Chinese population.

The oddity of China's diplomatic and trading position was clearly evident in its contacts with Britain. In the late eighteenth century, the British made a number of proposals to China for closer trading links. The Chinese initially rejected the overtures, declaring that they had no need of anything Britain could offer. However, they eventually relented and in 1794 allowed a delegation, led by Lord McCartney, to enter the Forbidden City in Beijing. McCartney's refusal to prostrate himself before the emperor in the time-honoured 'kowtow' created bewilderment and anger among his hosts. The incident can now be seen as presaging the antipathy and hostility that developed between China and Europe in the nineteenth century.

The first major affront to China's concept of its superiority among nations occurred in 1839 when Lin Lexu, acting as representative of the Emperor Daoguang, who had been angered by increasing British demands for unlimited trading rights in his country, ordered the seizure of all British-owned opium and forbade further Anglo-Chinese trade. Britain responded by sending warships to shell the port of Canton. Realising that they were totally outgunned, the Chinese signed the humiliating Treaty of Nanjing in 1842, in which they agreed to increase their opium imports and cede the port of Hong Kong to Britain.

Such humbling of China was the cue for other European powers to impose themselves. In a series of 'unequal treaties' signed over the next half-century, China opened some fifty 'treaty ports' to foreign powers, most notably France, Germany, and Britain. The ports were key strategic or commercial sites, dotted along China's coastline and rivers. In addition a number of Chinese cities witnessed the creation of 'concession' areas; these were defined parts of cities and ports within which European law and customs held sway. The Chinese were treated as strangers in their own land. The concessions functioned as a series of foreign mini-states within China's borders. Embittered by these depredations, the Chinese were also dismayed by their own inability to offer effective resistance. What excited their particular resentment was that successive emperors, rather than working to prevent the Western violation of China, were seen to be collaborating with the occupying powers in a desperate attempt to maintain Qing authority.

The natural reaction of Chinese nationalists was to look for ways of ridding China of the 'foreign devils' who occupied it. But achieving this presented a dilemma. Such was the obvious military and technological superiority of the West that the Chinese realised that in order to drive out the foreigners they would have to be able to match them in fighting strength. Unless they adopted Western techniques they could not hope to defeat the West. Nor was this simply a matter of physical resources and scientific expertise. There was a critical political dimension to it. Western dominance raised searching questions about the nature and character of China. The march of events was forcing China to recognise that its erstwhile belief in its own greatness was a fallacy and that the imperial system was moribund. If the system could not or would not be reformed, the only alternative path for China was revolution that would be both anti-foreigner and anti-Qing.

Map 1 Foreign treaty ports established in the nineteenth century

THE CHINA OF MAO'S YOUTH

The decade into which Mao Zedong was born was a time of particular suffering for the Chinese. During the 1890s a combination of droughts and floods led to a series of harvest failures that caused widespread hunger. Significantly, the Chinese blamed their plight on the foreigner as much as on the forces of nature. They had reason. It was the late 1890s that witnessed the so-called 'scramble for concessions' during which the Western powers imposed themselves even further on China. An interesting example of this was the gaining by Britain in 1898 of a ninety-nine year lease on the territories around the port of Hong Kong, which was then formally declared to be a British Crown Colony. The Qing government hoped that such grants would satisfy Western demands. But appetite grew by what it fed on. This was the high age of Western imperialism; the scramble for concessions was part of the same European competition for overseas territories that had produced the scramble for Africa. However, China was not colonised in the same way as Africa. With some exceptions, such as the British in Hong Kong and the Portuguese in Macao, the Europeans did not directly govern China, which formally remained a sovereign state. The pattern adopted by the European powers was to establish their own enclaves within China. Nevertheless, although formal Western domination may have existed only in pockets, it exerted a pervasive influence over the whole of China. The evident power wielded by the foreigners was a scandal to Chinese nationalists.

What rankled most with many Chinese was that the scramble for concessions had been begun by their Asian neighbour, Japan. Rivalry between China and Japan had existed for centuries. But the two countries had shared the view that their oriental cultures were superior to those of the Western 'barbarians'. Japan, therefore, had undergone as deep a trauma as China when it, too, had fallen prey to Western imperialism in the nineteenth century. The initial impact had been very similar. Around the middle of the century, Japan had been forced to open its ports to European and American ships and to sign disadvantageous agreements with foreign traders. That, however, was where the similarity ended. Japan rose swiftly to the Western challenge by embarking on a large-scale modernisation programme, modelled on Western lines. Within two generations it had reached economic and military parity with the Western powers. This remarkable recovery was organised from the top. The Emperor Meiji

(1869–1914) took the lead in the restructuring of Japanese society. The incipient unrest occasioned by the breathless pace of the enforced changes was suppressed by the powerful military forces whose development Meiji made an integral part of the reforming process. Indeed, militarism became an outstanding feature of the new Japan. How strong its land and naval forces had grown was dramatically revealed in 1895 when they inflicted an overwhelming defeat on China. Ten years later Japan won a still more impressive victory over Russia. These triumphs united the Japanese people, glorified the concept of martial glory, and attracted foreign investment.

The striking aspect of Japan's regeneration was the way it had been able to achieve what China seemed incapable of – modifying its traditional culture to meet the demands of modernity. Moreover, in doing this Japan had strengthened, not weakened, its sense of national identity. By the end of the century, it had acquired such confidence that its thoughts turned towards imperial expansion. The territorial rewards for its 1895 victory over China included large parts of Manchuria, the peninsula of Korea, and the island of Taiwan. Japan then proceeded to join the European powers in 'the battle of the concessions'; between 1895 and 1900 it set up enclaves in four Chinese cities.

Humiliation at the hands of the neighbour whom they had tradition- ally despised cut very deep with the Chinese. Japan entered the twentieth century recognised internationally as a united and thriving nation. China in contrast remained ill-led, fragmented, economically weak, and at the mercy of foreign occupiers. The Chinese leaders did make some attempt to rouse the nation. In the 1898, Emperor Guangxu gave his approval to a 'self-strengthening' movement which aimed at introducing reforms into China as a means of preventing further foreign seizures. But the truth was that the Qing, led nominally by Guangxu, though in reality dominated by the reactionary Dowager Empress Cixi, were not genuine reformers. Cixi's detestation of the 'foreign devils' was real enough, but the Qing record of collaboration with the occupiers compromised any effort the imperial government might make to lead resistance. Nevertheless, such an effort was made when the Qing chose to give their support to a remark- able anti-foreigner movement, known as the Boxers.

Map 2 The provinces of central and eastern China with their main towns and cities

THE BOXER RISING, 1898–1901

The Boxer movement can now be seen as a product of religious fervour, national bitterness, and starvation. It was essentially a peasant movement and in that sense it belonged to the series of desperate peasant rebellions that had occurred sporadically and always unsuccessfully throughout the history of imperial China. What made the Boxer rising distinctive was that it was joined by the Chinese gentry. This small but ambitious class, increasingly angered by the barbarous foreigners, who blocked their progress, were eager to reclaim China's independence.

The hopes of all three groups – peasants, gentry and Qing – proved illusory. The attempt to end fifty years of foreign domination never became a national movement. Most of China's provincial and military leaders ignored the Qing government's appeal for a united Chinese resistance. Acting out of self-interest, they chose instead to co-operate with the foreign powers by protecting them against the Boxers. Beyond a desire to get rid of the foreigner there was no unifying purpose or strategy to the Boxer movement. In spite of its slogan 'support the Qing, attack the foreigners', Cixi was as fearful of peasant rebellion as of Western domination. Yet, in the end, the factor that destroyed any chance of Boxer success was not internal division but Western strength. Once an international army representing eight of the occupying powers – Britain, Germany, France, Japan, the USA, Russia, Italy, Austria – had been put into the field in 1900, Chinese resistance crumbled. Cixi and the emperor ran for their lives.

In their physical attack upon Westerners and pro-Western Chinese, the Boxers had been guilty of some savage acts, particularly against Christian missionaries, for whom they had a special loathing. But what was to live in Chinese memory was not Boxer excess but Western brutality. In putting down the rising, the German commander of the international forces acted upon explicit instructions to be utterly ruthless. His troops subjected the areas they occupied to a reign of terror; Chinese civilians were raped and killed, premises were razed. Needless severity continued even after the rising had been suppressed. In the Boxer Protocol of 1901, China had to pay $45 million in reparation, and to accept the permanent stationing of foreign troops in China. Leading government officials had to give themselves up for trial and sentencing. Heads rolled figuratively and literally. The imperial court was allowed to return to Beijing a year later but the credibility of the Qing as rulers had been fatally weakened.

QING WEAKNESS

Cixi struggled to maintain imperial authority by again colluding with the foreigners, and by fiercely suppressing Chinese dissidents. However, appreciating that suppression alone would not stem the tide of mounting opposition to the Qing, she allowed a number of changes to be introduced. Among these were the formation of provincial assemblies and the dropping of the requirement that civil-service entrants pass examinations in Confucianism. But the alterations did not bring the political credit Cixi had hoped for; they were seen by opponents as concessions reluctantly wrung from a government that had no real intention of relaxing its authority. Moreover, they cost money, which the government could raise only by recourse to taxation. Since this fell on the commercial and financial interests, the Qing were alienating the very class the reforms had been aimed to placate.

One of the dynasty's biggest failings was its blindness to the importance of the economic changes that the Western presence had brought. Between 1890 and 1910, China experienced something approaching an industrial revolution. As a consequence of the unequal treaties, foreign companies enjoyed low costs and high returns in the their trade with China. This encouraged major investment by Western financiers. China both gained and lost from this. Capital resources expanded and numerous Western-owned businesses and factories, employing Chinese workers, were established in China's cities. The downside was that in order to develop its own industrial programme, China had to take out large foreign loans. The impact of this on internal Chinese politics was strikingly evident in regard to the question of the railways.

China's industrial lift-off had created a railway boom which provided many provinces with substantial foreign investment. This worried the Qing; they feared that if the provinces were enriched in this way it would lessen Beijing's central control over them. To prevent this, the government decided to nationalise the major rail lines. However, to raise the capital to buy out the existing owners and shareholders Beijing had first to borrow heavily from abroad. This served to emphasise that China under the Qing had became a debtor nation, dependent on the West. The government then made things worse for itself by bungling the nationalisation programme and leaving the dispossessed railway owners without compensation. The result was increased disaffection among China's commercial class, which although still small in relation to the country's population of half a billion, was growing in influence as a result of rapid industrialisation.

Despite the swelling dissatisfaction with the imperial system among Chinese nationalists, it was still difficult for them to challenge the government openly. In the aftermath of the Boxer rising, government troops were quick and invariably vicious in crushing disorder. This had the effect of increased Japanese influence in China. Japan was both a reproach and an inspiration to Chinese progressives. They hated it for the way it had joined the European occupiers in lording it over China. Yet they admired it for regenerating itself as a nation and so becoming a model of Asian resistance to Western imperialism. It was no accident, therefore, that revolutionary ideas made their greatest initial headway among the 10,000 Chinese living in Japan.

THE INFLUENCE OF SUN YATSEN

After China's defeat by the Japanese in 1895 nearly all the Chinese provinces began sending students to Japan to be educated there. The expatriates were deeply impressed by their direct experience of Japan's successful adoption of modern ways. In Tokyo in 1905, a number of Chinese nationalists formed the Alliance League under the leadership of Sun Yatsen, an influential figure among the nationalists since the early 1890s. Sun had qualified as a doctor at a Western medical school in Hong Kong and had travelled in Europe and North America. His conviction was that China had to modernise as Japan had done, and that this required the removal of the obsolete imperial system and the creation of a Chinese republic. Such views meant that Sun spent the greater part of his time after 1895 in exile. Whenever possible, he returned to Japan, which he considered an ideal base for organising a radical anti-Qing movement.

Sun Yatsen drew on his foreign experience to develop his revolutionary policies for China. His programme was based on 'the three principles of the people', which he defined as nationalism, democracy and socialism. He was well aware that these Western political terms did not translate easily into the Chinese context but he was untroubled by this. He asserted that 'the merit of an ideology does not lie it its logic; whether it is good or bad depends upon its suitability to a certain circumstance. It is good if it is beneficial to both China and the world; otherwise it is bad.'[3] This attitude was very much in keeping with the pragmatic nature of traditional Chinese thinking. The value of an idea depended upon its practicability. Sun Yatsen defined nationalism as the determination to eliminate Western imperialism and restore China's independence as a sovereign state. By socialism, he meant the government-ownership of major enterprises and their protection from foreign competition. His most interesting definition was of democracy, which was very much in tune with Chinese collectivism rather than Western individualism:

> There is a difference between the European and Chinese concept of freedom. While the Europeans struggle for personal freedom, we struggle for national freedom. As far as we are concerned, personal freedom should never be too excessive. In fact, in order to win national freedom, we should not hesitate to sacrifice our personal freedom.[4]

As the imperial government began to totter, the Alliance attracted an increasing number of supporters. The uncompromising character of Sun's anti-Qing stance appealed to those nationalists who had become convinced that China could not advance until the imperial system was overthrown.

THE END OF THE IMPERIAL CHINA

Fortune served the revolutionaries well and the Qing ill. In November 1908, the Manchu dynasty entered its final crisis when, within the space of a day, both Emperor Guangxu and Cixi suddenly died. Pu Yi, destined to be the last emperor of China, came to the throne at the age of two, with his uncle, Prince Chun, as regent. To those whose wishes were father to their thoughts, it was now only a matter of time before the imperial system collapsed. Nevertheless, Chun struggled to preserve it. He continued with the reforms introduced under Cixi but let it be known that he would not suffer slights to the imperial dignity. To show his sense of purpose he dismissed Yuan Shikai for using his position as commander of the Beiyang army to encroach upon the authority of the imperial government. It was done in a very Chinese way. On the pretext that Yuan's war-wounds, which had left him with an awkward limp, made him an undignified presence at court, the regent instructed him to take early retirement. Yuan hobbled away, vowing to be revenged.

Such shows of Qing strength were effective only within the court. Outside, opposition was mounting. The government-led reforms had come too late. Crucially, no effort had been made to lessen the economic restrictions, particularly the high levels of taxation, on the entrepreneurial classes in China's cities. In the event of a crisis, the Qing had forfeited their claim to civilian support. This left them ultimately dependent on the army to preserve their position. Should the military turn against the Qing their fate would be sealed. This is indeed what happened in a sequence of events that led to the Chinese revolution in 1911. On the 10 October, the 'Double Tenth', a rising among a detachment of imperial troops at Wuhan in Hubei province rapidly spread into neighbouring provinces. It was as if a rebellion had been waiting to happen. The rising soon became a full-scale mutiny, supported by local political revolutionaries, who encouraged the troops to defy orders from Beijing. By the end of November, the majority of China's provinces had declared themselves to be no longer under the authority of the imperial government. In an attempt to give legality to these events, representatives from the rebellious provinces met in Nanjing to proclaim the creation of a Chinese republic. Sun Yatsen, who had played no direct role in all this, returned from the USA to be installed as president on 1 January 1912.

The Qing knew they could no longer rely on the loyalty of the provincial armies and administrations. Their only recourse was to send an imperial army south to suppress the insurrection. They turned once again to Yuan Shikai and appealed to him to lead the forces. It was a desperate move. After being disgraced by the Qing, it was unlikely that Yuan would show absolute devotion to them. But there was no one else on whom they could call. Yuan accepted the commission, but events were to show that his motives were personal not dynastic. As they moved south, his troops had no difficulty in retaking the rebellious regions, but when they arrived at Wuhan, the scene of the Double Tenth, Yuan chose not to seize the city as he could easily have done. Instead he did a deal with the republican rebels. He told them that, if they were prepared to accept him as president in place of Sun Yatsen, he would use his influence to persuade the Qing to abdicate without a struggle.

The republicans eventually agreed to Yuan's proposal. He then went back to Beijing and presented the Qing with a stark choice: abdicate or be removed by force. To preserve what remained of their dignity, the regent and Longyu, the dowager empress, chose the former course. On 12 February 1912, Longyu issued a formal abdication decree on behalf of the five-year-old Pu Yi. Observing the niceties of tradition, the decree announced that, in accordance with the mandate of heaven, power had passed from the Qing to the new Republic. Yuan Shikai was recognised as having full authority to oversee China's transition from empire to republic.

The fall of the dynasty was only a partial revolution. A total break with the past had not been made. A number of democratic trappings appeared but the representative principle was not introduced. Many of the imperial officials retained their posts, and corruption continued to dominate Chinese public life. China's middle classes had certainly been prominent in the spread of anti-Qing feelings before 1911 but the Wuhan rising was a rising of the military. It is true that the republicans then joined them, but the military remained in control. What can be claimed is that the events of 1911–12 were clearly a revolution of the provinces against the centre. The Double Tenth was another round in the perennial contest between central autocracy and local autonomy, a contest that was to condition much of China's history during Mao's time.

THE FAILURE OF THE REPUBLIC, 1912–16

Sun Yatsen's Alliance League, which after the Qing abdication had changed its name to the Guomindang (GMD or Nationalists), had had misgivings about offering Yuan Shikai the presidency. What had finally convinced them to go through with it was the belief that in order to establish his new government Yuan would have to come south to Nanjing, the main centre of the republican movement. The GMD calculated that this would effectively leave him under their control since he would be detached from his power base in Beijing. Yuan found their reasoning impeccable, which is why he refused to budge. When a Nanjing delegation arrived in Beijing to provide him with a presidential escort for his journey, they were peremptorily told that he would not be coming back with them; the new Republic would be run from Beijing.

The GMD knew they had been used, but there was little they could do. Their influence did not extend beyond the southern provinces. They were a national party in theory, but a regional one in fact. Moreover, as Sun Yatsen acknowledged, they had yet to outgrow their conspiratorial triad mentality. They were used to plotting in opium dens and brothels. Their lack of understanding of practical politics on a national scale was a major handicap. This explains why Yuan was able to outflank the Nationalists at all the key moments.

A typical example of this was the GMD's failure to exploit a serious financial crisis in 1913. In that year Yuan, leader of a Republic that was desperate for cash, raised a £25 million foreign loan. One of the conditions laid down by the international consortium that advanced the capital was that China pledge the greater part of its national revenue as security. Yuan thus opened himself to exactly the same charge as had been levelled at the Qing, that of sacrificing China's independence. The GMD tried but failed to impeach him for misusing his presidential authority. They also attempted to raise rebellion among the armies of the southern provinces. But Yuan reacted decisively. He swiftly removed the military commanders in the troublesome provinces, and then brought the officers and men into line with a mixture of bribes and threats. Such civilian resistance as remained was then easily scattered by Yuan's own northern army. Sun Yatsen heeded the lesson. He told his followers that until the republican parties were better organised they would be incapable of mounting a real challenge to Yuan as president. Sun returned to Japan intent on restructuring and retraining the GMD.

While Yuan appeared powerful in relation to his internal enemies, the underlying insecurity of his position was revealed by external events. The outbreak of war in Europe in 1914 was of great moment for both China and Japan. The two countries had good reasons for supporting the Allies; each hoped to gain the territories which Germany held in the Far East. Japan actively joined the Allies from August 1914 onwards. China, however, did not enter the war until 1917. In the Allied view, this gave Japan an obvious precedence over China. The struggle in Europe also gave Japan a freer hand to interfere in China while the Western powers were preoccupied. In 1915 the Japanese government presented Yuan Shikai with the 'Twenty-one Demands'; these required China to recognize Japanese supremacy by ceding key rights and territories. Official Chinese protests led to some of the demands being dropped, but those that remained still represented an affront to China's sovereignty

Yuan gave in to these demands, a capitulation that provoked a series of violent demonstrations in Beijing and other cities. Significantly, resentment was directed as much against the new republican government as against Japan. All the main sections of the Chinese community currently dissatisfied with the Republic came together in open defiance. Yuan Shikai appeared to ride the storm. Rather than concede to the protesters, he introduced measures to increase his power as president. He suspended parliament, axed the regional assemblies, and centralised the tax system so that the revenue flowed directly into the presidential treasury. Late in 1915, Yuan took the step towards which all his other moves had been tending. He announced that for the sake of national harmony he intended to restore the imperial system with himself as emperor. On New Year's Day 1916 he was duly installed.

The enthronement was accompanied with full ceremonial rites, but the trappings belied the reality. Yuan had over-reached himself. He had not inherited the mandate of heaven; he had grabbed it. Far from uniting the nation, his reclaiming of the imperial title aroused even greater opposition than his presidential manoeuvrings had done. Provincial revolts against him began to spread. Once again, Yuan instructed his northern army to suppress the risings. But his own generals now turned against him. Deprived of the loyalty of his army, he had no other resources on which he could rely. Acknowledging that his position had become impossible, the ailing Yuan renounced the throne in March 1916 only three months after taking it. Within another three months he was dead.

Yuan Shikai's career provides a lesson in Chinese history. It may have been vaulting ambition that inspired him, but he had made some effort to address China's problems. His attempted reforms showed an awareness of how cripplingly outdated the nation's administrative and financial systems were. His civil war against the southern provinces also made perfect sense from a national viewpoint. Given its history, China could not develop into an integrated and independent modern state without the existence of a strong central authority able to lead the nation. While Yuan Shikai did not have the answer to China's problems, he had provided some degree of cohesion. With his passing, republican China slid rapidly towards the fragmentation and misery of the warlord period.

THE WARLORDS

Nominally, the republican government continued to function in Beijing after Yuan's death, but its authority was very limited. It was split between rival factions bidding for power. Its most serious weakness was its inability to maintain a loyal army; it had no force strong enough to impose control over the provinces. The result was that the local areas fell under the domination of a series of regional armies, whose commanders took over the reins of civil as well as military authority. These 'warlords', as they became known, were answerable only to themselves. They created their own laws, issued their own currency and imposed their own taxation. Warlord China has been likened to England during the Wars of the Roses and to Renaissance Italy in the time of the warring city states. The common Chinese experience of warlord rule was one of oppression and terror.

China's weakness, during the warlord era, which lasted for a decade after 1916, revealed the failure of the Republic to replace Qing autocracy with effective central government. Regional ties had proved too strong. The hope that the 1911 revolution would lead to the introduction of representative government in China had proved illusory. The roots of democracy were too shallow for it to take hold. Central despotism was replaced by regional tyranny. This proved crucial politically. The disunity and distress that characterised the warlord years intensified nationalist feelings in China and stimulated radicalism. The grim times gave direction to a revolutionary movement that otherwise might have continued to dissipate itself in factionalism. Although their ultimate objectives for China might differ, all revolutionary groups shared the basic view that an essential first step was the removal of the two evils that characterised the warlord period: warlordism itself and the continued subjection of China to foreign imperialists.

The anomaly was that while the political leaders professed a deep animosity towards the foreigners, they were not above colluding with them when in need. Sun Yatsen frequently sought help from Japan and took sanctuary in the foreign legations. His attempt to set up a rival Nationalist government in Guangzhou in opposition to Beijing only added to China's divisions. Neither the Republican government in the north nor the Nationalist one in the south could operate independently of the warlords in those regions. Both bodies negotiated with local warlords in an attempt to enlist their military support. The strength of Zhang Zuolin, warlord in the Beijing area, was such that a number of foreign countries chose to deal with him rather than the official Republican government in the capital. Similarly, the power of Wu Peifu in central China made him independent of the rival government in Guangzhou.

Violence holds a critical place in the history of China in the early twentieth century. The traditions of antique China which survived beyond the fall of the Qing were so deep-rooted that they could not be wrenched up without violent consequences. China lacked the philosophical beliefs, the social tradition, the scientific knowledge, and the political flexibility to make an easy transition from the old to the new. Modernity came upon it too quickly. Moreover modernity could not come by a following a purely Chinese path. It could come only by the adoption of foreign ways. This made an ordered development impossible. Chinese progressives were excited by Western notions of democracy and socialism but when they tried to apply these to China they did not take root or, if they did, they produced a very different crop from the one expected.

Unable to make the journey from authoritarianism to an ordered, peaceable alternative, China returned to authoritarianism. It was the only political pattern it had ever known. The difference after 1911 was that the authority was no longer centralised. Instead, conflicting groups and interests now struggled to impose themselves on China. A number of writers have referred to Chinese history in the first half of the twentieth century as a story of misrule, not simply in terms of incompetent or ineffective government, but in the deeper sense of China's being trapped in a state of chronic disorder.[5] Civil society had collapsed. Misrule accompanied by violence became the norm. It was in such a setting that the career of Mao Zedong was to unfold. Violence was not simply a background to his times; it was the determinant of them.

1

THE YOUNG MAO

I lament the foolishness of the people of our country, I lament the wasted efforts of the rulers of our country, and I lament the fact that for several thousand years the wisdom of the people has not been developed and the country has been teetering on the brink of a grievous disaster.

Mao Zedong, 1912

FAMILY BACKGROUND

The evidence for Mao Zedong's earliest years comes largely from his own remembrances, as recorded in conversations he had with Edgar Snow, an American communist who stayed with Mao in the 1930s and was one of the first Westerners to get to know him. Obviously, the recollections give only Mao's side. There are one or two early biographies written by members of the Chinese Communist Party, but these tend to be panegyrics and unreliable. Similarly, the anecdotal evidence about Mao's youth comes largely from sympathetic associates who were recounting what he had told them and who were careful to say nothing to his detriment. As a consequence, what can be pieced together about his early background is sketchy, though fascinating. A family tree does exist which traces Mao back to Prince Mao Bozhang, son of the emperor Zhou Wen. However, Mao did not allow the genealogy to be published during his lifetime. One reason may be that as the leader of the great proletarian revolution he was anxious not to reveal his privileged descent. But it is more likely that Mao regarded the tree as largely fictitious. Like the family name Smith in the English-speaking world, the patronym Mao was one of the commonest among the population of 1.3 billion in China at the end of the twentieth century. In Shaoshan, the village where he was born in 1893 and where he was brought up, all the families bore the name Mao and were closely related.

What is reliable fact is that Mao Zedong's family were Han, the race which, according to a late nineteenth-century official census, made up 90 per cent of the Chinese population, the other 10 per cent being drawn from the Manchu, Tibetan, and Mongol peoples. It is also well established that Mao's father, Mao Rensheng, was a self-made man. As a rice and grain merchant, he acquired sufficient capital to dabble in moneylending as a side line. Maoist historians later made efforts to suggest that Mao Zedong had risen from the humblest of origins. This was not so. It is true that, like four-fifths of the population, his family were peasants. But by the time of Mao's birth, his father had already acquired some 30 acres of land, which needed hired labourers to assist the family in working it. In good years, the paddy fields, which took up most of the acreage, produced a bountiful rice crop and brought in a comfortable income. The sprawling farmhouse in which Mao grew up was a substantial building by rural standards. In the 1960s, its mud walls and thatched roof were renovated and it was turned into a shrine to which 3 million Chinese came every year in pilgrimage. By the beginning of the twentieth-first century the numbers had dropped to a trickle, but it was still maintained as a museum.

At the age of seven Mao began working on the family farm, and he continued to do so while at the local primary school, which he attended until he was thirteen in 1906. The school curriculum was largely based around the Confucian programme of ethics. Mathematics and language were also studied, but the main object of the school was to educate the children into ways of good behaviour and deference. They were being trained to play their part in a society whose lineaments had been very clearly marked and maintained over millennia.

What was extraordinary in historical terms was that Mao's period of schooling coincided with the time when these antique values were being challenged and rejected elsewhere in China. There was a possibility that Mao, being a bright lad, might have gone on to one of those schools for the training of the mandarin class that had been the mainstay of China's conservatism for over two thousand years. But that tradition was ended while Mao was still at school. In 1905, in one of the belated Qing attempts at modernisation, the passing of examinations in classical law and ethics was abolished as a requirement for entry to government service. It was no longer necessary for somebody hoping for a public career to be trained in Confucian principles. The irony was that all the signs suggested that Mao would have made an ideal Confucian scholar. His initial reading was in the Chinese classics. At first, he found them difficult and preferred to read the romances of old China, such as *The Water Margin* and *The Three Kingdoms*, tales of adventure, rebellion, and derring-do. However, in time the classics came to impress him and they became a lifelong interest. Nor were they merely of academic concern. Throughout his career Mao turned to them for practical guidance.

Rensheng seems to have been unimpressed by his son's scholarship. He wanted him to use his abilities to do the accounts and prepare himself to become the farm manager. The official guides at Mao Zedong's shrine used to inform visitors that Mao hated his father, who beat him regularly. They would describe how on one occasion Mao threatened to jump into the village pond if the beatings continued; the message to the father was that not only would he be responsible for his son's death but that he would have reduced the family workforce by one. The guides claimed that the story, which Mao himself also related to Edgar Snow, illustrated Mao's early perception of the class struggle between worker and boss and his astuteness in sensing the power that lay in the worker's withdrawal of labour. The pond in question had particular significance in Shaoshan; the villagers believed it had been cursed ever since a young girl had drowned in it. Her death had not been an accident. It had been an execution watched by the young Mao and the other villagers. As punishment for taking a lover and rejecting the man she was betrothed to, the girl had been tied to a weighted plank and held underwater until she drowned. The tale was related with evident relish by the guides as a depiction of the social oppression and superstition that had prevailed in imperial China.

Mao's fraught relations with his father are an absorbing theme. Late in life, Mao said that had Rensheng been alive during the Cultural Revolution he would doubtless have been 'struggled against', the euphemism used in that period to describe the verbal and physical abuse meted out to those who were considered to be reactionaries. As a landowner, Rensheng would obviously have been in line for purging, but Mao may also have had in mind what he regarded as his father's feudal attitudes towards him. On one occasion, Mao criticised his father in front of his friends. An angry Rensheng demanded an apology. Mao gave one but only grudgingly and only after his mother pleaded with him. He was prepared to go down on one knee but refused to prostrate himself in a full kowtow with his forehead touching the ground.

This was the sort of tiff between parent and child that might be said to be common in most cultures. However, it took on a more serious tone in a Chinese context. A powerful and frequent theme in classical tradition was the reverence and dedication of children towards their parents. Indeed, the father–son relationship was regarded as one of the *san gang*, the 'three bonds' that held society together, the others being emperor–minister and husband–wife. In Chinese tradition, a dutiful child was looked upon with special admiration, a dishonourable one with deep distaste. The classics were replete with edifying accounts of filial devotion, involving such sacrifices as children selling themselves into slavery in order to raise money for their father's burial. In one story, a child ate his dying father's excrement in the hope that this would inspire the old man's recovery. Unfortunately, the picture we have of Mao's father comes only from his son's critical perspective. There may have been more to Rensheng than Mao was prepared to grant. Mao appeared not to appreciate the hurt which his disloyalty caused his father or to understand the natural disappointment felt by Rensheng when his son would not conform to his wishes. Perhaps father and son were too alike for them ever to be close. The tension between them became acute when Rensheng tried to marry Mao off at the age of fourteen. In imperial China it was customary for marriages to be arranged by the parents. The motive was invariably economic. The girl's family gained a negotiated bride-price, based on an estimation of her value as a potential breeder of children, while the groom's family immediately gained an extra domestic servant since the custom was for the bride to work under her mother-in-law's orders. Mao rejected the arrangement his father had made, even though this meant forfeiting the dowry money that Rensheng had already paid.

Mao's motives for rejecting the betrothal are not entirely clear. Perhaps he regarded the arrangement as his father's way of tying him down. It is possible that he found the intended bride, Miss Luo, who was six years his senior, unattractive. It may be that he was sexually unawakened and found the prospect of intimacy distasteful. If this was the case, it is wry, since Mao later in life was to become notorious for his insatiable sexual appetite. Whatever his reasons, Mao declined to indulge in *yuan fang*, the traditional first night copulation that consummated a marriage. Miss Luo, however, did move into the Mao household. This raises doubts about Rensheng's motives in arranging the betrothal. It may be that he wanted Luo for himself as a concubine, for that is what she subsequently became. It is certainly the case that his wife, Wen Qimei, left Shaoshan soon after and went back to live with her own family in another village.

Mao's stand against his father is instructive since it suggests that in the China of the new century filial respect and obedience were as capable of being honoured in the breach as in the observance. This is not to suggest that the old values and social certainties had already broken down as if in keeping with the momentous political changes taking place in China. That would be to pre-date events. Social convention was still a powerful force. The liberal developments that were occurring at this time in the West, such as the growing challenge to the class structure, the movement for women's emancipation, and the general argument for greater individual liberty, had yet to make any real impact upon rural Chinese society. That is why Mao's rebellion against his father would still have shocked his contemporaries. The strength of the conservatism that prevailed in Mao's youth was well defined in a caption to a photograph in the 'Mao Zedong Youth Period Revolutionary Activities Exhibition', mounted in the 1990s in Changsha, capital of Hunan:

> Mao had personally felt the four thick ropes binding the peasantry. In 1912 the political rope was already fraying, but the ropes of clan, control, religious superstitions and the exploitation of women were the same as they had been for hundreds of years.[1]

Mao, who ran away from home on at least two occasions in order to spite his father, described the household as being divided into two parties; his father represented, 'the Ruling power', with the rest of the family forming 'the Opposition united front'. Mao used these terms in retrospect in 1936 and it is likely that he was being humorous. Yet it would be fitting to regard the strain between him and his father as Mao's first experience of the dialectic. The lesson that he took from it was that 'when I defended my rights by open rebellion my father relented, but when I remained meek and submissive he only cursed and beat me the more.'[2]

MAO'S EARLY ATTITUDES

Despite his rebellious attitude towards his father, Mao remained conservative in his thinking until his late teens. His schooling and his private reading gave him a strong respect for Confucianism, from which he drew the conviction that to function effectively a society had to have a moral base, by which he meant a sense of order and propriety, and that the individual had to shape his life within the confines of the ordered society. Mao frequently quoted Confucius and other Chinese classics in order to make a point or to prove an argument. This was common practice in imperial China. Legal cases were often decided by reference to Confucius. If, for example, two claimants were in competition for a piece of land and one could back his claim with an apposite quotation from the ancient master he might well swing the magistrate's decision in his favour.

Intellectually bright, Mao Zedong was nonetheless a late starter politically. At the time they occurred, the young Mao knew little of the dramatic developments that preceded the Chinese revolution of 1911. Information was slow to reach Shaoshan in the inland province of Hunan where Mao was raised. Details of the Boxer rebellion were not known until months after the event, while Mao did not learn of Dowager Empress Cixi's death in 1908 until a year after it had happened. However, if Shaoshan was a backwater, the same could not be said of the province of Hunan itself. During the greatest rebellion in Chinese history, that of the Taipings between 1850 and 1864, the loyalty of the Hunanese, led by Zeng Guofang, to the Qing dynasty had been a major factor in the defeat of the rebels. The province had also figured prominently in a reverse role in 1898, when Tan Sitong had led an anti-Qing reform movement, and in the first decade of the new century, when Huang Xing had been a co-founder with Sun Yatsen of the republican Alliance League.

In 1909, when Mao was sixteen, Rensheng grudgingly allowed him to join his cousin at school in neighbouring Xiangtan. Initially, Mao was despised by the other pupils because they were richer and better dressed, but this intensified his desire to learn. The school had acquired a reputation for imparting what Mao called the 'new knowledge'. This was a reference to Western science subjects, such as chemistry and biology, but the curriculum also provided a grounding in Western history and politics. Mao was introduced to the achievements of such major figures as Washington, Napoleon, Lincoln, and Gladstone. He also learned a great deal more about contemporary events in his own country. One teacher who

particularly impressed Mao was a young man who, having recen
returned from Japan, enthused about the great strides the Japanese wei
taking towards modernisation and urged his students to agitate for China
to follow a similar path.

It was at school in Xiangtan that Mao quickly imbibed the bitterness
felt by his outraged compatriots towards both the foreign intruders and
the inept Chinese leadership. He later said that two particular works
had aroused his anger: *Words of Warning to an Affluent Age*, and a pamphlet
whose opening sentence read 'Alas, China will be subjugated!'[3] The first
of these described how backward China was in comparison with the West;
the second deplored the loss of Korea and Taiwan to the Japanese, and
bemoaned China's vulnerability in the face of Western expansion in Asia.
Mao said in recollection: 'After I read this I felt depressed about the future
of my country and began to realise it was the duty of all the people to
help save it.'[4] He also showed intense local Hunanese loyalty. Among his
earliest recorded writings are tributes to the province's three recent heroes
Zeng Guofang, Tan Sitong, and Huang Xing.

FAMINE AND THE DOUBLE TENTH

Mao's Confucian belief in the necessity of good order and strong government infuses his earliest surviving composition, an essay he wrote in 1912
when he was aged nineteen. Written in the year of the Qing abdication,
it was a study of Yang Shang, a powerful regional ruler of the fourth
century BC. In praising Yang for his wisdom and inspiring exercise of
authority, Mao expressed himself very forcibly about the current situation
in China.

> I lament the foolishness of the people of our country, I lament the
> wasted efforts of the rulers of our country, and I lament the fact that for
> several thousand years the wisdom of the people has not been
> developed and the country has been teetering on the brink of a grievous
> disaster.[5]

Since it was submitted as a school essay, the piece may have been written
for effect, but Mao's emphasis on the need for strong leadership in China
tallies with what we know of his attitudes up to that point. By the time
he wrote it, he had witnessed two remarkable events, which, by his own

description, had left a deep mark upon him. In 1910, when he was seventeen, a severe famine struck the Hunan province. Famines were recurrent in Chinese history, but the one of 1910 was particularly horrific. Some of the peasants resorted to cannibalism. Although harvest failure was the basic reason for the starvation, locals blamed it on grain hoarders. Serious disturbances occurred. Some 30,000 people were involved in protest; lives were threatened and property was attacked. The Mao family farm escaped the troubles, but Mao himself witnessed violent scenes in Changsha, the provincial capital. Eventually, the Qing authorities reimposed order by arresting a selection of the more prominent protesters, who were then wheeled through the streets in wooden cages before being publicly beheaded. Mao recorded his reaction to what he had seen:

> It made a deep impression on me. Most of the other students sympathised with the 'insurrectionists' but only from an observer's point of view. They did not understand that it had any relation to their own lives. They were merely interested in it as an exciting incident. I never forgot it. I felt that there with the rebels were ordinary people like my own family, and I deeply resented the injustice of the treatment given to them.[6]

Mao interpreted the failure of the Qing authorities to deal with the famine other than by repression as proof of the incompetence and corruption of the imperial government. His sense of injustice was sharpened the more he read; his thoughts turned to revolution as the only means of reversing China's decline. Quite when he came to that realisation is impossible to tell and it is doubtful whether Mao himself knew precisely. Damascene conversions are rare; ideas usually develop over time. What can be said is that by the age of eighteen he had become a radical. He was appalled when he learned how China had suffered at the hands of the foreigner. He was equally angered that the ruling Qing had not only failed to challenge the foreign oppressors but had colluded with them. He joined in a symbolic protest against the government by cutting off his queue, the braided mane of hair that Chinese males were required to wear in Manchu China. It was also about this time that he became excited by the ideas of Sun Yatsen, whom he later acknowledged as having been China's first great revolutionary of the twentieth century. 'China's bourgeois-democratic revolution against imperialism and feudalism was begun by Dr Sun Yatsen.'[7]

The second formative event was the fall of the Qing. Mao's own involvement in the revolution begun by the Double Tenth in 1911 was marginal and inglorious. He was caught up in the excitement of it, but missed the major action. By his own account, he first learned of the events in Wuhan from a talk by a revolutionary who came to Mao's school in Xiangtan seeking recruits. A number of fellow-students rushed to Wuhan immediately, but Mao delayed. His lame explanation was that the city was flooded and he did not possess a pair of weather-proof shoes. It is doubtful that he ever intended going to Wuhan. However, this ceased to matter when Changsha was occupied by revolutionary forces; the attention of Hunanese activists was redirected to their own capital. The rising in Hunan was led by Jiao Dafeng and Chen Zuoxin, supporters of Sun Yatsen. Although the two leaders gained a large following among peasants and poorer workers, they were unable to win over the local businessmen or government officials. This left them vulnerable to counter-revolution; their opponents, having infiltrated the army that Jiao and Chen had raised, organised a mutiny which resulted in the assassination of both leaders. Their bodies were put on public display in Changsha's main thoroughfare. Mao went to view them. The lesson he took from their grim fate was that revolutionary fervour was not enough; it had to be based on political realities:

> They [Jiao and Chen] were not bad men, and had some revolutionary intentions, but they were poor and represented the interests of the oppressed. The landlords and merchants were dissatisfied with them. Not many days later, when I went to call on a friend, I saw the bodies lying in the street.[8]

Soon after the suppression of the Changsha rising, Mao became a soldier in the republican army. This was not as radical a step as it might appear. The republican forces at this stage were largely made up of remnants of the imperial army. When the Qing had abdicated, the greater part of their forces had gone over to the new republic. Thus, insofar as there was a central authority after 1911, the army was loyal to it. However, Mao's decision still carried some risk. The situation was volatile, and mutinies were frequent. He could easily have been caught on the wrong side. Reprisals were invariably savage; Mao recalled witnessing suspected Qing spies being spread-eagled on wooden frames and used for rifle practice. As events turned out, Mao was not called on to do any fighting during his period of military service. He was in a garrison unit assigned to keeping order in Changsha. Apart from putting on a show of strength at the gates of the city, which deterred an attack by rebellious troops, his unit did not see action. Yet Mao considered that his time as a soldier had had its benefits. Among his fellow troops had been a number of urban workers; it was the first time he had got to know people who were not peasants. He had helped write their letters and they had looked up to him as a young man of learning. Commentators have sometimes read much into this. There is a view that the regard in which Mao was held by his illiterate comrades contributed to a growing sense of superiority that characterised him from his late teens onwards.[9]

MAO THE STUDENT

When it became apparent in 1912 that the Qing were finished and that there would be no imperial fight-back, the hastily recruited armies began to demobilise. After six months in the army Mao returned to civilian life, determined to improve his formal education. His method was simple. He scanned the Changsha newspapers that carried advertisements from a range of schools and colleges. He then registered with a number of them and sampled what they had to offer. Among the topics he studied at different schools over a period of six months in 1912 were soap-making, law, police training, and commerce. He raised the tuition and accommodation fees by writing home to ask for funds. In his twentieth year, Mao was still not above tapping his father for money. What is equally interesting is that his father obliged. Clearly, the breach between them had not been irrevocable. Indeed, Mao recorded that his father was pleased with his son's efforts to learn something useful. 'My father readily appreciated the advantages of commercial cleverness.'[10] However, Rensheng's appreciation was limited to practical education; he could see little value in purely academic learning.

The brevity of Mao's stay at the schools suggests that he found them unsatisfactory. The commercial college disappointed him because its courses were taught in English, a language he did not know save for its alphabet. After this period of pick 'n' mix schooling, he came to the conclusion that self-education was his best means of intellectual advancement. He went daily to the main library in Changsha, where he studied from opening until closing time, breaking off only at mid-day to eat two rice cakes. Apparently his hunger was assuaged by the literary fare he consumed. Among the texts he worked through in translation were Adam Smith's *Wealth of Nations*, Darwin's *Origin of Species*, and John Stuart Mill's writings on ethics. He also read outline histories of Russia, America, France, and England, and pored over maps of these countries.

The nineteen-year-old Mao was now desperately short of money, his father having refused to support him further until he resumed training for a proper job. He lived in what were little more than doss houses in Changsha, sharing rooms with poor students and low-rank soldiers who were billeted there while waiting to be demobbed. Fights between the students and troops were frequent. In one instance, Mao avoided being beaten up only by hiding in a latrine. In quieter moments, he helped the students by writing the essays that they had to submit when applying for college entrance. It was these endeavours that led the students to urge him to become a teacher. Their advice coincided with his own judgement. 'I had been thinking seriously of my career and had about decided that I was best suited for teaching.'[11] This time he wrote an essay on his own behalf, which gained him entrance into Hunan Provincial First Normal School. Despite its name, which translates oddly into English, the School was a comprehensive institution which included a teacher-training department, into which Mao enrolled in 1912. There he stayed for the next six years.

He was a gifted but difficult student. He ignored or ridiculed the compulsory subjects which bored him, and deliberately failed the exams in them. He found the drawing course a particular waste of time. In one class, when asked to compose an imaginative piece, he drew a straight line with a circle over it, entitled it 'half-sun, half-rock', and walked out early. In contrast, he devoted intense efforts to the subjects which engaged him. He was absorbed by philosophy, history, and Chinese language and literature. He became proficient enough in *wenyan*, a form of classical Chinese, to be able to write what he called a 'passable' essay in it. A full set of the notes which Mao made during his first year of study have survived. They were grouped under such headings as 'Self-Cultivation', 'The Philosophers', 'Literary Works'. The notes and comments indicate a very serious mind in the writer and a close attention to detail. The following extracts suggest their quality:

When we select literary works to read, it is best if we pick those with object lessons, which are appropriate for our times. . . .

If you neglect farming, you will not know how difficult it is to sow and reap. If you stop raising silk worms and weaving, you will not know how our clothes are made. . . .

Mencius said: 'Flowing water is a thing that does not proceed till it has filled the hollows in its course. The student who has set his mind on the doctrines of the sage [Confucius] does not advance to them but by completing one lesson after another.' Shallow people should reflect on this.[12]

In 1915, Mao was diverted from his studies by another twist in the unfolding story of the young Republic. The reactionary policies followed by Yuan Shikai as president had convinced many radicals that they had been let down by the revolution of 1911. The Republic was not what they had expected. Yuan's willingness in 1913 to forfeit China's financial independence in return for an international loan aroused dismay. Two years later this turned into anger when Yuan accepted Japan's Twenty-One Demands. Mao and his fellow students shared in the widespread feelings of outrage. Mao held Yuan in contempt, describing him as 'a bandit' who had betrayed China 'in order to pursue his own desires'.[13] In a letter to his closest companion of these years, Xiao Zisheng, Mao bewailed the scandal whereby China, which dwarfed Japan in size and whose population of 400 million was fifteen times larger, gave in cravenly to Japanese threats. He also helped raise funds for the printing of a pamphlet *Essays on the Sense of Shame*, written by one of the school's professors, which denounced Japan's aggression and China's cowardice, and called on the nation's students to exact revenge.[14]

The collapse in the spring of 1916 of Yuan Shikai's brief reign as emperor brought with it the end of the tenuous order that had existed since 1912. Conflict between the centre and the regions and within the provinces was renewed. It was again evident that no change or development seemed able to occur in China except through violence. In Hunan, the situation was especially confused and desperate. Tang Xiangming, whom Yuan had previously appointed governor of the region, tried to cling to power by leading a Hunanese breakaway movement, but was deserted by his military supporters and forced to flee; not, however, before he had purloined the bullion reserves from the provincial treasury. Tang's departure left Hunan in chaos. Troops from various factions roamed the streets, shooting at will and subjecting the cowed civilian population to what Mao called a 'Reign of Terror'. Beatings and killings were commonplace; within a fortnight of Tang's flight, over a thousand people had been executed in Changsha.

However, it was not the violence but its intensity that was novel. During his years as governor between 1913 and 1916, Tang Xiangming had imposed his own reign of terror. His brutality in carrying out Yuan Shikai's orders to crush the Guomindang in Hunan had earned him the sobriquet 'Butcher Tang'. He had ordered over 10,000 executions of criminals and political opponents, had sanctioned the use of torture to extract confessions, and had subjected the press to the tightest form of censorship. Yet Mao, despite his GMD sympathies, persisted for some time in defending Tang's record as Governor. Writing to Xiao Zisheng, he expressed regret that Tang had been deposed. Consistent with his views on the importance of strong authority, Mao surveyed Tang's years in office and praised him for maintaining order in troubled times. He exonerated him from the charge of excessive cruelty, claiming that hard times necessitated hard measures. 'The fact that he killed well over ten thousand people was the inescapable outcome of policy.' Moreover, Mao argued, the virtue of Tang's measures was evident in the lawlessness that had ensued once his strong hand had been removed. 'The police scattered and fled. . . . Gamblers are emerging, and the atmosphere is white hot with debauchery. . . . The disorder is extreme.' Mao confessed to being 'truly frightened' by the anarchy that prevailed. He feared that his critical views on the current situation might land him in trouble and begged Xiao to burn the letter once he had read it.[15]

Mao was over-dramatising the danger he was in; there is no other evidence to suggest he had been picked out by the authorities. He survived and returned to his college in Changsha, which had been closed down during the recent troubles. Despite the pressure of his immediate concerns, Mao still found time to look at wider events. In letters, he commented informatively on the war in Europe, Russo-Japanese relations, and the Mexican revolution. It is possible to detect a growing tendency in Mao to set developments in China into an international perspective. He appeared to sense that he was living in momentous days not merely for China but for the world at large. It added to his seriousness and stimulated his wish to analyse his times and his place in them.

Mao told Edgar Snow in the 1930s that a number of teachers at the Hunan college had impressed him by their knowledge and integrity. This was contrary to what Mao had written to a friend in 1915. Then he had complained that the standards at the school were unacceptably low and that the teachers were uninspiring.[16] He had certainly fallen out with the staff. He had often exasperated them in the lecture room by challenging their ideas and refusing to co-operate in their study programmes. Matters were so tense at times that he was threatened with dismissal. Yet, despite his low estimation of his teachers, it was they who helped to expand and direct his understanding of Chinese politics. One teacher made a point of passing on to Mao copies of the GMD journal *Min Pao* (The People's Paper), whose pages kept him informed about the activities of Sun Yatsen and his followers. Mao later claimed that there was not a day between 1911 and 1927 when he did not read the newspapers from Beijing, Shanghai, and Hunan.

It was *Min Pao* that prompted Mao to undertake his longest journey yet. Having read articles describing the experiences of student travellers who had walked across China as far as Tibet, Mao persuaded a fellow student, Xiao Yu, to give up his summer vacation and join him in a similar journey. In the event, their travels proved far more modest than those that had first inspired Mao. He and his companion walked across five counties, but never actually left Hunan province. Nonetheless, the journey had its significance. Mao and Xiao took no money with them. They relied on the generosity of the locals, which was invariably forthcoming. Mao later claimed that wherever they went they were well received and given food and shelter for the night. In most cases, however, this was provided not by the peasants but by monks in the Buddhist temples.[17] In one village, Mao had his future read by a young peasant girl whom locals believed to have the power of prophesy. Eerily, she told him: 'You could kill ten thousand or even a hundred thousand people without blinking an eye.'[18]

The same expansive feelings that had led Mao to undertake the tour led him to form a student discussion group. His aim was a very serious one; he wanted companions with whom he could examine and debate the major issues in Chinese life. Initially, only 'three and a half' students responded to his newspaper advert calling on 'young men interested in patriotic work' to contact him. In the light of later events, his reference to 'a half' has a special irony. The student in question was Li Lisan, who, twenty years later, was to be a determined rival of Mao's within the Chinese Communist Party (CCP).[19] After its disappointing start, the group grew in number to around a hundred members. Collectively, their outstanding feature was their high-mindedness. They excluded the trivial; Mao insisted that everything they said or did 'must have a purpose'. Under trivial, Mao included all talk of romance and women. He declared that 'the times [are] too critical and the need for knowledge too urgent to discuss women or personal matters.' Instead, they must deliberate on great matters – 'the nature of men, of human society, of China, the world, and the universe.'[20]

Not content with intellectual rigour, these young puritans deliberately embraced physical suffering. They followed Mao in training their bodies to withstand heat, cold, and hunger. They climbed tortuous hills, swam in ice-cold rivers, marched stripped to the waist under the hottest sun, and slept under the stars on the frost-hardened ground. Mao later claimed that such privations had prepared him for the hardships he experienced as a guerrilla leader resisting the Nationalists and the Japanese. In 1917 he wrote a long article extolling the virtues of physical education, not simply as a path to individual health but as means of regenerating the Chinese nation. The body was a metaphor for China.

> It is the body that contains knowledge and houses virtue. . . . Physical education really occupies the first place in our lives. When the body is strong, then one can advance speedily in knowledge and morality and reap far-reaching advantages. . . . The principal aim of physical education is military heroism.[21]

The article was published in *New Youth*, a radical journal jointly edited by Chen Duxiu and Li Dazhao, who were to be among the founding members of the Chinese Communist Party. Mao later acknowledged that Chen, who believed passionately that a new China had to be restructured out of the remnants of its traditional culture, had had a profound influence upon the development of his own political thought. By the time Mao came to write the article, which he signed as '25 Characters' (the number of brush strokes which made up his name), his discussion group had turned itself into the New People's Study Society. Its title expressed its aim of spreading ideas and knowledge to a much wider audience. The society organised night classes in a range of subjects from basic literacy to advanced philosophy and ethics. The goal was not merely to encourage ordinary people to improve themselves but to enlighten them about the true nature of the political situation in China and reveal to them how subservient their country was to foreign authority.

The more Mao studied, the more convinced he became of the need for China to adopt Western ideas in order to make genuine progress. This conviction pre-dated his eventual conversion to Marxism by at least three years. His writings and correspondence in 1917, when he was twenty-three, showed that while he had not abandoned his respect for Chinese learning he had become fascinated by Western scholarship. He confided to a friend that he was particularly impressed by its logical structure and its clear distinction between the theoretical and the practical:

> The defect of our country's ancient learning lay in its disorganized and unsystematic character . . . no differentiations were made between the abstract and the empirical. That is why we have not made any progress, even in several millennia. As for Western studies, they are quite different. Each field of study is further divided into pure and applied. . . . The classifications are so clear that they sound like a waterfall dashing against the rocks. . . . Today, anyone who is resolved to pursue learning, and yet does not follow this principle, will not be able to gain excellence.[22]

Mao's analysis had important implications for his political thinking. As he grew increasingly impressed with Western notions of individualism, he felt a need to reconcile this with his basic belief in the necessity of authority and order. The tension between these two ideas was a constant theme in the voluminous notes he made on the texts he studied. The conclusion that Mao struggled towards was that individualism, even selfishness, was acceptable in great men, but not in lesser mortals. Individualism in the generality of men could not be tolerated since it would destroy the structured society. In a remarkable synthesis, Mao attempted to incorporate Confucianism and Western philosophy. He argued that the attaining of righteousness, which Confucius had seen as the purpose of life, could best be achieved by the enlightened hero leading the mass of the people towards the Tao, the truth. Mao's idea of the hero was influenced by his reading of Nietzsche's concept of the superman. Mao judged that great men were those who understood and represented 'ultimate principles'. He venerated the Chinese sages, Confucius and Mencius, because they had mastered ultimate principles, which he defined as 'deep understanding of heaven and earth, and insight into the present, past, and future'.

> Those who wish to move the world must move the world's hearts and minds, but . . . to move people's hearts one must have great ultimate principles. . . . Although details are indispensable, they are at most details, and ultimate principles are required. Without ultimate principles, such details are merely superfluous.[23]

> The superior man and the petty man are one in their egos; it is just that their understanding and experience may be higher or lower. . . . Our judgements of human character consequently also distinguish between higher and lower.[24]

Mao's analyses suggest that his reading was beginning to provide him with an intellectual explanation for the violent times he was living through. He interpreted life and history in dialectical terms, as an unending struggle between opposed forces. He wrote of 'the natural alternation between order and disorder, and the cycle of peace and war' and noted that people always hated disorder and hoped for order, 'not realising that chaos too is part of the process of historical life.' It is clear that even before he met the theory in Marxism-Leninism Mao had already accepted the dialectic as the dynamic of history. He gave a striking definition of the dualism of the dialectic as he understood it:

> I am the universe, life is death, death is life, the present is the past and the future, the past and the future are the present, small is big, the yang is the yin, up is down, dirty is clean, male is female, and thick is thin. In essence the many are one, and change is permanence. I am the most exalted person, and the most unworthy person.[25]

The seriousness with which Mao faced the world often expressed itself as a brooding melancholy. He declared himself to be lonely, lacking friends who were capable of stimulating his intellect or imagination:

> There is nobody here with whom I can discuss scholarly issues, or talk about weighty affairs of state . . . when one's aspirations are

continuously frustrated and when one gets lost in a maze of twists and turns, one's bitterness is too much to describe. For a very young man, all this represents a world of bitterness.[26]

Although Mao described himself as 'a very young man' it would be wrong to regard his musings simply as adolescent angst. He was twenty-three when he wrote this. His dismal view of the world and his place in it derived logically from what he had read and observed up to that point. It was as a moralist and a nationalist that Mao was depressed. He felt that his compatriots had betrayed China's great traditions by becoming sluggish in their thinking and by losing their sense of morality through their neglect of truth and honesty. 'The thought and morality of our country can be summed up as false rather than authentic, illusory rather than real.'[27] Yet Mao could be buoyed up as well as cast down by his own thinking. His optimism broke through as a sense of a greater vision for China and its people. The nation would throw off its oppression. When that happened: 'the reform of the Chinese people will be more profound than that of any other people. . . . Our golden age, our age of glory and splendor, lies before us.'[28]

In June 1918, Mao graduated from his Changsha college as a qualified teacher. Soon after, he left with a group of fellow graduates for Beijing. He had taken on the task of organising their visit to France to take part in a 'work and learn scheme', started by the French government during the First World War as a means of recruiting foreign workers for the war effort. It was around this time that a number of young Chinese radicals had chosen to work in France; among them were Zhou Enlai and Deng Xiaoping, destined to be Mao's close colleagues in the CCP, although he did not know them at this juncture.

Mao did not go to France with the Hunan graduates. He had other plans. By this time he had committed himself to the Hunan independence movement, which had developed as a reaction against the rule of the warlord, Zhang Jingyao. Zhang and his brother, Jingtang, had led a loose coalition of northern marauders which had defeated an army of southern warlords in Hunan in the spring of 1918. Thereafter, the Zhangs had imposed a harsh regime over Hunan and a number of surrounding provinces. Mao announced himself 'disgusted' with what he called 'the Northern Government', the remnant of the Republic which had been re-established in the place of Yuan's empire. A local event that concentrated

Mao's mind was the forcible billeting of Zhang Jingtang's troops at the Hunan First School in Changsha in March 1918. Mao was in the forefront of a resistance movement that developed. He contributed to a range of hurriedly published and clandestinely distributed pamphlets which demanded that the Zhangs end their tyranny and remove themselves from Hunan. Among the charges that Mao directed at the oppressors was that of drug running.

It was the aim of raising funds for the cause of Hunan independence that took Mao to Beijing 1918. It was his first visit to China's northern capital. His time there proved eventful. Penniless when he arrived, he was helped by one of his former Changsha teachers, Yang Changji, now a professor at Beijing University, to obtain a post in the library, working under Li Dazhao. Mao described his position as a registration clerk as being so menial that the readers whom he served did not acknowledge his existence. Nonetheless, he used the opportunity to attend university classes in philosophy. He became fascinated by the ideas of the Russian anarchist, Peter Kropotkin. News of the Russian Revolution of 1917 had excited Chinese radicals, but Mao had yet to be greatly influenced by Marxism or Bolshevism. He acknowledged the impact Marx had made in Russia, but at this stage he was much more interested in anarchism and how it might be applied in China.

The feature of Kropotkin's ideas that impressed Mao was the central notion that the people represented the creative force of history; if they acted together in good will they made government unnecessary. This was at variance with Mao's original belief in the necessity of strong government and leadership. The truth was that Beijing was a heady experience for Mao and he would in the space of two years swing between a number of different radical theories. For a brief period he turned against Confucianism. He later admitted that at this time his mind had been 'a curious mixture of ideas'. Among these, he listed liberalism, democratic reformism, and utopian socialism, but added that what basically inspired him was anti-imperialism.[29] What we can now see is that he was searching for a programme by which to work towards his vision of a new China. The programme would have to encompass the destruction of warlordism and the end of China's subjection to foreign control. It was the second of these objectives that provided the dynamic for the movement that took its name from the drama that began in Beijing in May 1919.

THE 4 MAY MOVEMENT AND HUNAN INDEPENDENCE

The 4 May marked the first day of violent reaction in Beijing to the news that China had been humiliated by the Versailles Treaty. The Chinese had expected that the post-war settlement would give them back the areas in Shandong province previously controlled by Germany. Indeed, the recovery of Shandong, which included the vital port of Qingdao, had been China's principal motive in entering the war on the Allied side in 1917. However, in April 1919 the peacemakers at Versailles had informed the Chinese delegation that the German concessionary rights in Shandong would revert not to China but to Japan.

The intensity of the Chinese reaction at home matched that shown two years earlier when Yuan Shikai had capitulated in the face of Japan's Twenty-One Demands. Demonstrators took to the streets in all of China's major cities. Boycotts of Japanese goods and premises were hurriedly organised. In Beijing, university and school students formed processions and protested outside government buildings. Japanese personnel and Chinese officials known to be pro-Japanese were abused and in some cases physically assaulted. The attempt by the authorities to control the troubles by using strong-arm tactics simply added to the demonstrators' fury and made martyrs of those who were arrested or beaten by the police. In a dramatic gesture of defiance, one student gnawed through the flesh of his arm and used the flowing blood to inscribe a banner with the words, 'Give Us Back Qingdao'. After some weeks, order was eventually restored, but the situation remained tense.

The atmosphere created by the events of 4 May 1919 imparted a sense of purpose and direction to those radicals and revolutionaries who considered the destruction of foreign imperialism to be the essential first stage in China's rebirth as a nation. This nationalistic reaction became the basis of a broad anti-Western and anti-Japanese movement that could be said to have lasted until 1949 when China's independence was finally established. Mao himself had not played a direct role in the May happenings in Beijing; he had returned to Hunan the previous month on learning of his mother's fatal illness. Yet Mao was greatly affected by the events in the capital. He identified Japan as the 'international aggressor' and called for a mass boycott of Japanese goods. In what may be taken as his first contribution to the May Fourth movement, Mao launched a new journal, *The Xiang River Review*. The river of the title was a metaphor for 'the propagation of the newest currents of thought'.

> What is the greatest problem in the world? The greatest problem is that of getting food to eat. What is the greatest force? The greatest force is that of the union of the popular masses. What should we not fear? We should not fear heaven. We should not fear ghosts. We should not fear the dead. We should not fear the bureaucrats. We should not fear the warlords. We should not fear the capitalists.[30]

To his newly found anarchism had been added a belief that the people must be organised to fulfil their role as saviours of China. He appealed to them to 'question the unquestionable. Dare to do the unthinkable.' It is noteworthy that at this stage Mao did not advocate violent action. 'We will not pursue that ineffectual "revolution of bombs," or "revolution of blood."'[31]

For the next two years, he threw himself into political action. The scale of his hectic activity can be measured simply by listing the various organisations he either founded or joined: the Association for Assisting Hunanese travellers in Beijing, the Hunan Students' Association, the Problem Study Society, the Hunan Peace Preservation Society, the Association for Promoting Reform in Hunan, the Association of Hunanese Scholars Residing in Beijing, the Cultural Book Society, the Strengthen Learning Society, the Xiangtan Society for the Promotion of Education, the Russian Studies Society, the New People's Study Society, the Women's Work-Study Mutual Aid Group (Beijing), the Work-Study Mutual Aid Society (Shanghai). His involvement was never merely nominal; he played an executive role in nearly all these groups and was frequently their secretary. One example of his prodigious energies was his composition and drafting of the Statutes of the Problem Study Society, a list of seventy-six issues 'which have not yet been solved yet influence the progress of contemporary human life.'[32] Among these were education, women's rights, racial equality, self-rule for India, economics, Japanese expansionism, industrial relations, and transportation.

Mao's listing of such problems had a wider significance, relating to a dispute which had broken among the editors of *New Youth*, the leading radical journal of the May Fourth movement. By 1919, Chen Duxiu and Li Dazhao had become convinced Marxists, arguing that China should push towards a revolution on the lines of the 1917 Bolshevik coup in Russia. Their fellow editor, Hu Shi, had openly challenged this view; he urged China's revolutionaries not to lock themselves into a prescriptive ideology, but to deal in a directly practical way with the problems confronting the Chinese people. The dispute which split the ranks of the radical intellectuals was often defined in the short-hand form of 'problems versus isms'. All three men greatly influenced Mao, but his commitment to the Problem Study Society suggests that at this stage of his development it was the ideas of Hu Shi that most affected him.

Elsewhere, Mao made a direct reference to the violent, proletarian anti-capitalism advocated by Karl Marx, but asserted that Kropotkin's theories were a superior interpretation of the role of the masses in changing history. As Mao understood it, Kropotkin believed that there was no need to kill the capitalist oppressors since they were capable of being reformed. They could then contribute to a great world movement 'to unite the human race in a single family, and attain together peace, happiness and friendship'. With the needs of the Hunan independence movement uppermost in his mind at this time, Mao asserted that the ultimate goal of 'the great union of the masses' could best be achieved by first forming 'small democratic unions'. He called on individual classes and groups in China to organise themselves so that they could then contribute to the reconstruction of the whole nation.[33]

Beginning with the peasants and workers, Mao listed specific examples of China's oppressed. These included women, students, teachers, policemen, and rickshaw boys. He appealed to them to follow the example of those workers in the West who had created unions to defend their interests and in so doing had helped the masses acquire a consciousness of their revolutionary destiny. It was the duty of the Chinese people to create a similar 'raging torrent' in China by demanding liberation. Yet he was insistent that before China could rediscover its greatness it had to be unified, and that this required China's regions first achieving their own independence. He called for 'a Monroe Doctrine' to protect the provinces from warlord oppression and from meddling by the incompetent central government of what he called the 'false republic'. 'We must strive with all our might, first towards the goal of establishing a Republic of Hunan, and then, by realizing our new ideals, creating a new life, and a new world . . . to give an example for the other twenty-seven small Chinas to follow.'[34] Mao now sensed that developments in Hunan and China were part of a worldwide movement. 'A storm of change', he wrote, 'is rising throughout the entire world; the call for "the self-determination of nations" echoes to the heavens'.[35]

> Everything must be changed, from thought and literature to politics, religion, and art. Even such questions as whether or not to retain the nation, or the family, or marriage, whether property should be private or public, are all issues that are open to examination. And even more important are the great European war and the Russian Revolution it sparked, the waves of which are moving from West to East.[36]

Mao's efforts on behalf of the Hunan resistance movement did not end with rousing words. During the autumn of 1919 he devoted himself to organising a province-wide strike aimed at challenging the Zhang tyranny. In December, thousands of workers and students went on to the streets in Changsha. Their protest met the customary response. Soldiers, led personally by Zhang Jingtang, surrounded the strikers, who were made to kneel and submit to being punched about the head and face. Those not sufficiently subdued by this were arrested and hauled away. Mao was not among the victims. Well aware that his activities were making him a marked man, he had kept on the move, interspersing his organising work in Changsha with visits to Beijing. Soon after the strike had been broken, he again slipped away to the capital. His aim was to spread information about the corruption and brutality of the Zhangs' regime and gain wider support for a concerted attack against it. However, much of his time in Beijing was taken up with looking after the family of his mentor, Professor Yang, who died soon after Mao arrived. Before returning to Hunan, Mao also found time to visit Shanghai. En route he visited the village of Qufu to pay homage at the shrine of Confucius.

By the time he returned to Hunan to pick up the reins of the independence movement, events had overtaken him. The Zhangs had been overthrown. For all the considerable efforts of Mao and his colleagues to organise popular resistance, when the regime did fall it was primarily because of warlord intrigue. Zhang Jingyao was ousted in a rising plotted by a group of military rivals. It was further evidence that in Republican China political agitation was of little consequence in itself. Rule was by the sword. Mao was made conscious of this when, after a period of uncertainty during which various attempts were made to establish civilian rule in Hunan, another military commander, Zhao Hengti, appointed himself provincial governor. Although Zhao's rule was less despotic than Zhang's, it was still military rule. Mao had to face the fact that his years of political activism and journalism had had little tangible effect. The power of ideas to influence events in China seemed minimal. This had the result of pushing Mao towards a programme in which actions, not words, were paramount. He quoted Tolstoy approvingly: "'To earn your living through labour is true happiness". I think it is extremely miserable to lead a life in which you only use your brain and your mouth.'[37] Mao was now convinced that what was required was a politics of action. He was expressing the traditional Chinese attitude that the value of ideas lay not in their intellectual cogency but in their practicability as guides to action.

Yet if Mao was depressed over political developments, he could take some consolation from an upturn in his personal life. Such was his reputation in Changsha after the fall of the Zhangs, that he was able to use his contacts to gain an important public post. He was appointed head of the primary school attached to the Hunan college from which he had graduated two years earlier. He now had a regular salary, which was supplemented by fees from his writings and from his share of the profits from the Cultural Book Society. Although this book-selling business, which he had helped to found in 1920, was aimed primarily at the dissemination of cheap revolutionary literature, it proved to be remarkably profitable. This was partly because it was subsidised by local businessmen who believed that Hunanese independence would serve their interests. But its success was also due to Mao's meticulous attention to the running of the enterprise. Within a few years, the Cultural Book Society had opened seven branches in Hunan. For Mao at the age of twenty-seven, life seemed to hold out the prospect of a relatively comfortable existence.

But comfort is seldom a priority for visionaries. Mao was so possessed by the conviction that China had a great destiny that he was prepared to subordinate all other considerations to working for its fulfilment. His belief in 'ultimates' had brought him to that position. The greater Mao's exposure to the barbarities of his contemporary world, the harder he became in outlook. He could be moved by what he saw, as his reaction to the Hunan famine and to the savagery of the warlords showed, but what activated him was the idea that the suffering could be ended only by destroying the system that had created it.

Greatly influenced by Western ideas though Mao was, he did not think in Western humanitarian terms. His compassion was not of the type that leads people to commit their lives to the relief of the poor and the afflicted. Mao was no latter-day Francis of Assisi or precursor of Mother Theresa. He saw poverty and suffering as the products of a social system which, being based on power and privilege, would never reform itself. The role of revolutionaries, therefore, was to speed the historical process by which such systems were overthrown. Mao believed that the dynamic of history meant that China was destined for regeneration; the task of Chinese revolutionaries was to clear away the encumbrances that blocked the path. That is what, after his initial hesitations, drew him to Marxism and led to his being a founder-member of the CCP in 1921.

2

MAO THE COMMUNIST AND NATIONALIST, 1921–30

The freedom and unity of China must be based on an ideology that has been produced in Chinese conditions. Academic thought and academic research is worthless dross unless it is in the service of the demands of the masses.

Mao Zedong, January 1926

MAO EMBRACES MARXISM

Mao Zedong did not become a revolutionary because he was a Communist; he became a Communist because he was a revolutionary. The 4 May movement in China created a political and intellectual clamour in which the dominant theme was the regeneration of the nation through collective endeavour. It was an atmosphere which excited Mao and into which Marxism easily fitted. The first detailed reference in China to Marxist theories had been in an article by a British missionary in the *Globe Magazine*, published in Shanghai in 1899. A number of Chinese progressives had subsequently alluded to it, but it was not until the period of the First World War that Marxism began to be considered seriously. This was largely due to the writings of Chen Duxiu and Li Dazhao, the leading lights in New Culture, an organisation which sought the rebirth of China through democracy and science. Chen, whom Mao later acknowledged as 'the supreme commander' of the 4 May movement,[1] argued that the 1914–18 war had raised large question marks against the value and durability of Western capitalist culture. He held that science, which for him included political science, was the key to the transforming of China from a feudal to a modern society while avoiding the failings of capitalism. He believed that events in Russia had shown how this could be done. Democracy, the establishment of the will of the people, had been achieved by Lenin's Bolshevik party by applying the scientific principles of Marxism. Chen saw the Russian Revolution of 1917 as the first sign of the breakdown of the West's stability and dominance.

New Youth, a radical journal which may be regarded as the voice of the 4 May movement, committed itself to the Marxist cause in 1919. Its chief editor, Li Dazhao, explained why the journal had taken this momentous step. His reference point was also the October Revolution, which he viewed as primarily a blow against imperialism. One of the first declarations of the Bolsheviks after taking power in 1917 had been to renounce all claims to non-Russian territory. This vivid demonstration of anti-imperialism resonated powerfully in China. It appealed to all those radicals who believed that the first step towards real change in their country had to be its liberation from foreign domination. For them, the finer points of Marxist ideology were less important than the central thrust of the Marxist message as presented by the Bolsheviks; namely, that by collective effort the existing social and political system could be overthrown and China liberated.

Mao Zedong's commitment to Marxism as a distinct ideology can be quite accurately dated. He had come into contact with both Chen Duxiu and Li Dazhao while at Beijing University, but it was under the promptings of his friend, Cai Hesen, that he began to give close attention to Marxist theories. Since 1919, Cai Hesen, in whose house the New People's Study Society had been founded in 1918, had consistently urged Mao to become a Communist and had recommended key Marxist texts to him. Mao studied these and was particularly impressed by the *Communist Manifesto*, which he read in 1920. Yet late in December of that year, he still regarded 'a Russian-style revolution . . . [only] as a last resort when all other means have been exhausted.'[2] However, writing again to Cai on 21 January 1921, Mao declared that he had abandoned the anarchism to which he had previously been drawn and now accepted that the Marxist revolutionary path was the only way forward for China. It was necessary to struggle for the establishment of a proletarian dictatorship, for 'without achieving political power, it is impossible to launch, maintain, and carry through the revolution'.[3]

By revolution, Mao understood the process by which China would be purified through the destruction of its internal and external enemies. From the beginning, therefore, Communism for him was a universal means adapted to a Chinese end. Mao had found a philosophy and a programme that fitted the violent times in China. It is interesting that Mao specifically rejected the argument of Bertrand Russell, the British philosopher and pacifist, who had given a lecture in Hunan in 1920 in which he had claimed that communism could be established in China through education, not violent revolution.

The Marxism espoused by Chen Duxiu and Li Dazhao had a two-fold attraction for Mao: it was scientific and it was anti-imperialist. His own writings had begun to exhibit a growing conviction that China must embrace science. When Chen Duxiu had been arrested in Beijing in June 1919 for his outspoken attacks on the corruption of the Republican government, Mao had written a passionate article in his defence, describing Chen as 'a bright star in the world of thought'. Mao used the opportunity to define China's current predicament.

> China today can be said to be in an extremely dangerous situation. The danger does not result from military weakness. . . . The real danger lies in the total emptiness and rottenness of the mental universe of the entire Chinese people. They superstitiously believe in spirits and ghosts, in fortune-telling, in fate, in despotism. There is absolutely no recognition of the individual, of self, of truth. This is because scientific thought has not developed.[4]

Chen's emphasis upon the pattern underlying the Russian Revolution appealed to Mao's sense of historical order. Inspired though he was as a fighter for Hunan independence, Mao was eager to set events in China into a wider context. He was a looking for a bigger unifying cause. This was very evident in the discussions in which he participated in 1920 in the Cultural Book Society. Mao and his fellow members laboured for hours over defining their aims. The leitmotif of Mao's contributions was that the autonomy of Hunan, however worthy an objective, was as nothing compared with needs of China overall. He spoke of his desire 'to transform China and the world'.[5]

In an influential article of 1918, 'The Victory of Bolshevism', Li Dazhao had urged that the Russian Revolution be read as a defeat for imperialism. This found a ready response in Mao. His earlier sympathies had lain with Germany rather than Russia. Like most radicals in China, Mao considered that the defeated Germans had been unfairly treated under the Versailles Treaty in 1919. The loss of territory and peoples that Germany had been forced to accept was on a par with the foreign impositions that China had had to endure since the 1840s, culminating in the Allies' handing of Qingdao to Japan in 1919. However, Mao quickly came to accept that the Bolsheviks, by abandoning Russia's links with the Allies and making a separate peace with Germany in 1918, had struck what he saw as a historic blow against Western capitalism.

Mao's adoption of Marxism came at a point of personal crisis. His commitment to the new cause showed a resolve which he felt he had previously lacked. In 1921, he berated himself for having wasted too much time in unproductive thinking:

> I have a very great defect . . . I constantly have the wrong attitude and always argue, so that people detest me. You might call this my strong will, but in fact it is a manifestation of my weakness. I have long since learned that on earth only those who attain complete greatness can be most firm.
>
> In the past two and a half years virtually all the time I have spent in self-cultivation has been wasted. I have gone to extremes in reasoning, I have tended to be over critical in viewing people, and my attempts at thorough self-examination have been almost completely useless.[6]

Mao's breast beating anticipates the lacerating self-criticism sessions that were to prove such a terrifying feature of the rectification campaigns and the Cultural Revolution. (See below, pages 186–7.)

THE FOUNDING OF THE CHINESE COMMUNIST PARTY

The formal adoption of Marxism in China came in July 1921 with the creation in Shanghai of the Chinese Communist Party (CCP). For some two years prior to that, a variety of Marxist groups had been formed in Shanghai and Beijing, and in a number of other provincial towns. Mao's first practical contribution to the movement, once he had declared himself a Communist, was his setting up of two organisations in Hunan: the

Socialist Youth League and the Hunan Self-Study University. The purpose of both organisations was to spread Marxist ideas among students and intellectuals and to promote strikes and disruption among Hunan workers. It was in recognition of Mao's work in Hunan that Li Dazhao invited him to Shanghai in July 1921 to attend the 'First National Congress of the Communist Party of China'. Mao joined eleven other representatives from sundry provinces.

Also in attendance were two Comintern (Communist International) agents, Maring and Nicolsky. Their presence marked an early success for the Comintern, the Moscow-based agency, which had been created in 1919 with the purpose of promoting Soviet interests through international revolution. From its beginning, the Comintern had taken a close interest in developments in China and Maring had been instrumental in persuading the Chinese Marxists to form themselves into a party. The Comintern was to continue to play a significant role in the development of Chinese Communism.

According to the fragmentary minutes of its inaugural meeting, the CCP resolved:

> to overthrow the bourgeoisie by means of the revolutionary army of the proletariat . . . to establish the dictatorship of the proletariat in order to attain the objective of class struggle, that is, the elimination of classes . . . to abolish private ownership of capital.[7]

These ambitious aims were not, however, accompanied by a programme for their implementation. The new party recognised that as yet it was too small; it would have to co-operate with the existing radical parties in the immediate struggle against 'the common enemy', its term for the warlords. For the moment, the CCP chose to concentrate its energies on agitation among the factory workers. Mao returned to Hunan to continue his activities as a strike organiser. He warned the employers that if they did not give in to worker demands they would be overthrown as the capitalists of Russia had been. In his relations with the Hunan unions, which consisted of such groups as railway workers, textile hands, masons, and printers, Mao urged that, besides fighting for better pay and conditions, their prime objective should be to develop their 'class consciousness'.[8] To encourage them in this, Mao told them to take inspiration from 'the establishment of a worker-peasant state in Soviet Russia'.[9]

Mao's efforts as a labour agitator had considerable success. He listed ten major strikes in which he had been the chief organiser, claiming than nine had been successful. The one failure was the '7 February Massacre' in 1923. This dramatic term described the crushing of a general strike of railway workers by pro-government troops led by a warlord, Wu Peifu, who had first befriended the strikers and then betrayed them. On behalf of the strikers, Mao addressed Wu Peifu, whose orders had led to the killing of thirty-five of the workers. He told him that the time would soon come when the soldiers who had fired on the strikers would turn their weapons on the warlords themselves. Did not Wu Peifu and the other warlords realise that '390 million of our 400 million people are rebels'?[10]

Despite these bold words, Mao knew that the 7 February Massacre had contained a number of hard lessons. It had re-emphasised the necessity of the CCP's working with other radical groups; the Communists were not yet sufficiently influential to succeed on their own. The failure of the strike had also shown that belief in a proletarian revolution was premature. China's industrial workers simply lacked the numbers and resources to offer a serious challenge to the existing system. Mao's conclusion was that given the residual strength of the Beijing government, the existence of powerful warlord armies, and the weakness of the workers, the only way of fulfilling Communist objectives was through armed struggle. To this end it was vital that the two major revolutionary forces in China, the Guomindang (GMD) and the CCP, should ally with each other.

THE CCP–GMD UNITED FRONT

What made the plan for a radical alliance realistic was that the hostility that later developed between the CCP and GMD was not apparent at this stage. In the early days, what united the Communists and the Nationalists was weightier than what separated them. Both were revolutionary organisations, whose essential first purpose was the same – the regeneration of China. That was why it was possible for a Chinese revolutionary to be a member of both organisations.

It was such reasoning that led Mao, early in 1923, to follow in the footsteps of Chen Duxiu and Li Dazhao and join the GMD. He thus demonstrated his belief that CCP co-operation with the Guomindang was a necessary prelude to a Communist revolution. This was also the line of argument being pushed by the Comintern. The succession of agents who were sent to China after 1921 consistently argued that, whatever the long-term hopes of the young CCP, the reality of the Chinese situation made alliance with the GMD a necessity. There were some CCP members who were unhappy with this. They voiced their objections at the Third Congress of the CCP in June 1923. Mao attacked the doubters, restating his view that a CCP–GMD alliance was needed for the achievement of 'a national revolution'. According to the notes which Maring, the Comintern agent, made at the congress, Mao accepted that the GMD was drawn from China's petty bourgeoisie of financiers and merchants, who were pursuing their own selfish interests, but he had no doubt that, once they had played their role in bringing down the existing system, they could be discarded by the true Communist proletarian revolutionaries.[11]

It was also at the Third Congress that Mao raised another critical issue – the CCP's relations with the peasants. Since 85 per cent of China's people were peasants, it was obviously essential that the party fashion a policy that defined the role to be played by them. The Russian model did not help here. The official Soviet line was that the peasants could not be a truly dynamic force in a proletarian revolution; that role was restricted to the industrial workers. Up to 1923, Mao, although a peasant himself, had been involved politically only with intellectuals and workers. Yet, at the congress, he declared that coming from Hunan, a province where peasants 'filled the mountains and fields', he was very conscious that throughout Chinese history all rebellions had had 'peasant insurrections as their mainstay'. The CCP, therefore, must enrol the peasantry in its ranks. Mao drew up a resolution committing the Communist Party not simply to accommodating the peasants but to making them central to its policies. He proposed that the CCP:

> gather together small peasants, sharecroppers, and farm labourers to resist the imperialists who control China, to overthrow the warlords and corrupt officials, and to resist the local ruffians and bad gentry, so as to protect the interests of the peasants and to promote the national revolutionary movement.[12]

As a member of both the CCP and the GMD, Mao worked to bring about a genuine alliance between them. As secretary of the CCP's Central Committee, he wrote to Sun Yatsen suggesting ways in which the two parties could develop closer ties and combine their recruitment methods.

He appealed to Sun to abandon the GMD's links with the southern war-lords, whose crimes Mao described as being as vicious as those perpetrated by their counterparts in the north. He went so far as to propose that Sun, in order to make himself a truly national figure, should leave his Guangzhou base and move to Shanghai. There he could convene a national assembly and become the leader of a centralised revolutionary army. There is no record of Sun's response.

The Comintern gave as much attention to the Guomindang as it did to the CCP. It was at the urging of Mikhail Borodin, who came directly from Moscow in 1923, that Sun Yatsen accepted the primacy of the Soviet revolutionary model and began to restructure the GMD along Leninist lines. The result was that Sun's party moved towards the notion of central-ised democracy which involved greater power going to the leaders and stronger control being exercised over the members. One of the important changes of direction that the Comintern had pressed upon the GMD was that it should concentrate its revolutionary activities in the urban areas of China. The GMD had thus begun to weaken its links with the peasants at the very time the CCP had chosen to cultivate them.

In January 1924, Mao travelled south to Guangzhou to attend the first congress of the reshaped Leninist GMD. His reputation preceded him. His work as a strike organiser and his political writings were making him known in radical circles throughout China. His opinions were beginning to carry weight. He had gained plaudits for a series of articles in which he had attacked the imperialism of the foreign powers in China. He had been especially scornful of the way the Beijing government's trading with Britain, the USA, and Japan left those countries free to 'squeeze out more of the blood and fat of the Chinese people'. Mao had quoted a current saying, 'The Chinese government is the counting house of our foreign masters.'[13]

The GMD congress, which was chaired by Sun Yatsen, issued a manifesto restating its commitment to the Three People's Principles – nationalism, democracy, and socialism. Sun in his keynote address declared that it was time to arouse the masses to fight for independence for China. Mao made a number of proposals to the congress, including a suggestion that the parties should combine to set up an alternative government to the one in Beijing. Mao was elected to the Central Bureau of the GMD, which meant that he now held executive posts in both of China's revolutionary parties.

The GMD–CCP united front was to hold for the next four years, 1924–27, a period sometimes referred by Chinese radicals as 'the Great Revolution'. The front's aim was conveyed in a popular song of the day: 'Let us overthrow the imperialist powers and eliminate the warlords.' Throughout the period, Mao worked for the development of the CCP and GMD both as individual and allied parties. This was not always easy. Despite the formal union, there were members in each of the parties who looked on the other with distrust. A complication was that the Guomindang began to divide into two distinct wings: the left GMD which favoured close links with the Communists, and the centre-right GMD, which felt no affinity with the Communists but was prepared to use them for the time being. This was a mirror image of the attitude that Mao had earlier expressed when saying that despite its bourgeois character the GMD should be accepted as an ally for the time being, but then abandoned when it no longer served a revolutionary purpose.

There is some uncertainty about Mao's real attitude. One Russian source suggests that Mao's first move, after he left Guangzhou for Shanghai in March 1924 to carry out recruitment for the GMD, was to assure a meeting of the Socialist Youth League that the Guomindang was a truly revolutionary force which merited its membership of the Comintern.[14] Another Russian source, however, has it that in July 1924 Mao had joined Chen Duxiu in urging the CCP to consider severing its connection with the Guomindang.[15] There is no surviving document to substantiate this. There is, however, a written CCP statement of the same month, bearing Mao's signature, which warned Communist Party members that a CCP–GMD split might well occur: 'overt and covert attacks on us and attempts to push us out have been mounting daily on the part of a majority of Guomindang members.'[16]

Whatever misgivings Mao may have had, he continued to work for the GMD. During the next eighteen months he travelled frequently between Shanghai and Guangzhou, and to Hunan and Anyuan, creating and liaising with worker and peasant unions. In October 1925, he took on the role of organiser of the Guomindang's peasant training department, which meant he also became editor of the *Political Weekly*, the GMD's main journal. In a four-month period, he wrote some twenty articles for it. This was in addition to his other work as propaganda agent with its demanding administrative duties. Such was the intensity of Mao's labours, that early in 1926 he wrote to the GMD requesting a period of leave, so that he could recover from what he called his 'mental ailment'.

It was a term he had used before; in May 1924, he had formally asked the CCP's People's Education Committee to be released from his work for a time. Some writers have taken the term as evidence that Mao suffered from a neurological disorder.[17] However, what is equally possible is that Mao simply cited his 'mental ailment' as a shorthand for saying that he had too much work to do. That was the view of his fellow editor of the *Political Weekly*, Mao Dun, who recorded that Mao claimed to be ill whenever he wanted a break from official duties. This was not out of a desire for leisure; Mao wanted to be away from work in order to involve himself in what he called the peasant question. He used his free time to study the peasants at first hand in his own province of Hunan. It was a sign, perhaps, of his growing conviction that only through the mobilising of the peasantry could a Communist revolution be achieved in China.[18]

THE 30 MAY INCIDENT, 1925

What gives added interest to the question of Mao's motives is that it had been during one of Mao's extended breaks that the 30 May Incident of 1925 had occurred. He was not, therefore, immediately caught up in the excitement that this event engendered. As a date, 30 May 1925 has a similar place among Chinese revolutionaries as 4 May 1919. The incident began with a demonstration in Shanghai against the shooting of a Chinese worker by guards at a Japanese-owned cotton mill. The British commander of the international settlement in the city ordered his police force to disperse the demonstrators by firing over their heads. In the confusion his instructions were misunderstood and some twelve protesters were killed by rifle bullets. As news of the tragedy spread across China, a series of further demonstrations and strikes broke out. An 'Avenge the Shame' movement sprang up in a number of provinces. Protest banners bore such slogans as 'Down with Imperialism' and 'Abolish the Unequal Treaties'. Foreign nationals and premises were attacked and Guangzhou and Shanghai were the scenes of serious disturbances. Order was eventually re-established but the authorities, Chinese and international, had been badly shaken.

The beneficiaries of all this were the revolutionary parties. They claimed that their anti-imperialist, anti-government stance had been vindicated. The incident also strengthened the case for the GMD–CCP alliance, by illustrating the need for unity and military strength if the forces oppressing China were to be overcome. By another remarkable coincidence, the 30 May Incident had occurred only two months after the death of Sun Yatsen. His successor, Chiang Kai-shek, thus became leader of the GMD at a critical, and for him, highly opportune moment. In 1924, Chiang had been appointed commander of the Whampoa Military Academy at Guangzhou, the GMD's military headquarters. The belligerent national mood created by the 30 May Incident meant that his military standing was a major advantage to him in overcoming his political rivals in the jockeying for power within the GMD after Sun's death.

Sun Yatsen's passing had another major consequence. With his moderating influence gone, the anti-Communists within the Guomindang became predominant. Chiang Kai-shek represented the centre-right, the wing of the party that, being drawn largely from the urban middle class, had never been happy with the social revolutionary policies of the Communists. Although personally loyal to Sun, Chiang had disapproved of his predecessor's tactic of absorbing the Reds into the GMD. Despite going to Moscow in the early 1920s for revolutionary training, Chiang had not accepted Marxism as an ideology or the Soviet Union as a political model. His particular sense of patriotism led him to believe that the nation's freedoms could best be won by cultivating China's contacts with successful Western capitalists. Such views meant that for Chiang the Chinese Communists were a threat that at some point in the development of the revolution would have to be destroyed. It followed that, once he had become head of the Guomindang, the days of the CCP–GMD alliance were numbered.

However, although his ultimate goal was the obliteration of the Communists, Chiang had a short-term use for them. The GMD's authority was restricted to the southern provinces. Large parts of central and northern China were still dominated by warlords. Any vestiges of authority that the Republican government in Beijing had held finally vanished in 1924 when the city had fallen to the armies of the warlord, Feng Yuxiang. Although the GMD often colluded with various warlords, including Feng, it was obvious that the Guomindang could not achieve full national power until warlord rule had been broken. The omens were propitious; the mood of national bitterness created by the events of 30 May made many Chinese willing supporters of a campaign against warlordism, which for over a decade had disfigured the nation. Chiang Kai-shek decided, therefore, to maintain the link with the Communists so that they could contribute to an allied campaign – the Northern Expedition – against the warlords.

These developments, which had occurred during Mao's temporary detachment from the centre of politics, did not lessen his commitment once he had returned. One of his first moves was to join the Hunan branch of the 'Avenge the Shame' movement. Such was the keenness with which Mao agitated that Zhao Hengti, the military governor of Hunan, sent a secret message to the police in Xiantan ordering Mao's arrest and execution. Fortunately for Mao, a clerk in the governor's office, who happened to be a friend of Mao's family, leaked the message to him, giving him time to hide. Having survived the scare, Mao continued to work enthusiastically for the GMD under its new leader. He shared the platform with Chiang Kai-shek at a number of Guomindang meetings in 1926, and although this did not betoken any real personal contact between them there were no signs at this stage of the mutual antipathy that would subsequently develop. Mao seems to have believed that Chiang in all key respects was continuing Sun Yatsen's policies. Mao also judged that by working closely with the Guomindang and its leaders he could keep it on a leftward course. Hindsight shows that this was a naive calculation, but it was also the orthodox Comintern thinking of the time.

MAO AND THE PEASANT QUESTION

There were two outstanding features of Mao's speeches and writings in 1926 after he had returned to full political activity. One was his plea that the struggle between the opposed wings of the Guomindang be ended. Mao claimed that the GMD split was an affront to the Chinese people who were demanding an end of factionalism. 'Wherever we go nowadays, the slogan we hear is almost always "Revolutionaries of the whole country unite."' For Mao there was but one solution. The rightist elements among the Nationalists, who wanted to break with the Chinese Communists and with the Comintern, must give way to the left, who wanted to preserve unity. Compromise was out of the question. 'There is absolutely no third way.'[19]

The second feature was the attention he gave to the peasant question. Clearly, his period away from the centre of politics studying the Hunan peasantry had given a powerful direction to his revolutionary thinking. He told his colleagues: 'We have concentrated too much on urban dwellers and neglected the peasantry.'[20] He was now convinced that the economic and social backwardness of China meant that its revolution had to be a peasant movement:

> China now has not yet gone beyond the agricultural economy and peasant production, and the peasants account for as much as 90 percent of the total productive output. If we wish to carry out [Sun Yatsen's] Three People's Principles, the first thing is to liberate the peasants. . . . China's national revolution is, to put it plainly, a peasant revolution.[21]

In a series of major reports and articles he wrote for the CCP and the GMD in 1926, Mao developed his argument that the monopoly of resources enjoyed by the landlords rendered them all powerful. They formed the ruling class and it was on them that warlordism and foreign domination ultimately rested. Consequently, a revolution aimed at modernising China had to begin in the countryside with war against the landlords. He did not discount the importance of revolutionary struggle in the urban areas but 'if the peasants do not rise and fight in the villages to overthrow the privileges of the feudal-patriarchal landlord class, the power of the warlords and imperialism can never be hurled down.'[22] He believed that once the peasants gained a true class awareness that their present desperate state was the result of centuries of landlord oppression, they would become an unstoppable force.

The climax to Mao's examination of the peasant question came early in 1927, when, building on the material he had amassed in a series of field studies over the previous three years, he produced his *Report on the Peasant Movement in Hunan*. The work was undoubtedly a major piece of social research and became part of Communist lore. It was first presented to the CCP Central Committee before being published in instalments in the magazine, *Soldier*. The report was a meticulously detailed Hunan domesday book. It classified the peasants into a range of economic categories and provided descriptions, often in tabulated form, of the resources, income, living and working conditions, local customs, religious and superstitions rites, and land distribution. It also examined the attitudes and expectations of the peasants and dwelt on the subjugation of women.

His report made no attempt to hide the harsh treatment meted out to the 'bad gentry' by the peasants when they had the opportunity. Mao saw the violent revolts in which the gentry were stamped underfoot as acts of retribution for centuries of landlord tyranny. Not merely was this to be condoned; it was an essential part of the revolutionary process. In a chilling passage, Mao introduced an argument that he was to repeat throughout his career whenever he wished to justify the use of terror:

> All excessive actions have revolutionary significance . . . it is necessary to bring about a reign of terror in every rural area; otherwise we could never suppress the activities of the counterrevolutionaries in the countryside or overthrow the authority of the gentry. To right a wrong it is necessary to exceed the proper limits; the wrong cannot be righted without doing so.[23]

Mao's purpose in producing so detailed an analysis was to give weight to what he then recommended. He told the CCP that the countryside was witnessing a rising against the landlords and local gentry in which the peasant masses were beginning to achieve their historical mission. 'What Mr Sun Yatsen wanted, but failed, to accomplish in the forty years he devoted to the national revolution, the peasants have accomplished in a few months.' In a notable passage, which the Communist editors of Mao's works were to omit in 1950 lest it put the urban revolutionaries in a bad light, the report stated:

> If we allot ten points to the accomplishments of the democratic revolution, then the achievements of the city dwellers rate only three points, while the remaining seven points should go to the peasants in their rural revolution.[24]

Mao cited the dramatic developments in the countryside to impress upon his Communist colleagues that they were out of touch with the revolutionary masses. He referred to the pioneering work of Peng Pai who, even before joining the CCP, had in the early 1920s led the peasants in a sustained campaign of land seizures against the landlords in Guangdong province. Mao urged his comrades to build upon such achievements. Let them look upon the peasantry as the vanguard of the revolution and work actively with the peasant associations, listening to their grievances, and reducing their rents and debts.

The significance that Mao ascribed to the peasants as revolutionaries represents a fascinating gloss on Marxist theory. Strictly interpreted, the dialectic of class conflict determined that revolution had to move through progressive stages, culminating in the anti-bourgeois rising of the proletariat. Notwithstanding the uncomfortable fact that Russian Revolution had not conformed to this pattern, the ern agents insisted that the bourgeoisie in China could be overthrown only by the proletariat, not by the peasants. Hence the agents' concentration on the need to organise the urban revolutionaries. Mao cut through such theorising with striking simplicity. He calculated the strength of the revolutionary impulse not in terms of abstract theory but as a measure of the oppression that real people suffered. As he saw it, the Chinese industrial workers, though abused by their employers, did have some means of alleviating their conditions; his experience as a strike organiser had shown him that. But no such possibility of improvement was available to the mass of the peasants. Their condition was wretched, made so by centuries of landlord exploitation. They lived 'a worse life than that of the tenant peasants in any other country in the world'.[25] Since they could not improve themselves within the system which enslaved them, their only recourse was to destroy it. Such was Mao's rationale for demanding that the CCP make the awakening of peasant consciousness the prime objective. It was an approach that was bound to lead to conflict with Chiang Kai-shek's Guomindang.

THE NORTHERN EXPEDITION, 1926–28

Within two years of the Northern Expedition's launching in Guangdong in March 1926, united front armies had imposed themselves on the eastern and northern provinces and broken the back of warlord resistance. By surrounding and isolating the individual warlord armies, the CCP–GMD forces were able to pick them off separately and defeat them, even though this sometimes involved savage and costly fighting. By the summer of 1927, the vital cities of Wuhan and Shanghai had been taken by united front forces. When Beijing fell in 1928, with the withdrawal of Zhang Zuolin, Chiang's Nationalists claimed that they were now the legitimate republican government of China. Nanjing was declared to be the new national capital. Mao had played his part in the GMD victory. The close relations that he had developed with the peasant associations in Hunan proved highly valuable when he was commissioned to organise the united front forces in the province. In 1926 he helped prepare the way for the western units of the allied army to sweep through Guanxi and Hunan, and drive the troops of the local warlord, Zhao Hengti, across the Yangxi

River. At a special reception in Changsha at the end of the year, Mao was honoured as 'a son of Hunan' for his efforts. He later observed that his success owed much to the quality and attitude of the troops who fought under the joint banner of the GMD and CCP: 'there was unity between officers and men and between the army and the people, and the army was filled with a revolutionary militancy.'[26]

Yet, whatever pride Mao and the CCP could take in their contribution to the Northern Expedition, the fact was that Chiang Kai-shek had outwitted them. His calculation had been that he needed the CCP in the countryside and in the urban areas to provide the organisation and to raise the necessary troops to fight the warlords. This support had been forthcoming. Whatever the reservations of some of its leaders, the CCP had played a vital role in the crushing of the warlords. As well as providing troops, the Communists had worked to destabilise the warlord areas by strikes, boycotts, and sabotage.

With the objectives of the Northern Expedition achieved, Chiang Kai-shek then began what proved to be a near-lethal assault on the CCP. He had made clear anti-Communist moves as early as March 1926 when he had demanded adjustments in GMD organisation so as to reduce the influence of the Communist members. Mao was one of those directly affected by this; he lost his post on the Central Bureau. But, since he still kept his position as peasant organiser, he seems not to have been unduly concerned. He viewed such reshuffles within the GMD as a response to the needs of the Northern Expedition. Yet, as the year wore on, Chiang's true intentions became increasingly evident. He began to purge the Guomindang of both its Communist and its left-wing members. The Comintern agents were told to leave or face arrest. Wang Jingwei, the GMD's leading pro-Communist and Chiang's main rival in the party, was ousted from office.

By the end of 1926 the Communists at last began to stir themselves into a response. Their major problem was that insofar as there was an orthodox line on the CCP–GMD issue it was the one dictated by Stalin and the Comintern. Even as they were being subjected to Chiang's fierce purges, the word from Moscow was to maintain the united front. Stalin stubbornly kept his faith in Chiang Kai-shek as a genuine 'revolutionary' even as the GMD began wiping out the Communists.

Chen Duxiu, the CCP leader, had been initially sceptical of the idea of a united front but he had faithfully conformed to Comintern instructions not to withdraw from it. He continued in this way in spite of Chiang's onslaught. Mao, for his part, was slow to the point of reluctance to give up on the united front. His preoccupation with the peasant question meant he played relatively little attention to the party debate. But he did broadly support Chen in continuing to co-operate with the GMD. The complication was that there was more than one GMD. Chiang and the centre-rightists were dominant in Guangdong, while the leftists under Wang Jingwei held sway in Wuhan.

Throughout the Northern Expedition Mao had remained committed to its victory. This made party disputes appear secondary; the need was to defeat the warlords and thus spread the revolutionary message across China. At this stage, the intricacies of the CCP debates were of less interest to him than his study of the peasants. This is worth stressing since the official CCP line later was that Mao had opposed the united front once he saw the way Chiang was tending and realised that Chen Duxiu was backing the wrong policy. But this rewriting of the record made Mao's position appear more consistent than it had been. The united front period was a confusing one; although there was the odd occasion in 1926 when Mao and the leading CCP members seemed willing to resist Chiang, the Comintern military agents advised against it. The result was that the CCP asked its members to overlook the apparent threats from the Nationalists. Mao co-operated by toning down the demands he had made when presenting his peasant reports to the party.

THE WHITE TERROR, 1927–28

On 5 April 1927, Chen Duxiu issued a formal statement telling the CCP not to believe rumours that Chiang intended to expel the CCP and crush the trade unions. Seven days later, Chiang did precisely that when he unleashed what became known as the 'White Terror', his attempted annihilation of the Communists. The centre of the attack was Shanghai. It was there that the CCP had helped organise a powerful trade union movement and a workers' militia, which had proved highly effective in sabotaging the local warlord's forces and thus easing the way for the advance of the Nationalist forces into Shanghai. Yet within days of his triumphant entry into the city, Chiang had turned on those who had helped prepare his path. To destroy his opponents, he exploited his close connections with the bosses of Shanghai's underworld. The city's gangsters and triads were offered immunity in return for information on the Communists. Chiang's troops then went on the rampage. Cheered on by Shanghai's businessmen and traders, who wanted the trade unions brought low, and applauded by the foreign nationals in the concession areas, who had been frightened by anti-imperialist demonstrations in the city, Chiang's forces hunted down and shot 5,000 known Communists and their sympathisers. A campaign to annihilate the Communists had begun.

In a repetition of what had happened in Shanghai, purges were carried out by Nationalist armies in a number of other cities, including Guangzhou. The most notable killing occurred in Beijing with the slow strangulation of Li Dazhao, Mao's Marxist mentor. Hunan suffered particularly savage attacks; deaths in the province during the White Terror were estimated at a quarter of a million. For Mao, the worst excesses occurred in his home city of Changsha during 'the Horse Day Incident'. The garrison commander, in retaliation for what he viewed as CCP-inspired terrorism, instituted a blood letting in which some 3,000 suspected Communists were killed. Mao related the events in stomach-churning detail:

> The brutal punishments inflicted on the revolutionary peasants by the despotic gentry include such things as gouging out eyes and ripping out tongues, disembowelling and decapitation, slashing with knives and grinding with sand, burning with kerosene and branding with red-hot irons. In the case of women, they would run string through their breasts and parade them naked in public, or simply hack them to pieces.[27]

The CCP's initial response to the launching of the White Terror in April 1927 was an angry statement, to which Mao was a signatory, condemning Chiang Kai-shek for behaving like the worst of the warlords. A traitor to the memory Sun Yatsen, Chiang was seeking power for himself. He had ordered his 'running dogs' to persecute and butcher CCP and left-GMD members. In league with the foreign oppressors of China, Chiang Kai-shek had become an arch counter-revolutionary. The statement ended with a call for the revolutionary popular masses to rid themselves of 'the scum of this party, and the swindler of the people'.[28]

THE AUTUMN HARVEST RISING, 1927

It was in a newly defiant spirit that the CCP took on Chiang's armies in a straight fight. Eight areas were chosen for counter-attack. It was an ambitious but hopeless venture. None of the campaigns launched against the Nationalists in the later months of 1927 succeeded. Having been instructed by the CCP's Central Committee to organise resistance in Hunan, Mao built his campaign on his knowledge of the peasantry. He originally intended to raise a force of 10,000. In the event, he gathered barely a third of that number. According to one Nationalist description, his force was a motley gathering, of 'riffraffs, desperadoes and deserters'.[29] The Autumn Harvest Rising, as Mao's Hunan venture became known, occurred in August and September. Although an assault on Changsha formed the centrepiece, the rising was not a single movement but a number of unco-ordinated skirmishes in which Mao's units were easily overcome.

According to Mao's own account of the rising, it was at the end of one engagement near Changsha that he came very near to being executed. He described how, after being captured by GMD troops, he was told that would be shot. Having first tried to bribe his guards to release him, he seized a moment to escape. He hid in tall grass and waited breathlessly until the search for him was called off. Befriended by a sympathetic peasant, he eventually found his way back to his comrades.

The Autumn Harvest Rising was an obvious failure militarily, but it was not entirely disastrous for Mao. It was his first direct experience of military leadership and he learned much from it. It confirmed the warning he had given to the Emergency Conference of the CCP that the party was too blithe in assuming that a mass movement somehow just happened, as if spontaneously. The defeat of the Autumn Harvest Rising, together with the crushing of the Communist insurrection in Nanchang in Jiangxi province, had shown the necessity of the CCP's possessing an effective army. 'One of the Party's mistakes in the past was that it neglected the military. Now we must pay sixty per cent of our attention to the military movement. Unless we preserve our own armed forces we shall be helpless.'[30] In one of his best-known sayings, Mao observed 'political power is obtained from the barrel of the gun'. He added 'it will not be enough to rely on the power of the peasants alone. There must be military support.'[31]

To Mao's enthusiasm for peasant action had been added the sombre realisation that unless the peasants were led by able officers they could not be successful. One of his difficulties was that in the early stages the officers invariably came from the bourgeois-landlord classes. The political problem of getting them to lead an essentially peasant movement was considerable, something which Mao had become especially aware of during the Autumn Harvest Rising. The party could not be simply a political body; it had to be an army and had to produce its own officers. Ten years earlier Mao had been certain that revolution was possible without recourse to violence: persuasion and education would be sufficient. Practical experience had changed his mind. Circumstances required that to be a revolutionary he also had to be a soldier. For the next two decades his understanding of revolution in China would develop within the context of constant, often desperate, military campaigning.

By the end of 1927, Communism was on the run. By that time even Stalin had accepted that the CCP's alliance with Chiang's Nationalists had not worked as a method of establishing Soviet-style socialism in China. But he was unapologetic. He simply suggested that the Communists switch their support to the left GMD in Wuhan. As the CCP retreated on all fronts, the recriminations within the party began. Chen Duxiu came in for the strongest censure for having compromised the CCP's existence by his readiness to make concessions to Chiang's Guomindang. At Moscow's insistence, Chen was dismissed and replaced as leader by Qu Qiubai. This was more than a touch unjust since Chen had invariably acted on Comintern orders. The later official CCP verdict on this episode was telling: 'the Comintern and its representatives in China ultimately failed to understand the actual conditions in China. . . . It was difficult for the immature Chinese Party to reject the mistaken guidance of the Comintern'.[32]

At the time, Mao Zedong was also severely criticised. A meeting of the Central Committee in November 1927 declared that he carried 'the most serious responsibility' for the failure of the Autumn Harvest Rising. His fault was 'military adventurism', a reference to what were deemed his rash offensive tactics and disregard of orders from the centre. To back its criticism, the Central Committee removed Mao from the Politburo and the Hunan Provincial Committee.

JINGGANGSHAN AND JIANGXI

Mao was not present to hear his dismissal. He had already 'gone to the mountains'. In October, he had led his straggling band of a thousand survivors from the Autumn Harvest Rising south to the remote Jinggang mountains that straddled the Hunan–Jiangxi border. He was helped in this by the contacts he made with Wang Zuo and Yuan Wencai, two ex-warlord generals who had developed Communist sympathies. They used their local knowledge to direct Mao to Maoping, a remote area which offered a temporary refuge. It was difficult terrain but for a year it provided Mao's forces with a defensible base from which they could make occasional sallies against the enemy. However, it was a hard area to keep provisioned and as the pressure of Nationalist attacks intensified, it became clear that another base would have to be found. In January 1929 Mao took his forces 150 miles south-east to Ruijin in Jiangxi province. By then he had already been joined by the troops led by Zhu De and Peng Dehuai.

This combined force took the title of the Fourth Army of the Workers' and Peasants' Red Army. Zhu De was a tough little fighter with an opium addiction. Having participated in the 1911 Revolution and then fought for various warlords, he had gone on to receive military training in Germany and the USSR, before joining the CCP in 1926. Zhu was recognised as commander-in-chief, with Mao as party representative, though he, too, was invariably referred to as commander. In the joint directives they issued Mao signed himself as 'political commissar'. They came to be regarded as working so closely together that many peasants believed that Zhu-Mao was one person. However, far from being as one, Mao and Zhu argued fiercely and frequently over troop movements and tactics.

In a contrary way, their disagreements helped to confirm Mao's growing conviction of his own correctness. This expressed itself in his readiness to disobey or ignore the instructions issued by the Central Committee or its various front committees which were set up to run the shifting and complex campaigns against the Nationalists. Mao's attitude was not mere perversity. Communications were poor, establishing contacts and maintaining clear lines of authority proved hugely difficult, and personnel and posts in the party were subject to rapid change. Qu Quibai lasted only eighteen months as leader between 1927 and 1928. While he was away in the USSR, the CCP replaced him. Changes were even more frequent lower down the chain of authority. Mao and other commanders in the field often found they were receiving orders from officials who were junior to them politically and less experienced militarily. This did not make for party discipline or cohesion.

One of Mao's constant refrains was that those at the centre who sought to lay down policy simply did not understand 'the concrete circumstances' of armies in the front line of the war against the Nationalists. Mao's actions certainly suggest that he had no qualms about disregarding directives with which he disagreed. In the late 1920s, Zhou Enlai, later to be Mao's faithful lieutenant, was technically in charge of the CCP's armies, and drafted many of the official military documents. At this stage, he was very much a Central Committee man and so found Mao very difficult to deal with. When Mao did not wish to do something, he simply refused. In Philip Short's succinct description, 'he was unconformable'.[33] He could be courteous and disarming in his refusals, but they were refusals nonetheless. An interesting example occurred in 1928 when Mao declined to be posted from Hunan to Shanghai, on the grounds that the buildings there were too tall and he worked better at sea level.

Interestingly, his practice of ignoring orders contrasted sharply with his insistence on obedience from those under him. Mao was well aware of the difficulty of imposing authority. He did not find it easy to maintain control over the Fourth Army. After Zhu De had joined forces with Mao in April 1928, the army numbers swelled to around 10,000. While this obviously brought added numerical strength, it also increased the problems of discipline. In the mountain fortresses, the peasant soldiers often became homesick and Mao had to allow numbers of them to return to Hunan. However, in doing so, he used the opportunity to rid himself of unreliable or obstructive troops.

In the summer of 1929, Mao succumbed to a bout of malaria, which left him so enervated that he had to be carried about in a litter. He was taken to a remote village where, for over four months, he took to his bed in a bamboo hut, with his wife, He Zichen, beside him dosing him with quinine. He seemed so unwell that the Kremlin published his obituary. Confounding this somewhat premature prognosis, Mao began to recover. While recuperating, he read his way through what he described as 'a mountain of books', a detail which suggests that he may have again exaggerated his illness in order to withdraw temporarily from the constant political battles. He also took time to mix with the locals and prepare another first-hand study of the peasant question.[34]

His absence did him no harm. Without his leadership, the Fourth Army had not performed well. He received appeals begging him to come back. This put him in a very strong position when he did return. He dominated the Ninth Congress of the CCP held in December 1929 at Gutian in Fujian province. In a detailed resolution, he set out a list of demands calling on the CCP to correct the mistakes that had crept into the party. Challenging those who believed that military and political questions could be separated, Mao insisted that the whole purpose of the Red Army lay in 'carrying out the political tasks of the revolution'. CCP members, instead of enjoying comfortable lives in the fleshpots of the cities, interspersed with the occasional guerrilla foray, should embrace the hardship of war against the Nationalists. They should integrate with the peasants and learn the reality of revolutionary struggle. To this call for commitment and selflessness, Mao added a condemnation of 'individualism' and 'ultra-democracy'. These terms were broad enough to cover any CCP member of whom Mao disapproved or whose policies he rejected. What he was demanding was obedience to the party line. He seemed to be unaware of the irony of asking members to conform in ways which he was quite willing to transgress when it suited him.

THE LI LISAN LINE

Mao's resolution may be regarded as his first shot in the internal party battle over the policy advocated by Li Lisan, a Moscow-trained Communist, who was prominent in pushing the Comintern line on the primacy of urban revolution. Given the disagreements in the CCP over what revolution really meant in China and how it could be achieved, it was always likely that a major dispute would break out within the party. When this duly happened it was a consequence of Comintern pressure. Misunderstanding developments in China, the Comintern insisted in 1930 that the nation had entered a period of 'profound national crisis', which provided a perfect moment for the Chinese workers and peasants to rise up against the bourgeoisie and the landlords and establish the dictatorship of the proletariat 'in the Soviet form'. This view was largely based on the fact that one of Chiang's armies had been defeated the previous October by Russian forces in the border province of Heilongjiang following a Sino-Soviet dispute over railway rights. The Comintern then made a hopelessly inaccurate overestimate both of the weakness of the Nationalists and of the strength of the CCP.

However, such was influence of the Comintern that a number of CCP members rushed to do the Kremlin's bidding. In June 1930, Li Lisan, who, as Moscow's nominee, had become chairman of the Central Committee, persuaded the CCP's Politburo to endorse the Comintern's judgement by preparing military uprisings against the GMD in as many provinces as possible. He urged that the Red forces be concentrated for a planned attack on selected urban areas, not divided into individual units for guerrilla attacks in the countryside. This wholly unrealistic scheme was soon branded by the CCP doubters as 'Left adventurism' or 'the Li Lisan line'.

Li Lisan and Mao had been colleagues intermittently for over a decade, but they had never been friends. Li was the 'half' student who had joined Mao in founding the New People's Study Society in 1918 (see page 34). Their coolness towards each other suggested a clash of personality, certainly a clash of wills. Li had criticised Mao earlier for his peasant-based tactics and for being too ready to enlist Nationalist deserters and bandits into the Red army. He had even proposed that Mao be relieved of his command and be made to take a civilian post in the CCP base in Shanghai. Nothing had come of this. Mao had disregarded the order to leave his army and go to Shanghai, and there had been no way of forcing him to act against his will.

Despite their strained relations, Mao made an initial attempt to co-operate with Li's call for urban risings by preparing to attack Changsha in Hunan. But, when he realised how outnumbered and outgunned his army would be, he abandoned the plan and withdrew to Jiangxi. It was a similar story in all the other provinces selected for risings; the CCP forces were simply not strong enough. Where risings were attempted they were easily suppressed by the Nationalists at huge cost to the Communists in men and weapons.

The Li Lisan line might equally accurately have been called the Zhou Enlai line, for it had been Zhou's advocacy as much as Li's that had led the CCP to believe that China was ripe for revolution. Although Li Lisan was nominally the party leader in 1930, it was Zhou who had the greater influence. Zhou had joined the CCP in 1922 after working for the student movement in France. He had gone to Moscow in the mid 1920s and had become the Comintern's front man in China. In fact, he was in Moscow for further briefing when Li Lisan introduced the resolution claiming there was a 'new revolutionary tide' in China. Zhou's absence was his salvation. He was able to return to China, condemn Li Lisan for his impetuosity, and absolve the Comintern from any culpability in the failed adventurism of the left. Li made an abject self-criticism in which he took all the blame upon himself. By early 1931 Li had been replaced as leader by Wang Ming.

The failure of left adventurism left Mao in a far stronger position. It gave prescience to what he had written to the Central Committee a few months prior to the introduction of the Li Lisan line:

> In the revolution in semi-colonial China, the peasant struggle must always fail if it does not have the leadership of the workers, but the revolution is never harmed if the peasant struggle outstrips the forces of the workers.[35]

In the same letter, Mao had re-emphasised the importance of persisting in the struggle in rural revolutionary base areas. He did not dispute that the CCP's ultimate task was proletarian revolution, but he was convinced that in the conditions prevailing in China:

> the development of the struggle in the countryside, the establishment of soviets in small areas, and the creation and expansion of the Red Army are prerequisites for aiding the struggle in the cities and hastening the revolutionary upsurge.[36]

The defeat of the Li Lisan line sharpened the debate which had divided the CCP since the formation of the united front. The issue was both political and military. Did the Communists regard the revolution as achievable primarily through the actions of the urban proletariat or were the peasants to be the prime movers? The vital question that followed from this was whether the Communists should concentrate their forces into one large army or continue to rely on discrete and unco-ordinated groups. In short, would there be one Red Army or a number? Behind such questions lay the issue of party control. Could the Central Committee of the CCP, whose location had to be constantly changed to avoid Chiang's armies, effectively command its scattered forces or should decisions be left to the operational commanders in the field?

Mao understood the importance of obedience and discipline, but he drew a distinction between what was desirable and what was possible. On practical grounds, he doubted that in the current desperate situation the

CCP was capable of exercising central control. This reinforced his belief that not merely was he entitled to follow his own judgement but that there was really no alternative. Much as Mao loved ideological debate, he knew his revolutionary ideas were meaningful only if they provided the means of survival. The situation required real solutions, not the pursuit of theoretical answers, which, whatever their philosophical appeal, had no practical application.

3

TERROR AND SALVATION, 1930–35

The enemy advances, we retreat; the enemy camps, we harass; the enemy tires, we attack; the enemy retreats, we pursue.

Mao Zedong, 1930

THE FUTIAN INCIDENT, 1930–31

Mao's experiences in Jiangxi had convinced him that if he wished to dominate the party at top level it was vital that he first secure control over the lower echelons. This is the context in which to understand his involvement in the Futian Incident, a set of events in which he displayed a ruthlessness which he had hinted at before and which became a defining characteristic of his subsequent career. The incident was a continuation of the intra-party dispute over the Li Lisan line. Official Chinese Communist histories have either excluded any reference to it or have glossed over Mao's part in it. Some of the details are still obscure, but the main features of the story can be pieced together.[1]

By the autumn of 1930, two competing groups within the CCP had developed in Jiangxi; the South-west Jiangxi Special Committee, led by Li Wenlin, in opposition to Mao's General Front Committee.[2] The antagonism arose initially from a clash of local loyalties. The Red Army soldiers were peasants with strong ties to their localities. Factions tended to form representing particular regions; rivalry between them could become intense when, for example, it came to a question of leaving their own regions to fight in territory unknown to them. The Red Army's land seizures were another sensitive issue since the appropriations might mean the troops' own families or villagers were dispossessed. This raised the issue of the right line to take towards the rich peasants. Some CCP members argued for leniency towards them, since they were an indispensable source of food and supplies.

Mao's contribution to the debate was to assert that land distribution should be based on the principle of 'taking from those who have a surplus and giving to those who have a shortage, and taking from those who have better and giving to those who have worse'.[3] This was an uncompromising line, but in practice Mao was less rigid. His land seizures had been exercised with some discretion and understanding of local conditions.

The Li Wenlin and the pro-Mao groups met in a joint conference at which their disagreements over the Li Lisan line soon emerged. Mao was criticised for his policy of 'luring the enemy deep'; Li Wenlin claimed that this would result in prolonged guerrilla warfare and so delay the urban revolution. Mao countered by saying that luring the GMD to its destruction in the countryside was indeed his aim, but the purpose was not to delay the final revolution but to bring it closer. Each group began to charge the other with being a front for counter-revolution. The accusation was that certain units had been taken over clandestinely by pro-Guomindang troops. These were referred to as ABs (anti-Bolsheviks). Claiming that Li Wenlin was preparing to use the AB infiltrators to foment an anti-party rebellion in the Red Army, Mao ordered an immediate suppression. He sent in his own double-agents to expose the plotters. Around 4,000 troops were arrested. Torture was used to extract confessions and to force the prisoners to incriminate others. Half of those arrested were then executed.

This was simply the first stage of what became a violent purge. Acting on Mao's instructions, one of his political aides, Li Shaojiu, began rooting out of all those suspected of being ABs or anti-Maoists in the towns of Futian and Donggu. Despite the savagery of their treatment, which again included torture and maiming, some of those picked on fought back desperately. Their resistance, which led to the deaths of hundreds of Li Shaojiu's own men, and the execution of Mao's former wife, Yang Kaihui, was branded as rebellion against the party. This justified the harshest means being used to suppress it. In the fighting that followed between December 1930 and February 1931 some 5,000 troops and civilians were killed before Li Shaojiu's forces eventually prevailed. What enabled Mao to veil the unpalatable details of the Futian Incident was that the events became merged with a genuine victory over the GMD. In January 1931, an attempted encirclement of the Jiangxi base by government forces was successfully repulsed by the combined Fourth Army forces of Mao, Zhu De, and Peng Dehuai.

There is no evidence that Mao personally witnessed the torture in Futian. But he did approve its use. Indeed, he went further. He gave instructions that the torment was to be as severe as required in order to obtain the necessary information from the prisoners: 'Do not kill the important leaders too quickly, but squeeze out of them the information. . . . [F]rom the clues they give, you can go on to unearth other leaders.'[4] What was then wanted was confession of guilt. The official CCP investigation into the affair, published two years later, recorded the techniques employed by the Maoists at Futian

> [The] method used . . . was the carrot and the stick. The 'carrot' meant extracting confession by guile. . . . The 'stick' meant thrashing suspects with ox-tailed sticks and hanging them up by their hands. If that had no effect, next came burning with incense or kerosene lamp. The worst method was to nail a person's palms to a table and then to insert bamboo splints under the fingernails. . . . Torture ceased only after confession.[5]

Mao's sympathisers have sought to justify his behaviour at Futian on the grounds that torture was part of Chinese tradition, justified by the enormity of rebellion. Moreover, it has been argued, his apparent ruthlessness has to be set against the predicament he was in; without recourse to stern measures he and the Red Army would have been lost.[6] Edgar Snow accepted Mao's description that 'the fate of the revolution depended on the outcome of this struggle.'[7] Other writers dismiss this as special pleading and suggest that Futian shows how far Mao was prepared to go in removing challengers to his personal authority in the party.[8]

In his own justification for Futian, Mao rejected the charge of 'despotism' made against him. He claimed that the ABs had tried to drive a wedge between him and Zhou Enlai, the CCP's overall commander, and to separate the masses from the Red Army. He posed his own question, 'why should they seek to overthrow Comrade Mao Zedong?', and answered:

Precisely because Comrade Mao represents the correct revolutionary line, and is truly leading the struggle and promoting the Chinese revolution. . . . Chiang Kai-shek is shouting loudly 'Down with Mao Zedong' from without, and AB Corps . . . are shouting loudly 'Down with Mao Zedong' from within.[9]

When, in an effort to calm party tensions, the Central Committee sought to pass off Futian as a regrettable incident arising from misunderstandings, Mao would have none of it. He insisted that there had truly been a GMD-backed rebellion against the CCP. He accused his opponents of seeking to discredit him by misrepresentation and forgery. Mao was throwing back the very charges made against him. It was a clever tactic. Mao felt no compunction about doing the very things for which he condemned others. In his informed analysis, Philip Short calls the Futian episode 'a loss of innocence',[10] but the concept of Mao as an innocent before 1930 is difficult to accept, given all that he had already experienced. Futian is perhaps better understood as part of a logical progression in authoritarianism and terror that looks back to the crushing of the anti-Qing rebellion that Mao had witnessed in his youth in Changsha and forward to his own launching of the Cultural Revolution in his old age. He had already provided the justification for it all by claiming that 'all excessive actions have revolutionary significance. To right a wrong it is necessary to exceed the proper limits.'[11] It was no coincidence that Mao's historical heroes were those figures, Chinese and foreign, who exhibited firmness of will and sureness of purpose in pursuit of great goals.

Mao unashamedly condoned the use of terror. For him, violence was never arbitrary. Cruelty served a revolutionary purpose. Not to have used it would be the greater fault. This was where traditional Chinese authoritarianism and twentieth-century absolutism came together in him. The mandate of heaven had merged with the dynamic of class struggle. What is so fascinating about Mao is not just the willingness to acquiesce in barbarity but the cast of mind that saw the needs of party orthodoxy as overruling all other human considerations. Balance and clemency were not allowed to intrude. The genuine sympathy that inspired and infused his reports on the peasantry somehow became stifled when he suspected that those same peasants were betraying the revolutionary cause. Political considerations deadened the humanitarian impulse in him. He could be moved to outrage by accounts of the savage treatment of the peasants by the Nationalists and yet remain untroubled when sanctioning similar barbarities perpetrated in the name of the party. Though Mao did not acknowledge this, his attitude contradicted his guiding judgement that revolutionary struggle was to be understood not in terms of the abstract dialectic of class conflict but in relation to the degree of suffering undergone by real human beings.

However Mao's role at Futian is judged, the incident did show the huge problems he faced in trying to establish authority and control in a lawless land. Jiangxi proved more difficult to defend than Jinggangshan and throughout Mao's period there his forces suffered unrelenting attack from the Nationalists and the bandits that continued to roam the countryside. The scene was not dissimilar to the Wild West in the years following the American Civil War. It was this anarchic situation that provided Mao with the ultimate justification for tightening his grip over his Jiangxi stronghold by removing those whose opposition, if tolerated, would have destroyed the Red Army. Mao's was the familiar adage of all those who embrace violence as an unavoidable part of the revolutionary process: desperate times required desperate measures.

THE JIANGXI SOVIET, 1931–34

For Mao, the Jiangxi period was one of struggle on two fronts, one military, the other political. The most immediately demanding was the desperate battle to prevent the GMD's forces from crushing the Jiangxi base. Chiang's priority was still the annihilation of the Chinese Communists. He continued his White Terror by adopting an encirclement strategy. The broad aim, which was based on German military advice, was to surround the Red base areas, deny them outlets by blocking roads and waterways, and steadily choke them. This programme of what Chiang called 'bandit suppression' was a vast enterprise, involving cumulatively a million troops, and was phased in a series of campaigns of increasing intensity. In all, Jiangxi was subjected to five encirclement campaigns between 1930 and 1934. These threats preoccupied Mao and made the attempt to construct a Jiangxi Soviet dependent on sheer physical survival.

The conflict on the political front, while less dramatic than the military one, was equally significant in relation to the development of the Chinese revolution. It involved the fight to resist the USSR's domination of Chinese Communism. Despite the manifestly unrealistic advice of

Comintern agents in China since the early 1920s, Stalin and the USSR continued to be looked upon by the majority in the CCP as the party's true guides whose instructions had to be followed. In 1930, a number of young Moscow-trained Chinese Communists, led by Wang Ming and known as the 'Twenty-eight Bolsheviks' or the 'Returned Students', came back to China intent on imposing the Kremlin's ideas and strategies on the CCP. Mao's task for the next four years, and indeed in a sense for the rest of his career, was to prevent this takeover. He led an essentially nationalist enterprise devoted to establishing, first, a soviet and, ultimately, a nation in keeping with the conditions and history of China rather than in conformity to the alien notions of international socialism as advanced by the Soviet Union. Mao had chosen to be a deviationist.

As the world knows, he was eventually successful in this. Yet in the course of his struggle the rebuffs he suffered affected him deeply and he frequently withdrew to nurse his bitterness with only his wife, He Zichen, for company. During the Jiangxi period there were several occasions when he became a virtual hermit. This was in part because malaria continued to plague him; he suffered intermittently from weight loss and exhaustion. But there was also calculation in it. He never stayed away so long as to be unable to continue the struggle for power.

The pro-Soviet Central Committee realised that if the party was to be directed along Bolshevik lines Mao would have to be marginalised. It had been to that end that Xiang Ying had been sent from party headquarters in Shanghai to Jiangxi in January 1931 to set up a new party organisation, the Central Bureau of the Soviet Areas, which, without openly challenging Mao's position, would undercut his influence. It was hardly coincidental that this was the same month that the 'Returned Students' began promulgating the 'Wang Ming Leftist Line'. Xiang's problem was his lack of knowledge of how Red base areas actually operated. Mao, whom the Central Committee, in an effort to pacify him, had appointed head of the General Political Department, was thus able to outmanoeuvre Xiang while appearing to co-operate with him. Mao was quite prepared to counter Xiang by packing party conferences and committees with his own supporters. Mao's advantage, which he played on strongly, was that his own practical experience and success in the field made it hard for the Central Committee to pull rank on him. This was evident from Mao's declaration of March 1931, 'Eight Conditions for a Great Victory', which was essentially a restatement of his belief in the policy of 'luring' the enemy into the Red base areas in the countryside and defeating them.[12]

Mao backed his words with deeds. Despite facing 200,00 GMD troops in the second of Chiang's encirclement campaigns, his army was able to prevent Jiangxi being overrun in 1931. Nor was it solely a matter of defence. Mao led units of the Red Army through the enemy lines in raids on Nationalist bases as far east as the coast of Fujian province. It was such efforts that stimulated Mao's distaste for those party officials who had no knowledge of the peasants or of the fighting but still saw fit to dictate policy. Scathingly, he asserted: 'He who has not made an investigation has no right to speak.'[13] As he saw it, the Central Committee had not fully grasped the stark truth; the fate of the Reds ultimately depended on military strength. Revolution of whatever kind was impossible unless the Communists were successful in battle.

The issue during the Jiangxi years was whether, in the shaping of the Chinese revolution, the ideas of the Comintern-dominated Central Committee of the CCP or those of Mao would prevail. It became a struggle of the most desperate kind, which Mao was destined to win. At a critical stage in the development of modern China, when reason and rationality might easily be mistaken for weakness, Mao was toughness itself. He was a ruthless man in a ruthless age. China had seldom had sympathy for pure thought; ideas had to have utility. Mao's genius lay in seeing the implications of this in post-imperial China. With the old certainties gone, the Chinese were looking for new ones. Mao made it his mission to provide these. Such was the firmness with which he continued to suppress the remnants of the Futian rebel faction that it won the admiration of Zhou Enlai when he came from Shanghai to visit the Jiangxi Red base late in 1931. By then the base had been formally named 'the Chinese Soviet Republic' and Mao declared to be its chairman. His opponents in the party hoped that this would be no more than an honorary title. His apparent elevation was meant to give him position without authority.

In their struggle against encirclement, the Reds were given a temporary respite by another turn in the Chinese story. In 1931, Japanese forces entered the northern province of Manchuria, so beginning an occupation of China that was to last until 1945. This meant that after 1931 there were two wars going on in China: the continuing CCP–GMD conflict and the Chinese resistance to the Japanese occupation. At the news of the Japanese move into Manchuria, the GMD government at Nanjing immediately diverted units of its southern based armies to northern China. Yet this proved little more than a gesture. When, in 1932, Japan turned Manchuria into a puppet by declaring it to be the independent state of Manchuguo under the rule of Pu Yi, the last of the Qing emperors, the Guomindang troops seemed powerless to prevent it. Undoubted patriot though he was, Chiang Kai-shek appeared less concerned with the Japanese affront to his country than with the Red menace.

Recognising this, Mao appealed to the CCP to seize a golden moment. The Japanese occupation provided a chance for all Chinese revolutionaries to unite in a great national upsurge against the enemy. Here was the opportunity to strike a blow against imperialism and at the same time expose the Guomindang for the corrupt regime it really was, unwilling to defend the nation against the foreign aggressor. The propaganda value to the CCP would be immense. To emphasise this point, he wrote an open letter to the troops of the White (GMD) army, urging them to mutiny for the sake of China: 'Soldiers, our brothers! Unite! Turn your guns around. Fight for the overthrow of imperialism and the Guomindang, which exploit, oppress, and slaughter the toiling and impoverished Chinese masses.'[14]

The CCP's Central Committee were unimpressed by Mao's passion. He was told that he had misconstrued the situation. Japan's move was directed not at China but at the USSR; the occupation of Manchuria was intended to provide a base from which the Japanese could promote their border dispute with Russia. Moreover, since the Soviet Union under Stalin had chosen at this stage not to antagonise the Japanese further by reacting too aggressively, there was no necessity as things stood for the CCP to involve itself in Manchuria.

Dejected by the party's refusal to respond to his appeal, Mao, in January 1932, went off in a sulk on another of his breaks. With only He Zichen and a few personal bodyguards, he stayed in a remote abandoned temple outside Ruijin, a CCP base on the Jiangxi–Fujian border. He took with him the conviction that, as long as the CCP continued to conform to the whims of the Soviet Union, Chinese Communism would be compromised as a revolutionary movement. This reinforced his resolve to pursue a separate course.

The opportunity was not long in coming. In March 1932, the Central Committee managed with some difficulty to get a telegramme through to him pleading with him to return. A Red attack on Guangzhou had gone badly and they needed his advice. It was as if the party hierarchy found him unacceptable as strategist but indispensable as a tactician. When he did return, he entered into a long discussion on how best to carry the fight to the GMD. As before, Mao protested that the Central Committee was wrong in planning to attack the major provincial centres. He advocated a war of movement based on the strength of the Red units in the rural areas. His recommendations were ignored and a large-scale attack was prepared. Having initially gone along with this by committing his army to a march on Fuzhou in Jiangxi province, Mao broke away half-way through the march and redirected his forces to Fujian. It was only after he had done so that he informed Zhou Enlai of his change of plan. Mao's contempt for the misguided orders he considered he had received could not have been clearer.

To his actions, he now added uncompromising words. Mao had no doubts about the superiority of his own judgements. Writing directly to the Central Committee he declared, 'The political appraisal and military strategy of the Centre are wholly erroneous.'[15] It did not worry him that his obduracy undermined the principle of obedience to the party. Until the party adopted the right line, obedience was meaningless. Mao knew that as long as could keep his army together and avoid defeat his position was strong.

STRUGGLING FOR POWER

Between 1931 and 1933, the CCP held a series of party conferences, which Mao attended when not prevented by illness or military commitments. The conferences were invariably hurried affairs that took place under the shadow of the GMD threat. The difficulty of maintaining contacts between the centre and the scattered Red bases meant that conference discussions were largely concerned with passing on badly needed information about the Reds' true military position. Nevertheless, the direction of the political debate was clear enough. Beneath the arguments over strategy a power struggle was going on.

The Wang Ming faction strove to isolate Mao by imposing the concept of an urban revolution on the CCP. But they had no desire to lose his military skills. Everyone acknowledged that Mao and Zhu De were the Reds' outstanding commanders. The trick, therefore, was to continue using him as a soldier while denying him the political influence that would enable him to determine the grand military strategy. At a key conference in Ningdu, in October 1932, Mao came under fierce criticism for being a 'right opportunist', a reference to his habit of backing his own judgement in defiance of central orders. Although this charge was eagerly seized upon by his opponents in the upper ranks of the party, the original complaint against Mao had come from lower down. The fine details are obscure since minutes of the conference were either not kept or were lost, but Mao appears to have been attacked by a group of subordinate officials who resented his influence over the Red base areas.

In the hope that Mao had been weakened by the conference attacks, the Wang Ming group proposed that he be removed from any office where he could dictate strategy. However, Zhou Enlai, although regarded as spokesman for the Comintern-backed Wang line, put forward a compromise intended to give the faction most of what they wanted but without humiliating Mao. Zhou persuaded the party not to remove Mao from his military position permanently. In return for their forbearance, Mao's opponents were assured by Zhou that he would officially make Mao his assistant in front-line planning; in that way he would be brought under party control. However, it is unlikely that Zhou or Mao regarded the arrangement as lasting or binding. As part of the deal, Mao agreed to take a period of sick leave which, as had happened frequently before, removed him from the immediate political tussle. During the three-month break that ensued, Mao visited He Zichen in a hospital in Fujian where she had recently given birth to their second child. It was at the same hospital that Fu Lianzhang, the first Western-trained doctor to examine Mao, persuaded him to enter a nearby clinic to be treated for tuberculosis.

When Mao came back in February 1933, he found that the balance of forces in the party had swung very much against him. Late in 1932, the Central Committee of the CCP, facing mounting GMD attacks, vacated Shanghai and re-established themselves in Ruijin. Soon after arriving there, they began an organised assault on the rural deviationists. Bo Gu, one of the 'Twenty-eight Bolsheviks' and a close ally of Wang Ming, subjected Mao to a series of aggressive political onslaughts. The only future for the CCP, Bo asserted, lay in the centralising of its power and an end to the local autonomy of the Red bases. It was time to make Mao and his supporters conform.

Mao was not always directly named in the attacks, but there was no doubt that he was the chief target. The climax came in April 1933 when four of Mao's leading supporters, including his brother, Mao Zetan, and Deng Xiaoping, destined to be the leader of China after Mao's death, were denounced at a party conference. They were mocked as 'hillbillies' who lacked any real understanding of revolutionary theory. They retorted by accusing the ex-Shanghai officials of being dupes of Moscow. Not for the last time, factions in the CCP were engaging in the vicious game of name calling as a way of destroying the credibility of their opponents.

In the midst of his troubles, Mao took time out to gloat over the Depression, the series of capitalist crises in the Western world that had followed in the wake of the Great Crash in the USA in 1929. As chairman of the Central Government of the Chinese Soviet Republic, he addressed the world's impoverished masses:

> The deepening panic of world capitalism and the end of the temporary stability of post-war capitalism have forced the imperialist bourgeoisie to launch an even more frenzied attack against the proletariat and toiling masses in their own countries. . . . In Germany, Italy, Japan, and all the capitalist countries of the world, the mad tide of fascism is waging a life-and-death struggle at present with the revolutionary movement of the working class.
>
> Proletariat and oppressed nations of the world, unite! Oppose the imperialist wars! Oppose the imperialists' partition of China. Down with world imperialism![16]

Consoling as such thoughts might be for Mao, they did not alter the reality of the local situation. The ex-Shanghai clique had gained the upper hand in Jiangxi. By the beginning of 1934, Mao's devotees found them-selves excluded from party office. Although Mao himself retained his party rank, it appeared that the attempt to sideline him had worked. During what proved to be the last months of the Jiangxi Soviet his was not the dominant voice. This might have mattered more had the Reds' position not been so desperate. But the truth was that the CCP stood on the verge of extinction. Ironically, the worse the plight of the party, the better Mao's position. What all the talk and dispute came to was that the Reds were losing the military struggle. The encirclement campaigns were working as Chiang Kai-shek intended.

Despite his temporary detachment from the centre, Mao was far from inactive. He immersed himself in his studies of the peasantry. Officially he was carrying out party duties, since he had been asked to examine the land question in the soviet, but he often found himself at variance with the instructions he was given. He was accused of being too lenient in his proposals for land redistribution, but his worry was that harsher policies, involving widespread property seizures, might alienate the very peasants the party was hoping to win over. As was to be expected, the Bo Gu group saw the issue very much in Stalinist terms. Their understanding of peasant policy was influenced by the contemporary scene in the USSR, where Stalin was enforcing a sweeping collectivisation of the peasantry as a prelude to his industrialisation programme. The thought of the Chinese peasantry being similarly used as an instrument for the furtherance of urban industrialisation appealed to the Moscow-trained Communists. They wanted the Chinese peasantry to be classified along Stalinist lines in order to expose the rich exploiting peasants, equivalent to the Russian kulaks.

Mao was disdainful. In two long articles he pointed out that the subtleties of Chinese agrarian relationships defied attempts to fit them into foreign theoretical moulds. He drew a distinction between landlords, who should be dispossessed, and rich peasants who should be allowed the chance to reform by distributing their wealth and joining the peasant movement.[17] Mao's analysis led to more name calling. He was dubbed a 'rightist', peddling 'a rich peasant line'. Mao was undeterred by such taunts. As in military matters, so on the land question, he was an activist and a practitioner. The detailed knowledge of the peasantry that he had amassed over a decade was unmatched by any of the theoreticians in the party.

Despite the attacks upon him from within the party, Mao continued to put great energy into recruiting for the Red Army. He was aware that the party's fierce infighting over the correct line to follow and its prodigious struggles to construct a Chinese Soviet would mean nothing if it could not defend itself. Indeed, there was an air of unreality about the way the CCP rowed over the niceties of the correct party line at a time when Jiangxi Soviet faced imminent destruction. By the beginning of 1934 it was increasingly evident that the growing Guomindang pressure would soon force the CCP to abandon its Jiangxi base.

The demanding question was how to break out of the encirclement. Disagreements were constant over the tactics to be adopted. In September 1933, the arrival from the USSR of the German Comintern agent, Otto

Braun, had deepened the divisions. His presence confirmed the dominance of the CCP by the pro-Moscow element. Braun advised that the Red Army should remain in its base but take on the Whites in a series of pitched battles. Mao rejected this as suicidal. He urged an alternative; let the complete Jiangxi army break through the GMD's blockade by a rapid surprise movement and then turn and counter the enemy on ground of the Reds' own choosing. Braun and Bo Gu dismissed Mao's suggestion as 'flightist'.

The grip that the Bo Gu faction had on the CCP during what proved to be the last year of the Jiangxi Soviet was evident from two important party assemblies held in January 1934. The plenary meeting of the CCP's Central Committee took place without Mao. Whether he was excluded or whether he chose not to attend because he had not been invited to give the keynote speech is unclear, but it was an indicator of how little influence Mao had at this stage as nominal chairman of the Soviet. But he was present at the Second National Soviet Congress held a week later, at which he gave both the opening and closing addresses. In substance, these were detailed surveys of the work and success of party, protected by its Red Army, in giving the Jiangxi Soviet a workable economic and social structure. Being official statements, the addresses were broadly optimistic, but in the closing section Mao warned congress, that, contrary to what some members were saying, the Nationalist blockade had not been broken. That great task had still to be achieved.[18]

ENCIRCLEMENT

The prudence of Mao's warnings was shown by the news that came in as the congress was dispersing; Chiang Kai-shek's armies, having overthrown a breakaway GMD government in Fujian, were now free to concentrate on intensifying the blockade of Jiangxi. The forces at Chiang's disposal numbered over half a million. The Reds could muster barely a third of that figure. They were also markedly inferior in weaponry. Through February and March 1934, the Guomindang fanned out from their blockhouses and began taking large areas of Red territory. Panic occurred in many regions as news spread of the fierce reprisals inflicted on the local populations by GMD troops. Large numbers of Red soldiers deserted either through fear or in an attempt to get back to defend their homes. Desperate to check the Nationalist advance, the CCP accepted Otto Braun's recommendation that a stand be made at Guangchang. If this proved successful, it would save Ruijin and the main Red base to the south from being overrun. It failed. A three-week battle resulted in defeat of the Reds and the destruction of a third of their units. The Jiangxi Soviet was now indefensible. If the Chinese Communists were to survive it would have to be elsewhere.

Over the next six months the Communists prepared for a great evacuation. For the greater part of that time Mao absented himself from internal party matters. He spent the summer touring the battle zones and sending in reports on the military situation. Mao was now openly contemptuous of Bo Gu and Otto Braun. Even the Comintern had had to accept that Jiangxi could no longer be held. But Bo continued to demand that in the interim the Reds must defend every inch of Soviet territory. Such obduracy meant months of fighting, with the Reds invariably suffering heavy casualties. The hopeless resistance required a reign of terror in the Red-held areas to sustain it; brutal punishments were inflicted on army deserters and civilian defeatists. For Mao, the most significant development of this time was that he and Zhou Enlai drew closer together. Zhou was worth cultivating. Despite the Reds' recent military reverses, his reputation was unsullied since it had been Bo Gu who had taken over the planning of the Guangchang offensive after elbowing Zhou aside. An immediate mark of Zhou's usefulness was that it was through him that a handbook on guerrilla tactics compiled by Mao received the party's imprimatur and was issued to the Red Army. In August, Mao went down with another bout of malaria which incapacitated him for three months. As before, with He Zichen to minister to him, he took sanctuary in a disused temple, this time on Mount Yunshi 12 miles from Ruijin. He was thus uninvolved in the planning of the CCP's breakout from Jiangxi that began in October 1934, the event that was to take its place in Chinese history as the Long March.

THE LONG MARCH, 1934–35

By chance the March passed close to Yudu where Mao had gone after his convalescence. It was there that he and He Zichen joined it. Mao had persuaded the party to allow his wife to accompany him. She did so in the designated role of army nurse, and was one of only some twenty women who were permitted to join the March. She paid a high price for her dedication. Since her two-year old son, Xiao, was too young to travel she had to leave him behind. In the chaos of the final evacuation of Jiangxi after the marchers had left, the boy was lost. Neither Mao nor He Zichen saw him again. Philip Short makes the telling observation that with Xiao's abandonment 'another small part of Mao's humanity withered on the vine.'[19]

The Long March began as a rout. Its only object initially was to escape from Jiangxi. It made obvious sense for the Communists to think of going to another of the existing Red bases – but which one and by what route? It was by answering these demanding questions that Mao Zedong began the process of reimposing himself on the Chinese Communist Party. Once he had joined the March, he proposed that they head west into Guizhou province and establish a temporary base around the town of Zunyi; there they would have time to decide on their ultimate destination. Mao's suggestion was accepted by the three-man group – Bo Gu, Otto Braun, and Zhou Enlai – who had been responsible for the initial plan to leave Jiangxi. Thus for the first time in over two years Mao had been able to influence a top-level party decision. So, as he set out for the real wilderness, his days in the political wilderness appeared to be coming to an end.

The Long March was a prodigious event. A notion of the scale of it can gained from listing its physical proportions:

Number of marchers who set out: approximately 90,000
Number of survivors: approximately 20,000
Time span of march : one year – October 1934 to October 1935
Distance covered: 18,000 li (6,000 miles)
Average number of miles marched per day: 17
Number of provinces crossed: 11
Number of mountain ranges crossed: 18
Number of rivers crossed: 24
Number of towns and cities taken or occupied: 60
Number of major battles fought: 15

Mao described the Long March to Edgar Snow as the migration of a nation. Based on Mao's account, Snow went on to define the March as 'an odyssey unequalled in modern times'. His lyrical depiction has become the received understanding both in China and the West of the March's character:

> Adventure, exploration, discovery, human courage and cowardice, ecstasy, and triumph, suffering, sacrifice, and loyalty, and then through it all, like a flame, an undimmed ardour and undying hope and amazing revolutionary optimism of those thousand of youths who would not admit defeat by man or nature or God or death.[20]

Mao sought to capture the epic quality and political significance of the March in these terms:

> It is a manifesto, an agitation corps, a seeding machine. . . . It proclaims to the world that the Red Army is an army of heroes. . . . It declares to approximately 200 million people of 11 provinces that only the road of the Red Army leads to their liberation. . . . It has sown many seeds in 11 provinces, which will sprout, grow leaves, blossom into flowers, bear fruit and yield a crop in future.[21]

It was all the things that Mao and Snow said it was, but it was also a defeat. It acquired the adjective 'Long', only after the event. No one knew what its duration and dimensions were to be. The Reds did eventually find haven in Yanan in Shaanxi province, where they set about creating a new Communist republic. But this later achievement tended to hide the fact that the March had begun as a humiliating flight from Jiangxi. The Reds had been routed. They had had to leave behind nearly all their women and all those who through age or frailty could not undertake the rigours of the journey. When the Nationalists entered Ruijin three weeks after the marchers had left, they engaged in a frenzy of retribution against the 10,000 who had remained behind. It was said that there was not a tree in the area that did not have a body hanging from it. Mao's brother, Zetan, was one of those executed. Nor should it be forgotten that in their relentless year-long pursuit Chiang Kai-shek's armies picked off some two thirds of the fleeing Reds.

To any neutral looking on in late 1934, the chances of the Communists' surviving as a force in China appeared very slim. Divided in their own counsels, the Reds had been driven ignominiously from their major stronghold, and forced to undertake a desperate march to a destination yet undecided. GMD armies were in pursuit intent on destroying them. Chiang's Nationalist regime had been recognised as legitimate by most Western governments and now enjoyed a greater degree of central control than any authority had exercised in China since the fall of the Qing. While the Japanese occupation of Manchuria showed the limitations of Chiang's power and ambition, this did not seem to offer any immediate advantage to the Reds. It is true that the CCP claimed defiantly that the Red Army of workers and peasants had chosen to march north in order to take the fight to the Japanese. But only the most committed or the most deluded of its own followers genuinely believed that it had been a matter of choice rather than compulsion.

Soon after Mao joined the March he warned that the Red troops were too heavily laden. Packed into carts and onto mules or carried on the backs of the soldiers were not merely weapons and food supplies but all the accoutrements of a nation on the move. The Reds had taken with them what they regarded as the essentials for re-establishing a soviet wherever that might be. Among the burdens that weighed them down were filing cabinets, printing presses, kilns, sewing machines and film projectors. Much of this baggage would be cast aside as the journey progressed, but the early stages of the march were slowed down by the difficulties the encumbered troops had in negotiating narrow paths and heavy ground. A source of constant discomfort for the marchers was the poor quality of their footwear. The adequate boots or shoes that a few had set out with did not long survive the constant tramping. The troops had to make do with slippers of plaited straw, which, while easily replaced, gave little protection or grip.

Mao himself had set out with little more than a bundle of clothes and blankets, and even these were carried for him by bearers. Yet there were many stories later told of his readiness to take his share of the toil when the going became particularly hard. One of his bodyguards, Zhen Zhang-feng, who doubled as batman, described Mao's belongings:

> Two cotton and wool mixture blankets, a sheet, two of the ordinary uniform jackets and trousers, a sweater, a patched umbrella, an enamel mug which served as his rice bowl, and a grey brief-case with nine pockets. On the march he used to carry the brief-case himself and the umbrella, and I made a roll of the rest of the things. When we made camp I used to make his bed up with the blankets and sheets. he used the rest of his belongings as a pillow.[22]

Mao's fears concerning the weight the troops were carrying were shown to be well founded during the first major engagement of the March. Late in

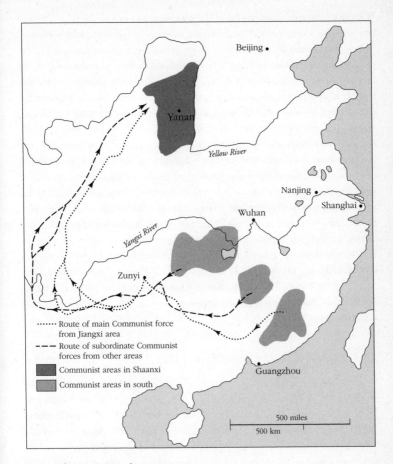

Map 3 The Long March, 1934–35

November, the main Red contingents reached the Xiangjiang river with the aim of crossing into Hunan province. What should have been a relatively easy fording was slowed down by the sheer amount of equipment the troops tried to ferry over. Learning of the Reds' predicament, the GMD launched a full-scale ground and air attack. For two days the Reds were battered on both banks of the river. When they eventually broke away to safety, they had lost over 50,000 men. Notwithstanding the uplifting tales of the sacrifice of those comrades who had died to protect the main body of the marchers, the crossing had been a blunder caused by the lack of foresight of those leaders who had followed the Wang–Bo–Braun leftist line.

The blunders were of benefit to Mao. Clearly, he was not to blame for any of the recent disasters since he had not played any part in the organisation of the break-out from Jiangxi. Luck had been on his side in this. Events had vindicated his position and undermined that of the Wang Ming group and their Kremlin backers. In an odd way, by doing little on the political front during the previous two years Mao had strengthened his standing. As a consequence, his voice during the Long March carried greater authority within the CCP than at any time during the four years of the Jiangxi Soviet. It was following the Xiangjiang debacle that Mao made his proposal that instead of marching north in the hope of linking up with other Communist forces, the Reds should go west into Guizhou, thereby avoiding the concentrated GMD forces in Hunan. In late November, the Politburo accepted Mao's advice, which ran counter to the plan originally drafted by Bo Gu and Braun, and re-routed the March accordingly. The sharp change of direction threw the GMD forces off the scent for a few weeks and allowed the marchers a brief interlude in which to relax and take stock.

THE ZUNYI CONFERENCE, 1935

In mid-January 1935, a full meeting of the Central Committee gathered in the town of Zunyi in Guizhou. The discussions lasted three days and proved to be one of the formative episodes in both the CCP's development and in Mao's career. In the weeks since the start of the March, Mao had been careful to canvass the support of a number of the Politburo members who had become disenchanted with those leaders whose mistakes had cost the CCP so dear. Among prominent members Mao enlisted were Zhang Wentian and Wang Jiaxiang, both of whom had been originally numbered among the 'Twenty-eight Bolsheviks'. Their willingness to co-operate with Mao suggested that the Comintern's hard anti-Mao line had begun to crack. Indeed, Wang Ming had let it be known that the Comintern had come to recognize Mao's considerable worth as a political and military leader. This admission by the pro-Bolshevik faction was not made out of largeness of heart. It was forced on them by the recent disasters suffered by the Reds.

When the Zunyi conference began, therefore, the lines of division among the twenty members in attendance were already established. Bo Gu opened the proceedings by admitting, without apology, that the strategies adopted in Jiangxi and at the beginning of the March had been unsuccessful. He ascribed this not to errors of planning but to GMD strength and the difficulty of maintaining links with the other Red areas. Zhou Enlai, who had been mainly responsible for military operations since 1932, was next to speak. He, too, defended the decisions taken by the troika of himself, Bo Gu, and Otto Braun. but acknowledged that mistakes had been made. If Zhou's apologetic style was intended to disarm his critics, it failed. In what was clearly a planned move, Zhang Wentian developed the attack. He condemned the flawed judgement of the March leaders that had led to the disaster at Xiangjiang. Mao then took up the cudgels. His argument was direct and simple. The centre had ignored the strategy which he had consistently advocated, and for which he had been sidelined, of fighting a war of movement and 'luring the enemy' into areas where they could be outflanked and defeated. Braun's alternative strategy of defending fixed positions had invited mass assaults by the GMD, which had so drained Red resources that Jiangxi had had to be abandoned. A bitter three-day discussion followed, but the tide flowed with Mao and his supporters. Zhou Enlai subtly manoeuvred towards a position where, without appearing to be blatantly disloyal to his co-leaders, he could begin backing Mao.

Although it is correct to regard the Zunyi meeting as a momentous event in the CCP's history, its significance is that it formally confirmed what had already taken place. There had been a shift away from the 'Twenty-eight Bolsheviks' towards Mao. His relative detachment from the centre of events during the previous two years had left him guiltless of the failure that now tainted the pro-Bolsheviks. This was the major reason why the assembled Politburo closed the Zunyi meeting by endorsing Mao's arguments and voting for major changes at the top of the party's hierarchy. The troika was dissolved and Bo Gu and Otto Braun were demoted. Zhou Enlai, however, reaped the reward for his subtleties by retaining his position as joint military commander with Zhu De. Zhang Wentian took Bo Gu's position as 'person with overall responsibility' for the party's affairs.[23] Mao was readmitted to the party's Central Committee. By early March 1935, he had resumed the position of political commissar in the reformed Frontline Headquarters and began to issue joint military orders with Zhu De.

Otto Braun, one the few non-Chinese to have taken part in the Long March, later commented that at Zunyi Mao had completely rehabilitated himself and regained control of the Red Army, 'thereby subordinating the Party itself to his will.'[24] Braun was being a little premature, but he had noted an essential truth. Since the White Terror in 1927, Mao had followed an increasingly independent course while the party centre had fallen in step with the Kremlin/Comintern line. It was evident that at some point the CCP would have to decide finally what its true character was. This decision was made at Zunyi. Mao's re-emergence as a major figure and the check to the Bolshevisation of the CCP meant that the party was now set on a Chinese course. It would develop a brand of Communism in which Chinese characteristics would predominate. This did not happen overnight. The Long March had still to be completed and many searing party battles lay ahead. But Zunyi was a confirmation that Mao Zedong would play a key role in the shaping of Chinese Communism.

MAO'S STRUGGLE WITH ZHANG GUOTAO

The forty-two-year-old Mao had little time to enjoy the political success he had won at Zunyi. The respite the Reds had earned by changing the direction of the March came to an end when GMD scouts relocated them at the end of January 1935. This prevented the Red units from following the route agreed upon at Zunyi, to go north, cross the Yangxi, and link up with the forces of Zhang Guotao in Sichuan. With Chiang Kai-shek's forces blocking the way, the March had to be re-routed; the plan now was for a wide swing south through Guizhou, then west into Yunnan, before turning north again into Sichuan. This broad sweep took three months and was interspersed with frequent zigzags in an attempt to throw off the pursuers. In Mao's words, 'The Long March took countless twists and turns, and the smooth parts were far rarer than the difficulties, so that our mood was gloomy.'[25] The fighting was almost constant and casualties occurred daily.

But there were successes, the most notable being the Reds' forcing of the Loushan Pass, an event which Mao commemorated in verse:

> Do not say that the strong pass is hard as iron.
> For this very day, we'll stride across its summit.
> Across its summit.

Where blue-green hills are like the seas,
And the setting like the sun.[26]

How sharp the CCP's internal disputes still were, despite Zunyi, became
evident at a party meeting in Huili in southern Sichuan, which the
marchers reached in mid-May 1935. Mao found that he had to defend
himself from charges made by Lin Biao and Peng Dehuai that the zig-
zag tactics had slowed the March and put the troops under needless strain.
Mao bore grudges; decades later he would make Lin and Peng suffer for
criticising him at Huili. However, at the time, he overcame their opposition with ease. Backed by Zhou Enlai and Zhu De, Mao won the meeting
round. The members formally thanked him for his leadership and approved
his plan for continuing the march north to join Zhang Guotao's army in
Sichuan province.

A month later this objective was realised when the main body of the
marchers reached Lianghekou in Sichuan, where they were rapturously
welcomed by Zhang's soldiers. On the way the marchers had achieved
two outstanding feats which were to become part of Communist legend.
The first was the crossing of the raging Dadu River, when, under continual
mortar' and machine gun fire, twenty Red volunteers had clawed and
crawled their way across a 120-yard chain bridge whose planks had been
destroyed. Having seized the opposite bank and dislodged the enemy, they
then made the bridge secure for the main body of the Reds by replacing
the burned planks with wooden doors taken from the adjoining town of
Luding. Mao considered the Dadu crossing to be 'the most critical single
incident of the Long March'; had the Reds failed there the whole army
would have been lost.[27]

The second feat was the crossing of the 16,000-foot Great Snowy
Mountain range from whose heights the marchers could see into Tibet.
The journey through the mountains proved a fearful ordeal. In the rarefied
atmosphere, the marchers gasped for breath and the baggage they carried
became impossible to bear. Thousands of the comrades died from cold or
slipped to their death off the narrow icy paths. Mao recalled that some
units lost two-thirds of their pack animals and supplies. He himself went
down with a mixture of malaria and altitude sickness and had to be carried
in a litter. But the March continued, morale held, and when the Reds
descended from the mountains they could justly claim that their losses and
privations had strengthened not weakened their resolve. When the two

Red armies met at Lianghekou the sense of achievement was palpable. Mao and Zhang Guotao hugged each other as comrades.

Yet troubles lay ahead. These stemmed from the same basic question that had caused division since the Red breakout from Jiangxi eight months earlier. What was the ultimate destination of the March? Mao and Zhang had conflicting answers. Behind their disagreement was a personal rivalry. They had first met in 1921 as founder-members of the Chinese Communist Party and had developed a mutual dislike. There was an interesting similarity in the strained relations between Mao and Zhang and those between Mao and Li Lisan earlier. Zhang in his published reflections accused Mao of having acted in bad faith by preventing his promotion within the CCP in the early years of the party's development.[28]

Whatever justification Zhang had for his sense of grievance, the situation in which he and Mao found themselves in the summer of 1935 necessarily made them rivals. Mao arrived in Lianghekou in a seemingly powerful position. He was the victor of the party struggles at Zunyi and Huili and had gained in stature by his leadership of the March. But Zhang also had influence and reputation. He had shown himself an able leader of the Fourth Front Army in the Henan-Hubei area. His greatest asset was that he was commander of a Red force of some 60,000 troops – five times larger than the depleted columns that had survived the March so far under Mao's command.

Zhang favoured the development of a Red soviet in the Sichuan-Gansu-Xikang region, an area far enough west to make direct contact with the USSR easier. Mao, however, preferred to continue to march north and establish a Red base in the Sichuan-Shaanxi-Gansu region. The competing views were aired at a number of party meetings. Late in June 1935, Zhou Enlai chaired a session of the Politburo called to discuss strategy. He proposed that whichever new Red base area was chosen it had to meet three basic criteria: it must be defensible, contain as large a population as possible, and have adequate food and resources. Mao strongly supported this proposal, adding the further requirement that the selected area should be in a part of China from which the Reds could sustain military resistance to both the Nationalists and the Japanese. He put it to the meeting that the region he had selected best fitted these needs. The Politburo accepted this by a unanimous vote in which they resolved 'to build a Sichuan-Shaanxi-Gansu Area.'[29]

Zhang Guotao, raised no objections at the meeting, but in the weeks following he made secret arrangements to lead his armies westwards to the Sichuan-Xikang border, this despite his having agreed to join up with Mao's troops in the move northwards. Zhang's intention was to sabotage the March by dividing its forces.[30] At a second Politburo meeting in early August, Zhang embarrassed the committee by reminding them that since the Long March was in fact a retreat forced on the Reds by the failure of the Jiangxi soviet to defend its base, the leaders were hardly in a position to dictate policy. Nevertheless, when the meeting closed it was generally understood that Zhang had suppressed his objections and agreed to march north.

So it was that in August 1935 Mao with his fellow commanders, Lin Biao and Peng Dehuai, led their divisions on what proved to be the last major stage of the Long March. They soon met one of the greatest natural hazards of the whole journey – the Grasslands of Qinghai and Gansu. The term grassland suggests, perhaps, verdant pastures and lush meadows. Nothing could be more misleading. These were fetid swamps, devoid of habitation and yielding little that was edible and nothing that was drinkable. Without guides, the troops could not move at night and only with the greatest difficulty by day. Bottomless quagmires waited to swallow the careless man or beast. As if the lethal terrain was not enough, the men's misery was compounded by foul weather. Bitter winds would suddenly spring up, bringing driving rain and hail. Shelter and rest were not to be had in such conditions; troops died of exposure. The only advantage was that the pursuing White armies were too terrified to follow them into such a place. It took ten days for the Marchers to traverse this deadly region. As so often before on the March, sheer survival was its own triumph. When the Red comrades touched *terra firma*, there was again a euphoria among them born of a sense that they were engaged on more than merely a forced March. Mao's claim that the journey was a nation on the move was a fitting description.

Having survived the Grasslands, Mao immediately restated his case that the route which he had chosen was the only genuine option. He called on comrades 'to unite under the correct line of the Central Committee, to destroy the enemy, and to turn Sichuan, Shaanxi and Gansu Red, thereby establishing a solid and unshakeable foundation for a soviet China.'[31] His words were principally intended as a reminder to Zhang Guotao. News had been received that GMD troops were massing for another campaign and Mao feared having to face attack without Zhang's army in support. However, Zhang had no intention of joining the First Army. For a time he equivocated, saying that floods prevented his forces from moving. But it soon became clear from an intercepted telegram to two of his officers that Zhang was preparing to abandon the northern marchers and follow his own western route. Not only that; he called on his supporters to do their best to cause disruption by promoting an inner-party struggle.

Zhang's attempt to undermine Mao's position nearly succeeded. There was a strong chance that, had the smaller First Army been left isolated, it might well have been destroyed by the GMD. Such a defeat would have crippled Mao politically as well as militarily. Acutely conscious of the difficulties he and the CCP were in, Mao even contemplated turning directly to the USSR for help, something he had never previously considered. At a party conference at Eiji in September 1935, he told the comrades that the reduced First Army simply could not fight through on its own. In the only recorded instance of Mao's wavering from his conviction that the CCP could achieve salvation by their own efforts, he suggested that it might be necessary for them to ask the Soviet Union for assistance:

> We are not an independent Communist party. It is wrong to refuse absolutely to ask for help. We are in any case one branch of the International. We can first establish a base area near the Soviet Union, and then develop towards the east. Otherwise we will have to fight a guerrilla war endlessly. We must not turn ourselves into a turtle inside an urn. The Central Committee must go to a place from which it can direct the revolution in the whole country.[32]

Mao was saved from having to take this drastic step by intelligence reports that came through around this time that there were substantial Red forces and CCP sympathisers located in Shaanxi province. This news had been delayed by the extreme difficulty of maintaining regular contact between the scattered Red units and bases. However, now that the Central Committee had learned of the existence of a strong Red base in Shaanxi, it gave the marchers a great lift of confidence. That region was now selected as the final destination. By late October, the First Army led by Peng Dehuai had fought its way into Shaanxi. Mao celebrated in verse:

The mountains are high, the roads are long, the gullies are deep,
Huge forces gallop through in every direction.
Who is it dares to ride on horseback with drawn sword?
None but our great General Peng.[33]

Mao entered the town of Wuqizhen in Shaanxi on 22 October 1935. At a formal meeting of the Politburo on the same day, Mao delivered a report stating that the proposal made at the Eiji conference for creating a Red base nearer the Soviet Union had been withdrawn. 'Now we must . . . direct the revolution in the whole country from the northern Shaanxi soviet area.'[34] The meeting accepted Mao's report and formally declared that the Long March was now finally at an end. After some months examining a number of alternatives in Shaanxi province, the CCP chose in 1936 to make the town of Yanan the centre of the new Chinese Soviet. Mao and the Central Committee took up residence there in January 1937. It was to remain their base for over a decade.

The threat that Zhang Guotao had represented rapidly receded. In October 1935 he had set up an alternative Central Committee. Events soon rendered this an empty gesture. His efforts to establish a western base in Sichuan foundered when his army was badly mauled by a combination of warlord troops, wild tribesmen, and GMD forces. In 1936, the remnants of his battered army limped into Shaanxi, only for their leader to be arrested by the CCP for his disloyalty. Moscow and the Comintern promptly turned their back on Zhang. He was obliged to admit his errors and disband his rival Central Committee. In 1938, Zhang left Shaanxi and deserted to the Guomindang. His challenge to Mao had long since been over.

4

MAO'S PATH TO POWER

THE YANAN YEARS, 1935–43

If our country is subjugated by the enemy we shall lose everything. For a people deprived of its national freedom the revolutionary task is not immediate socialism, but the struggle for independence.

Mao Zedong, July 1936

MAO AND CHIANG KAI-SHEK

The completion of the Long March and the fall of Zhang Guotao left Mao in a strong position. His military strategy had proved correct, he had chosen the route that saw the March through to ultimate success, and in the course of the journey he had overcome the various challenges to his authority and imposed himself on the party. Yet Mao was well aware of what a close-run thing the whole affair had been and how much was owed to chance and to Japan. He was wholly serious in 1972 when he told Kakuei Tanaka, the Japanese prime minister, that, far from being ill-disposed towards Japan, he looked upon her with gratitude since it had been the Japanese presence in China in the 1930s that had diverted and weakened the Guomindang and so saved the Communists from destruction.

What makes this ironic is that when Mao arrived in Shaanxi he made the struggle against the Japanese the centrepiece of his policy for developing the new Red soviet. This further vindicated the CCP's claim that the Long March had been undertaken not as a flight but as the first step in a crusade to lead the Chinese people against the invading enemy. Mao's declared aim was not merely to resist defeat by the Guomindang, but to unite all true Chinese revolutionaries and patriots in a national struggle. He spoke of 'combining civil war with national war' and winning over 'soldiers from the White armies and young students who are caught up in the anti-Japanese tide'. In regard to the GMD, he was careful to distinguish between Chiang Kai-shek 'the head traitor who is helping Japan destroy China' and Chiang's followers, who for the most part were dupes rather than evil people. If they could be shown the error of their ways they would be eager to enlist in the Red cause.[1]

The need for resistance was urgent. Late in 1935, the Japanese began to intensify their hold on northern China by moving more troops into the area and demanding that the Chinese accept the formation of a regional autonomous government, composed of pro-Japanese appointees, with authority over six provinces, including Shaanxi. Choosing not to challenge this, Chiang Kai-shek's northern commanders came to an agreement with the Japanese and withdrew from Beijing. This produced a reaction similar to the anti-Japanese demonstrations of 1915 and 1925. In what later became known as the 9 December movement, students took to the streets to protest against this new wave of imperialism. Beijing, Shanghai, and Wuhan witnessed marches, strikes, and violent clashes between protesters and police. Significantly among the banners carried were many declaring 'Stop the Civil War, Unite Against the Enemy': evidence that the protests were as much against China's internal divisions as against the Japanese occupation itself.

The event was a godsend to the CCP. It revealed that Chiang's anti-Communist campaigns and his inept resistance to Japan were alienating all genuine Chinese nationalists. Coinciding with the CCP's establishment of its base at Yanan, the 9 December movement gave point to Mao's own slogan 'Chinese do not fight Chinese'. If the Communists could exploit the mood of the times, they were in a position to undermine Chiang's position by leading the anti-Japanese movement. Mao claimed that 9 December marked a new period in the Chinese revolution; the CCP had begun to supersede the GMD as the true representative of Chinese nationalism. Strength was given to his claim by a remarkable set of events, known subsequently as the Xian Incident.

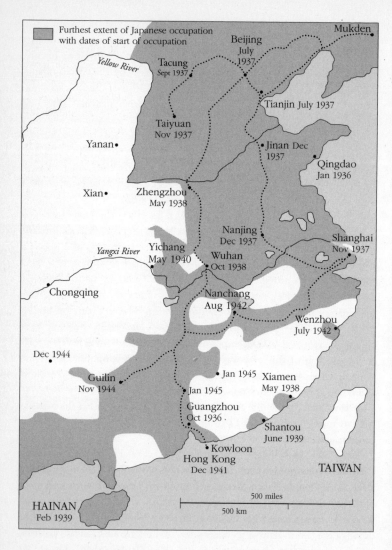

Map 4 The Sino-Japanese war, 1937–45

THE XIAN INCIDENT, 1936

During the twelve months following the 9 December movement, frustration with Chiang Kai-shek's less than resolute opposition to Japan began to mount. His style of warfare against the invader was summed up in the slogan 'trade space to buy time'. Chiang held that China was so vast that the Japanese would never be able to occupy it completely and would exhaust themselves in the effort to do so. The longer the war lasted the weaker the Japanese would become. This was a realistic but hardly inspiring judgement since it condemned China to a costly war of attrition, which strained the loyalty of Chiang's supporters. Splits began to appear in the Nationalist ranks and mutinies occurred in some of the GMD units.

A significant figure was General Zhang Xueliang, known as the 'Young Marshal'. In 1928 Zhang succeeded his father, Zhang Zuolin, as warlord ruler of Manchuria, following the elder Zhang's assassination by the Japanese. Although for expediency's sake Zhang Xueliang felt obliged to co-operate formally with the Japanese, he continued to act independently by expanding his power base in the northern provinces. He also accepted a post in the Nanjing government and pledged himself to the GMD. When the Japanese occupied Manchuria in 1931, Zhang's instinct was to carry the fight to the invader. However, Chiang Kai-shek ordered him to withdraw his forces rather than risk defeat. Zhang complied but was unhappy. By 1936, his disillusion with the GMD had been deepened by further orders from Chiang telling him to divert his resistance to the Japanese into an attack on the CCP forces in the Shaanxi region. During the same period, Zhang had become impressed by the dedication of the Communists in their war against the invaders. A campaign led by Mao Zedong into Hebei province in the spring of 1936, which Zhang witnessed, convinced him of the effectiveness of the Red army as a fighting force. This, coupled with Mao's willingness to negotiate with him as to how the GMD and the CCP might best combine their forces against the Japanese, strengthened Zhang's doubts about Chiang's anti-Communist strategy. He judged that Mao had a grasp of the seriousness of the Japanese threat to China that Chiang lacked.

Mao, indeed, placed the Japanese occupation in a world context. He told Edgar Snow that 'Japanese aggression is menacing not only China, but also world peace.' He added that if the foreign powers were prepared to assist China in its struggle to avoid being 'completely colonized' then 'the opportunities for foreign co-operation in China would become very great'. Mao also forecast that if Chiang continued his policy of 'compromise and retreat' the Guomindang would rebel against him. 'He must either oppose Japan or be overthrown by his own subordinates.' Chiang's only salvation was to accept his mistakes and heed the wishes of the Chinese people.[2]

In the remaining six months of 1936, the CCP, represented by Zhou Enlai, made frequent overtures to Chiang, urging him to act along the lines suggested by Mao and work for a common GMD-CCP resistance. But Chiang made no move to change his strategy. In November 1936, Mao complained to Zhang Xueliang that the GMD attacks on the Red bases were not lessening but mounting. A month later Mao wrote directly to Chiang in respectful but urgent terms. Addressing him as 'the honourable Mr Chiang', he appealed to him to recognize the fury that the Chinese people felt towards the Japanese occupiers. Instead of pursuing 'a civil war of mutual slaughter' let Chiang devote his energies to fighting the invaders. Were he to do so, he would become 'a glorious hero . . . respected by all and honoured forever by history'.[3]

The same plea was made by Zhang Xueliang, who begged Chiang Kai-shek to respond to the national mood by leading a combined resistance to the Japanese. But Chiang not only refused, he decided to force Zhang into line. He flew to Xian in central Shaanxi, where Zhang's army was stationed, with the intention of publicly reprimanding the Young Marshal and obliging him to obey the order to renew the extermination campaign against the Reds. However, Chiang had underestimated both the degree of disaffection among Zhang's troops and their commander's determination. Chiang had flown into a mutiny. The morning after he arrived, still in his pyjamas and minus his dentures, he was seized by a group of Zhang's troops. Zhang then telegraphed Mao and Zhou Enlai to inform them he had Chiang under arrest. The speed with which he contacted the Communist leaders led commentators to suggest that the Communists had helped plan the coup. This remained the GMD claim for decades despite the lack of hard evidence of CCP collusion. In any case, the question that mattered at the time was not whether Mao and his colleagues had plotted with Zhang to seize Chiang but how they would respond to the event.

In one obvious sense, Chiang's arrest provided a huge opportunity for the Communists. They now had at their mercy the man who for a decade had been trying to crush them out of existence, the Guomindang leader who had put a quarter of a million dollars on Mao Zedong's head. If retribution was their aim, now was the moment. Perhaps this was indeed Mao's first thought. He was quoted as advocating Chiang's execution, provided that Zhang Xueliang did the dirty work: 'the word "kill" must not come from our lips.'[4] But if that was his initial idea it was soon superseded by the realisation that Chiang Kai-shek was more valuable alive than dead. The humiliation of his arrest by his own troops put Chiang in a very vulnerable position. Now was the time to bend him to the CCP's will and impose a policy upon him. Zhou Enlai was immediately rushed to Xian to parley with Chiang and Zhang Xueliang. Since Zhang was willing to conform to any decision the CCP might come to, this effectively made Chiang the prisoner of Zhou and the Communists.

Moscow's interpretation of the incident was to see it as a piece of Japanese subterfuge. Stalin still held to the view that the GMD under Chiang remained the force best able to tie down the Japanese in China; he believed that was why Japan had been party to the mutiny and arrest.[5] Stalin, therefore, ordered the CCP to organise Chiang's release. Mao was reported to be outraged by this interference since it showed that the Soviet Union still regarded the CCP as incapable of running its own affairs. Yet it so happened that Stalin's demand was in keeping with the decision which Mao was moving towards. At a series of hurriedly called Politburo meetings chaired by Mao, it was agreed that if Chiang declared himself willing to accept a set of formal demands made by the CCP he should not be kept prisoner, let alone killed. Zhou Enlai negotiated over this with Chiang, Zhang Xueliang, and a number of other GMD leaders, including Chiang's vivacious wife, Soong Meiling.

The outcome was that in late December 1936 Chiang, in return for his freedom, accepted the Communist proposals. These included an end to the GMD's campaigns against the Reds, the recognition of the CCP as a legitimate party, and the re-forming of a GMD–CCP front to carry on China's anti-Japanese struggle. In a remarkable act of atonement for his original mutiny, Zhang agreed to fly back to Nanqing as Chiang's prisoner. His expectation was that, having helped Chiang Kai-shek save face in this way, he would be set free once he was back in the GMD capital. Chiang, however, did not forgive so easily; Zhang was to be held in custody by the Guomindang for the next fifty years.

In claiming credit for the successful resolution of the Xian Incident, Mao told the Politburo that the agreement with Chiang had brought an end to the civil war and 'marked the beginning of the War of Resistance'. However, even at the point of success it is unlikely that Mao really believed that Chiang would abide by his Xian commitments. It is true that in December 1936 Mao acknowledged that a declaration, published by Chiang after his release, in which he ordered GMD troops to begin withdrawing from the Red areas, was 'proof of his acting in good faith'. But Mao was also at pains to characterise the declaration as 'so ambiguous and evasive as to be a truly interesting masterpiece among China's political documents'. To his sarcasm he added a warning that should Chiang renege on the promises given at Xian he would be destroyed by 'the revolutionary tide of the people'.[6]

Yet if Mao harboured such doubts about Chiang Kai-shek, the question remains as to why he had not taken more drastic action against him when the Reds had him in their power at Xian. The answer lies in the propaganda value that the situation offered. Chiang's recognition of the CCP, albeit enforced, gave the Communists a legitimacy they had hitherto lacked. Moreover, set against a decade of the Guomindang's constant effort to exterminate them, the CCP's willingness not merely to spare Chiang but to recognise him as the leader of the Chinese resistance seemed an act of heroic selflessness. Party interests had been subordinated to national needs. The CCP's perceived restraint certainly gained them a rush of adherents. Yanan became a Mecca for those Chinese eager to be part of a genuine struggle against the occupiers of their country.

The ranks of the idealists were swollen by a mass of refugees who fled to the Red base area in Shaanxi following the events of 7 July 1937. It was on that day that, on the pretext of a Chinese assault on its forces at the Marco Polo Bridge in Beijing, Japan extended its occupation of China into a full scale expansionist war. It was these events rather than the Xian agreement that made a reality of the CCP–GMD united front. The day after Japan's attack, Mao telegraphed Chiang offering to place the Red Army under his direction in order 'to save the nation'. Chiang was forced by the sheer pressure of the Japanese advance to co-operate with the Reds. With the fall of Beijing, Shanghai, and Nanqing in 1937, the GMD capital had to be transferred to Chongqing in Sichuan province. As the Guomindang forces were pushed out of the northern regions during 1937 and 1938, the areas they left were defended in scattered pockets by Red detachments. The Communist guerrillas thus became the main front-line troops resisting the Japanese. They also provided the local government and administration of these regions. Through force of circumstance the Reds had begun to gain an influence in occupied China that would eventually see them achieve the very end which Chiang was dedicated to preventing – the displacement of the Guomindang by the CCP as the political power in the nation.

A major complication was the attitude of the Soviet Union. Stalin had never fully abandoned his belief that the Guomindang was the best bet for successful revolution in China. It is important to understand his reasoning. His call for a resumption of the GMD–CCP united front was far from being a disinterested one. He had become seriously disturbed by Japanese expansionism. The year 1936 had witnessed the signing of the anti-Comintern Pact, the agreement between Nazi Germany, Fascist Italy, and imperialist Japan, which opened up the prospect of a co-ordinated two-front attack on the USSR, on both its European and its Far Eastern borders. The primary purpose of Stalin's foreign policy had consistently been the protection of Soviet interests, not the advancement of international socialism. That was why the Comintern had become essentially a vehicle for subordinating the international Communist movement to the will of the Soviet Union. A fearful Stalin was hardly likely to put the interests of the nascent CCP before those of the USSR. His support for a resurrection of the GMD–CCP united front had little to do with the merits of the internal Chinese situation. He was concerned with how best to use China to lessen the Japanese threat to the Soviet Union.

MAO AND WANG MING

Soon after Japan began its full-scale war on China in July 1937, Wang Ming was sent from Moscow to bring the CCP into line. Mao found himself in yet another power struggle. Again, this was not openly acknowledged. When Mao went to meet Wang on his arrival at the airstrip in Yanan in November, the two men exchanged cordial greetings. The same evening a banquet was held in Wang's honour. However, in accordance with Comintern instructions, Wang immediately set about pressing the demand, 'everything for the united front'. He asked that the CCP accept the supremacy of the GMD and the leadership of Chiang Kai-shek. Mao responded by arguing that to do so would be to throw away all the advantages the CCP had gained by the Long March, by their skilful handling of the Xian Incident and by their establishment of the Chinese soviet at Yanan. Mao had already taken steps to counter Moscow's demands. In a meeting in August 1937 in Luochuan called to discuss the war crisis, he had gained the backing of the CCP leaders for a resolution he had introduced stating that while the Japanese threat made military co-operation with the Guomindang necessary, 'the CCP must be independent, and we must keep the initiative in our hands'.[7]

An initial worry for Mao was that, as had happened at Jiangxi, his CCP colleagues would be overawed by Moscow and desert him. He declared on one occasion after the arrival of the Moscow Reds in 1937 that his authority ended at the mouth of his cave. He was being unnecessarily pessimistic. The fact was that, while Wang Ming might be Moscow's man, he had overestimated the strength of support he could rely on from the Soviet Union. It was also the case that, faced with the increasing severity of the Japanese campaigns in 1937 and 1938, few Chinese Communists were willing to act on Wang's suggestion that they abandon their guerrilla tactics and confront the Japanese in a mass rising. Wang was showing the same misunderstanding of the situation as he and Bo Gu had in Jiangxi.

Mao clarified his ideas in a series of lectures and essays which laid down the basic strategy followed by the Communists during their remaining years in Yanan. He characterised the current war as a blatant Japanese attempt to turn China into a colony, an outrage that had aroused all classes and political groups in China to resistance. Such a national momentum would undermine the Guomindang. 'When the national crisis reaches a crucial point splits will occur in the Kuomintang camp.'[8] If the Reds stuck to their task by continuing guerrilla warfare, they would accomplish three things: hold down the Japanese forces, win over all true Chinese patriots, and fatally undermine Chiang Kai-shek and his robber bandits.

It was evident from Mao's analysis that he anticipated that the united front between the Communists and the GMD would not long survive. The soundness of his judgement became clear in 1938. Chiang had paid only lip service to the alliance. By 1938, he was already contemplating renewing his attacks on the Communists. It was this that further undermined Wang Ming's position. Not only had Wang failed to grasp the reality of the military situation, but his insistence on maintaining the GMD–CCP front, with the Communists in a subordinate role, made little sense in the light of Chiang Kai-shek's animosity.

Wang's greatest handicap was the failure of his patrons in Moscow to back him fully. While they did not formally abandon him, they let it be known that they now recognised Mao as the CCP's leader. Mao's photograph appeared for the first time in *Pravda*, the newspaper's tacit acknowledgement that its earlier obituary of him had been a touch hasty. The Comintern secretary-general, Georgi Dimitrov, openly accepted that in order 'to resolve the problem of unifying the party leadership, the CCP leadership should have Mao Zedong as its centre'.[9]

Mao had also won over to his side the principal Chinese Politburo members. Among these were Zhou Enlai, who had initially supported Wang Ming's pro-GMD line but who from 1938 on was to prove Mao's loyal lieutenant, Wang Jiaxiang, who had been one of the Moscow-trained 'Returned Students' but who had committed himself to Mao at Zunyi, and Kang Sheng, a sinister figure from Shanghai's violent underworld, who had travelled from Moscow with Wang Ming but who became a staunch supporter of Mao. Kang was appointed Mao's security chief at Yanan. Bereft of allies in the CCP and deserted by the Comintern, Wang Ming was further weakened in October 1938 when his base, Wuhan, fell to the Japanese. He could no longer mount an effective challenge for leadership. At the end of 1938, Mao was in the strongest position he had yet occupied in the Chinese Communist Party.

LIFE IN YANAN

The Yanan years were something of an interlude for Mao. While it was not a restful period – the Japanese and Nationalist threats prevented that – it was a time of relative stability. Mao was less on the move than he had been for a decade. Now in his mid-forties, he even had time to gather in some of his scattered children. Mao Anying and Mao Anqing, aged fourteen and thirteen respectively, came to Yanan to stay with their father for a time. It was scarcely conventional family life, but it did provide Mao with a chance to commune in his cave home with the sons he barely knew. For most of the Yanan period Mao and the Communists lived in caves. This was not as primitive as it might sound. Cave dwelling was the norm for most people in that part of northern China. The caves were man-made or man-modified structures, dug out of the loess hillsides. They were often spacious by peasant standards. Mao's own three-roomed cave contained a large round wooden bath in which he would lounge for hours in water drawn from a well and heated in cauldrons. Outside the cave entrance, Mao cultivated a tobacco patch which provided him with the leaves from which he hand-rolled his own cigarettes, a substitute for the American brands he chain-smoked when supplies allowed. (In the 1960s, he added further sophistication to his tastes by smoking Havana cigars, presents from the Cuban leader, Fidel Castro.)

The caves offered relief from the summer sun and shelter from the winter's rages. More importantly, they offered protection from the GMD and Japanese air raids on Yanan which began in 1938 and continued on and off until 1944. Mao had moved into his cave home after his first house in Yanan was bombed in 1938. Some of the caves, such as the one used as a hospital, boasted electric lights powered by portable generators. The caves which housed the 'Anti-Japanese Military and Political University', which was set up to train the comrades and cadres, contained open-fronted lecture rooms and even theatres and assembly halls.

In many respects, life for the Yanan Reds was an improvement on what most of them had known previously. The caves were certainly no worse than the straw and wood, mud-floored huts in which the peasant soldiers lived in their own provinces. Even Mao's family house in Shaoshan, considered a desirable residence by the locals, had boasted only an earthen floor covered with rushes. As Mao's many detailed studies of the land question recorded, the lot of the Chinese peasant was invariably grim and insecure. In the year in which the Yanan base was created, one of China's recurrent famines was taking its toll. The International Red Cross calculated that between 1935 and 1936 over 30 million Chinese were ravaged by severe malnutrition and disease, half of them fatally. The Communists did not live like princes at Yanan, but most of them had never had it so good. Complementing their material improvement was the camaraderie and feeling of achievement shared by the survivors of Jiangxi and the Long March. There was a sense of mission about what they were doing. This was mixed with some hard-headed economics. In their base areas the Reds developed a flourishing industry in the growing and marketing of opium. It has been calculated that during the Yanan years the CCP raised between 25 and 40 per cent of its revenue from opium exports.[10]

Mao sought to develop the system he had used in Jiangxi for creating and consolidating CCP authority. After a village or region had been taken over by the Communists, their practice was to drive out the landlords and form it into a soviet. Red troops and officials prepared for this by going around inviting the inhabitants to attend meetings and gatherings. At these, committees were elected representing various districts or activities. These might include land distribution and cultivation, health provision, and education. The Reds spelled out the benefits of co-operation and mutual aid. At its smoothest, this enterprise worked effectively and offered the local peasants something they had not known before – a degree of self-organisation and protection. However, all the smaller committees were ultimately subject to the authority of an over-arching revolutionary committee. Since this larger body was under the direct control of the CCP, the overall structure was democratic in appearance only. Communist rule prevailed.

Some Western observers were greatly impressed by the Yanan soviets. Edgar Snow, who saw the system working at first hand, described it as a study in representative government: 'committees were found in every branch organ of the soviets, right up to the Central government, where policies were co-ordinated and state decisions made.' Yet, sympathetic as he was to the whole enterprise, he had to admit that at all major points it was 'directly under the guidance of some Communist'.[11]

However, as a public-relations exercise, it worked. It was an extension of the policy begun in Jiangxi and carried on through the Long March of using the Red Army as, in Mao's words, 'an agitation corps and a seeding machine'. Mao did not see the troops simply as the protectors of the CCP and its Red bases; their purpose was as much political as military. They were the chief instrument by which the revolution was to be spread through China. They were the vanguard carrying the party's message. It would be the Red Army who would convince the peasants that the Communist revolution was their revolution. This was a remarkable development. Customarily in China, soldiers of whatever army had been regarded with dread by the population at large. The troops of the emperors, the warlords, or the foreign occupiers had all terrorised the Chinese people. More pertinent still, the Guomindang and the Japanese forces were currently behaving savagely in the areas they overran. The rape of Nanjing by a Japanese army in 1937 was one of the most barbarous acts in twentieth-century warfare.

All Chinese armies, of course, were composed largely of peasants. Mao seized on this obvious truth and turned it to the Communists' advantage. Peasant would understand peasant. True to his belief in the importance of practical action, he instructed the Red troops not to brutalise the people but to win them over by showing them understanding and decency. To this end, Mao in Jiangxi had already formulated a set of rules to guide the troops in their dealings with the peasants. These had to be learned and repeated regularly by every soldier:

1   Replace all doors when you leave a house. [doors also doubled as beds in many peasant homes]
2   Roll up and return the straw matting on which you sleep.
3   Be courteous and help out when you can.
4   Return all borrowed articles.
5   Replace all damaged articles.
6   Be honest in all transactions with the peasants.
7   Pay for all articles purchased.
8   Be sanitary, and especially establish latrines at a distance from people's houses.
9   Don't take liberties with women.
10 Don't kill prisoners of war.[12]

The disarming simplicity of these rules may seem out of place in the midst of the bitter and protracted war in which the Reds were engaged. But the reality was that for the first time the peasants experienced an army in their midst that took their feelings into account. It is unlikely that many of the peasants grasped the subtleties of Marxist revolutionary theory. What concerned them was the struggle against the landlords. It has to be remembered how bitter landlord–peasant relations in China traditionally were. As Mao frequently emphasised in his peasant reports, landlords invariably abused the peasantry. This was true especially in Shaanxi, one of the poorest areas in rural China. Although there might have been the occasional landowner who showed some compassion towards the peasants, the landlords as a class were simply concerned to exploit those whom they controlled. The reaction of the peasants was one of two kinds, either total subservience or extreme violence. Peasant risings were dotted through the history of imperial and republican China. When they occurred they were desperate affairs, invariably involving the murder of landowners followed by savage retaliation against the peasants before the risings were crushed.

Plate 1 Mao at Yanan in 1937
Source: © Bettmann/CORBIS

Plate 2 Mao at Yanan in the 1930s. To his left are Earl Leaf, a Western press correspondent, Zhu De, and Jiang Qing
Source: © Bettmann/CORBIS

Plate 3 Mao toasts Chiang Kai-shek in 1945 during one of their fleeting moments of co-operation

Source: © Bettmann/CORBIS

Plate 4 Mao in Beijing declaring the creation of the People's Republic of China in October 1949

Source: © Bettmann/CORBIS

Plate 5 Mao and Nikita Khrushchev in 1958. Their smiles belie the deepening antipathy between them

Source: © Bettmann/CORBIS

Plate 6 Mao makes a return to his old school in Shaoshan in 1959

Source: © Bettmann/CORBIS

Plate 7 Mao swimming in the Yangxi in 1966

Source: © Bettmann/CORBIS

Plate 8 Mao welcomes US President Nixon to Beijing in 1972
Source: © CORBIS

MAO AND THE PEASANTS

Reds like Mao and Deng Xiaoping showed an astute understanding of peasant frustration. They knew that, outside the infrequent and brief periods of rebellion, the hard and unrelenting life of the peasants made them an inert mass. Party cadres often spoke of the passivity of the peasants and how difficult it was to arouse them to action. Mao made it the Reds' task to wake them from their torpor and show them that rebellion when properly organised and led could be their salvation. To tackle the problem, Mao deliberately set out to attract people on the fringes of society, those who in modern Western terms might be termed drop-outs. He aimed to attract such groups as beggars, petty criminals, and prostitutes to the party's cause. He judged that once passive peasants were enthused and the marginalised were given a sense of worth and purpose, they would become activists and devoted supporters of the CCP. 'These people can fight with great courage, and, led in the right manner, they will become a genuine revolutionary force.'[13]

'The battle for the hearts of the people' was how Mao described the Reds' sympathetic policy towards the peasants. This battle was eventually to give the Reds a hold over rural China. The Communists did not gain their adherents through ideological conversion. There may have been some among the better informed peasants who were interested in the Marxist theories presented by Mao, but they would have been the exceptions. In the main, the peasants followed the Reds because of the way they were treated by them. One measure of Red success was the growth of the CCP. Between 1937 and 1945 formal membership of the party rose from 40,000 to 1 million. This provided the pool from which the party recruited its expanding Red Army.

It has to be said that some of this growth was the result of coercion. In Red-controlled areas it was obviously expedient for the local population to appear to support the CCP. The Reds were not chivalric knights. Where peasants did not see the light and declined to co-operate, they were treated severely. One method used to enforce compliance was to impose heavy taxation in kind. Cases were recorded in 1941 of villages in the Red controlled regions being forced to hand over a third of their gathered harvest. Such seizures created violent reaction. In some areas there were denunciations of Mao and calls for his assassination. Red repression followed. Yet, when due allowance has been made for these examples of terror, the fact remains that Yanan marked a major propaganda ory for the Chinese Communists.

That people will support those who treat them well is such a simple formulation that its significance can be easily overlooked. Here it is vital to emphasise the Chinese context. Mao had grasped an aspect of social relationships that had eluded all Chinese governments and one which Chiang Kai-shek had also failed to grasp. One of the things about Chiang that puzzles Western commentators is why he was so uncaring towards the Chinese peasants. Why, they ask, did the Nationalists not show the same sympathy towards the peasants that the Reds did? It was surely the obvious policy, given the political and military benefits that would follow.

The basic answer is that it was not the Chinese way. In Chinese tradition, authority was its own justification. It did not require a demo-cratic sanction. Those who held power did not need to condescend to winning support for their authority. Rulers did not have to woo those they ruled but to command them. Obedience was required of the people. Those who disobeyed were suppressed. It was a distillation, some might say a corruption, of the Confucian ethic: an ordered harmonious society required that legitimate authority remain unquestioned. From time immemorial the peasants had been the great despised of China. Though they made up four-fifths of the population, their numbers did not give them rights. Representative government had never been practised in China. Chiang saw no necessity to break that tradition. The peasants were there to be directed and used. Chiang's political strength lay elsewhere. His public avowal of the Three People's Principles was largely rhetoric. The fact was that 90 per cent of the Guomindang's finance came from China's business and commercial world. Save only as conscripts for the GMD's armies, China's rural poor counted for little in Chiang's scheme of things. The treat-ment of the enforced recruits by the GMD officers became legendary for its brutality and helps to explain why the Nationalists were so often ineffectual as a fighting force.

Mao's embracing of the peasantry whom Chiang despised should not be misunderstood. His humanitarianism was not of the Western liberal kind. Indeed, he specifically condemned liberalism because it put the interests of the individual above those of the revolution: 'Liberals look upon the principles of Marxism as abstract dogmas. They approve of Marxism but are not prepared to practise it.'[14] Mao's approach was primarily a hard-headed calculation: since a mass revolutionary movement could come about in China only by organising the peasantry, it paid the Reds to pursue policies that attracted rather than repelled the adherents they sought.

MAO AND THE RED ARMY

The humanity shown towards the peasants by the Red armies during the Yanan period was an extension of the practices which Mao had introduced into the training and treatment of his own soldiers during the Jiangxi years. It followed from his conviction that, whatever other factors might be involved in revolution, in the end it was achievable only through military force. He repeated his mantra that 'political power grows out of the barrel of a gun'. Rather than being simply the military wing of the CCP, the Red Army was the means by which Chinese Communism would eventually triumph. This made it vital that the peasant soldiers of that army looked upon themselves as the instruments of history that they were.

A critical step towards this was to instil into the troops a sense of self-worth by dealing with them as human beings not as cannon fodder. In contrast to the mixture of ferocity and indifference with which rank and file soldiers in Chinese armies had invariably been treated by their superiors, the Red Army commanders sought to inculcate brotherhood. The troops were trained in basic literacy and numeracy as first steps towards self-awareness and class consciousness. The notion of fighting for a cause was constantly put before them. One is reminded of the New Model Army trained by Oliver Cromwell in seventeenth-century England. The customary beating of troops by officers was forbidden and the soldiers were encouraged to hold meetings at which they might raise questions and put forward ideas. While this may not have been the perfect democracy which some apologists claimed, it was an extraordinary development in Chinese military terms. Enemy POWs were invited to defect and become part of an army that was truly fighting for China and its people. Despite the constant shortages from which the Red armies suffered, Mao made sure that the troops received a daily allowance to enable them to buy food:

> All this gives great satisfaction to the soldiers. The newly captured soldiers particularly feel that our army and the Guomindang army are worlds apart. They feel spiritually liberated, even though material

conditions in the Red Army are not equal to those in the White army. The very soldiers who had no courage in the White army yesterday are very brave in the Red Army today; such is the effect of democracy.[15]

By democracy Mao meant the people's rights – something very close to the second of Sun Yatsen's Three People's Principles. Sun had been careful to stress that democracy did not mean individualism in a Western sense; it referred to rights held collectively and protected by proper authority. Mao developed this concept. Using the same term that Lenin had applied in revolutionary Russia, he expressed it as 'democratic centralism', the notion that, through obedience to the legitimate authority of the CCP, the party members and troops would gain genuine representation and have their grievances settled. Mao knew that a peasant army largely uninformed in political matters would have to be educated to understand this:

Education in democracy must be carried on within the Party, so that members can understand the meaning of democratic life, the meaning of the relationship between democracy and centralism, and the way in which democratic centralism should be put into practice. Only in this way can we really extend democracy within the Party and at the same time avoid ultra-democracy and the laissez-faire which destroys discipline.[16]

He insisted that such training be extended to the Red Army. During the Jiangxi and Yanan years, Mao issued thousands of orders and instructions to his troops. These were often detailed analyses running into many pages. They were concerned not merely with military details but with guiding the soldiers on how best to order their day-to-day lives: what to eat and how to cook it, how and when to wash themselves and their clothes, how to keep healthy. To the Western eye this is a naive stuff. But Mao was for the most part dealing with simple peasants and if he treated them like children the paternalism was appropriate. It was certainly appreciated by the troops and helped form a remarkable bond between them and him. Yet it was a matter of respect rather than affection. From the accounts of people who met Mao personally he was not an easy man to get to know. He seldom opened himself to others, preferring to listen. While he could joke or utter peasant scatologies, he remained withdrawn. An American correspondent, Agnes Smedley, found herself deeply attracted to him in the 1930s, but it was his mystique rather than his humanity that appealed to her. She spoke of a dark brooding quality about him that was both impressive and frightening.[17]

MAO AS THINKER

Mao's basic view of life was dialectical; what he called 'contradictions' were a recurring theme in his writings.[18] From the beginning, his reading and experience had reinforced the notion that life was struggle, not simply in the obvious sense of the effort to survive, but in the scientific sense that conflict was the dynamic that made things happen socially and politically. Marx had, of course, provided a structured analysis of this phenomenon, which Mao had embraced in his late twenties. But Mao did not need a theory to convince him that progressive change could be achieved only by the overthrow and destruction of opponents. Everything he had been through so far in the forty-five years of his life by 1938 had taught him that violent conflict was not an accompaniment to the revolutionary process – it was the process. With this realisation went a conviction that the outcome of conflict was not accidental. Success or failure were pre-determined by the correctness or error of the combatants. Two conflicting interests could not both be right. Correctness was not a matter of debate; philosophical give-and-take played no part in it. Those who were correct succeeded, those who were wrong failed. It was a close variant on the Chinese concept of the mandate of heaven. Mao's belief that he and the party he led were on history's winning side provided the justification for the stringent means he used to enforce his will on the political deviants who opposed him.

It was at Yanan that Mao, aided by Chen Boda, one of the CCP's major intellectuals, began to establish a body of revolutionary thought that was to become the received wisdom of the party. Desperate though the struggle was in the Red areas during the Yanan years, it provided Mao with the opportunity to express himself as the great guerrilla leader, military strategist, and ideologist. His writings, which he worked on almost daily, formed the corpus that became 'the Thoughts of Chairman Mao'. He presented his ideas in a stream of essays and articles, and in lectures which he gave to students in the Red University.

Despite the veneration in China of Mao as a thinker, he was not, and never set out to be, a pure philosopher. His aim was the traditional

Chinese one of providing a set of ideas that had practical utility. He emphasised that the task of revolutionaries lay in 'seeking truth from facts'.

'Facts' are all the things that exist objectively; 'truth' means their internal relations, that is, the laws governing them, and 'to seek' means to study. . . . And in order to do that we must rely not on subjective imagination, not on momentary enthusiasm, not on lifeless books, but on facts that exist objectively.[19]

Mao wished to provide a framework of thought into which the current Chinese revolution could be placed and within which the key questions of political and military strategy could be answered. He honoured Marx and Lenin as the great pioneers of Communist ideology, but he insisted that the Chinese revolution had to be understood in its Chinese setting. 'We must plant our backsides on the body of China.' The context was everything. China's revolution would be a peasant revolution, because the Chinese situation, in which four-fifths of the population were peasants, dictated it. That was the reality of things. To force China to conform to an abstract theory of revolution would be 'cutting the feet to fit the shoes':

China's revolutionary war is waged in the specific environment of China and so it has its own specific circumstances and nature. . . . Some people say that it is enough merely to study the experience of revolutionary war in Russia. . . . [However] although we must value Soviet experience . . . we must value even more the experience of China's revolutionary war, because there are many factors specific to the Chinese revolution and the Chinese Red Army.[20]

Such views brought him into conflict with the Moscow-trained Reds and the Comintern. Their interpretation was that, in the absence of a substantial class-conscious proletariat, the CCP could best advance revolution in China by making common cause with the Nationalists. To pursue peasant revolution as an end in itself was to defy the dialectic. Mao refused to be bullied by the dialecticians. He told the comrades that they should regard Marxism not as dogma but as a guide. In the crude peasant terms he often employed, he described dogma as having 'less use than dogshit', which could at least fertilise the fields. Mao rejected the detached intellectualism which put theory before reality. 'Marxism-Leninism has no beauty, nor has it any mystical value. It is only extremely useful.'[21] He explained that revolutionary terms took their meaning from the context in which they were used. Earlier, he had defined class as a measure of human suffering; the revolutionary classes were those who were subjected to the greatest oppression. He now defined the proletariat not primarily as a social class but as a collective of like-minded revolutionary activists. Under this dispensation, all those truly struggling for revolution qualified as proletarians.

> Today, whoever can lead the people in driving out Japanese imperialism and introducing democratic government will be the saviours of the people. . . .
>
> Therefore, the proletariat, the peasantry, the intelligentsia and the other sections of the petty bourgeoisie undoubtedly constitute the basic forces determining China's fate. These classes, some already awakened and others in the process of awakening, will necessarily become the basic components of the state and governmental structure in the democratic republic of China, with the proletariat as the leading force.[22]

Mao made a special attack on the errors of the 'Right opportunists', his term for those who wanted to stop the CCP following a separate Chinese line. He acknowledged the correctness of the policies pursued by the Communist parties in the capitalist countries. They were right to model their uprisings on the 1917 Russian October Revolution by planning to seize the cities first.

> China is different, however. The characteristics of China are that she is not independent and democratic but semi-colonial and semi-feudal, that internally she has no democracy but is under feudal oppression and that in her external relations she has no national independence but is oppressed by imperialism. It follows that we have no parliament to make use of and no legal right to organise the workers to strike.
>
> Basically, the task of the Communist Party here is not to go through a long period of legal struggle before launching insurrection and war, and not to seize the cities first and then occupy the countryside, but the reverse.[23]

It is notable that while urging the Chinese Communists not to be overawed by the Soviet revolutionary model Mao was careful to avoid antagonising the USSR. In his public statements, he praised Stalin's leadership and acknowledged that China in its struggle against Japan needed the support of the Soviet Union. Yet, consistent with his notion of the primacy of action over theory, Mao stressed that it was the Soviet leader's practical achievements, not his ideas, that made him pre-eminent. In a formal tribute to Stalin on his sixtieth birthday in 1939, Mao wrote that 'Stalin's deeds are the materialization of his words. Marx, Engels, and Lenin did not build a socialist society but Stalin has. This is unprecedented in human history.'[24]

In an interesting anticipation of the Cultural Revolution of the 1960s, Mao broadened his analysis to cover writers and artists. He was anxious that the comrades should understand that culture did not exist as a separate activity governed by different values. Culture was as integral a part of the revolutionary process as politics and economics. It must not be regarded as a vehicle for the self-expression of the artist: 'Art for art's sake which transcends class or party, art which stands as a bystander to, or independent of, politics does not in actual fact exist'.[25] He quoted Lenin's dictum that the purpose of literature and the arts was to serve the people. Mao defined the people in China as: 'workers, peasants, soldiers and the urban petty bourgeoisie', who made up 'more than ninety per cent of the population'. Culture was not the province of a self-regarding artistic coterie. The duty of artists was constantly to criticise their works so as to avoid mere self-indulgence and individualism. Their output must be meaningful to a mass audience, so as to increase the revolutionary consciousness of the people:

> One who has a truly good intention must take the effect into con-
> sideration by summing up experiences and studying methods, or in
> the case of creative work, the means of expression. One who has a truly
> good intention must criticise with the utmost candour his own short-
> comings and mistakes in work, and make up his mind to correct
> them. That is why the Communists have adopted the method of self-
> criticism.[26]

Mao extended his argument by urging the party's intellectuals to live and work among the peasants. Only by directly experiencing the virtue of real labour would they develop true understanding and integrity as revolutionary artists. At the height of the war with Japan, Mao made this appeal: 'Revolutionary Chinese writers and artists, the kind from whom we expect great things, must go among the masses; they must go among the masses of workers, peasants and soldiers, and into the heat of battle.'[27]

As interesting as Mao's views on culture and revolution was the steely resolve that accompanied their development. He wanted to impose them on the party. Mao loved intellectual jousting, but he did not like persistent challenge or opposition. He shared with Lenin and Stalin the conviction that once he had discovered a particular truth or settled on a particular conclusion there was no gainsaying his judgement. It was the notion of a correctness that could not be challenged that led to Mao's tightening his hold over the party in a series of fearful moves known as 'rectification'.

THE RECTIFICATION MOVEMENT

The movement is best understood as the process by which Mao finally destroyed the challenge from the pro-Soviet wing of the CCP. It exhibited in him the same ruthlessness that he had shown at Futian. Known in Chinese as *Zhengfeng*, rectification, which operated between 1942 and 1944, was a system of self-criticism intended to free the individual from error. In practice, it became a way of isolating and removing those Communists who were real or potential opponents of Mao. It grew naturally out of the notions that he had developed in his writings at Yanan, particularly the concept of democratic centralism. Since the CCP was the repository of truth, it was the duty of its members to adhere to all the party's decisions and instructions. Those who declined to conform could expect no sympathy.

In the spring of 1942, Mao invited the comrades to point out mistakes in the way the party operated and to suggest improvements. Those who responded by offering criticism were then rounded on and condemned for their individualism in daring to put themselves above the party of the masses. This was a clear extension of Mao's attack on artists and intellectuals. The principal scapegoat singled out for exposure and humiliation was Wang Shiwei, a young writer hitherto admired for his intellectual brilliance. He had written a withering article denouncing those leading members of the CCP who lived a life of luxury in Yanan while their heroic comrades in the Red Army were fighting to the death against the Japanese and GMD enemies. He was particularly bitter about those in the upper echelons of the party who ate good food, wore fine clothes, and chased young women, while the lower ranks had to survive on 'congee', the water left over after rice has been boiled in it.

In the early stages of Wang Shiwei's persecution, other writers came to his defence, but, confronted by Mao's evident determination to undermine the intellectuals, they backed off. For a time Wang was supported by a respected feminist writer, Ding Ling, who had joined the CCP after the murder of her husband by the Guomindang. She attacked the hypocrisy of party leaders who, in public, professed their belief in female equality but who, in private, treated women members with either disrespect or indifference. However, when faced by the stern opposition of the party, Ding Ling made an admission of her errors at a public session, and abandoned Wang Shiwei.

Arraigned before the public in the Chinese equivalent of a Stalinist show trial, Wang was accused of Trotskyism and 'anti-Party thinking'. Chen Boda, Mao's chief political adviser, amused the spectators by playing on the characters that made up Wang's name to call him a 'shit-house'. Despite such humiliating treatment, Wang refused to retract his charges. For this he was incarcerated until 1947 and then executed.

In the wake of the assault on the intellectuals and individualists, which Wang's case represented, the party hierarchy queued up to engage in self-criticism. Eager to express regret for past errors and to avow absolute loyalty to the party and to Mao, a succession of prominent figures made public confessions. Between 1943 and 1944, all the leaders in party and government openly acknowledged their former wrongs and accepted admonition from their assembled colleagues. Even Zhou Enlai admitted to having supported Wang Ming and the erroneous 'left line'. The only exception of note was Liu Shaoqi; he denied making serious political misjudgements and maintained that he had been consistently loyal to Mao. It is unlikely that Mao was impressed by Liu's stand. The vicious treatment meted out to him twenty years later, during the Cultural Revolution, can be read as Mao's delayed retribution on him for his refusal to play charades at Yanan.

Interestingly, Mao's only concession to self-criticism on his own part came in April 1944, when he bowed low three times before a full assembly of the party, a token of his acceptance that 'excesses' had marred the rectification campaign. These had occurred when the purge had been imposed across the whole party. This had been largely the work of Kang Sheng, Mao's security chief. Garbed in black, carrying a black whip, mounted on a black horse, and accompanied by a growling black dog, Kang cut a fearsome figure. Claiming that 70 per cent of the party were crypto sympathisers with Wang Shiwei, Kang undertook a wide-ranging purge. Mao himself did not like the term purge; he preferred such descriptions as 'rectification', 'rescue', or 'redemption' since these suggested that the Chinese Communists were concerned not to punish errant members but to re-educate them.

Yet, however defined, Kang Sheng's assault remained a deadly affair. Acting on Mao's assertion that 'spies were as thick as fur',[28] Kang claimed that the party was riddled with conspirators; pro-Chiang, anti-revolutionary cells were at work throughout the party. Given complete licence by Mao, Kang set a terror campaign in motion. Arrests, followed by imprisonment and torture to extract confessions, became commonplace. Over a thousand CCP members suffered this fate while another 40,000 were dismissed from the party on suspicion of wrongdoing, despite no evidence being produced. Mao even permitted the Politburo's Secretariat to be cleansed: around 20 per cent of its officials were removed. Kang put to fearsome use the NKVD terror techniques he had recently studied in Moscow, a point emphasised by a Russian Comintern agent who described the 'tragic reality' of what he saw in Yanan:

> Party discipline is based on stupidly rigid forms of criticism and self-criticism. The president of each cell decides who is to be criticised and for what reason. In general it is a Communist who is attacked each time. The accused has only one right: to repent his 'errors.' If he considers himself to be innocent or appears insufficiently repentant, the attacks are renewed. . . . The cruel method of psychological coercion that Mao calls moral purification has created a stifling atmosphere inside the Party in Ya'nan. A not negligible number of Party activists in the region have committed suicide, have fled or have become psychotic. . . . Under the protocol of criticism and self-criticism, the thoughts and aspirations and actions of everyone are on full view.[29]

The agent was not exaggerating. So pervading was the atmosphere of repression that some sixty top officials in the Party took their own lives rather than undergo public disgrace. Clearly things had gone too far. In October 1943, Mao stepped in. He gave instructions that illegal methods were not to be used against suspected members: 'We should not kill anyone; many should not have been arrested at all.'[30] After purging the party for over a year, the rectification campaign was called off. Mao could afford to appear merciful; the process had done its work. There was now no doubting how far he was prepared to go to enforce his authority. Members now held him in awe or in terror. Mao Zedong had become the Red emperor whose words and wishes were to determine the fate of China for the next thirty years.

What all this suggests is that the sweetness and light which, according to Communist legend, had prevailed at Yanan was only part of the story. Behind the amity and comradeship that undoubtedly did exist was a darker, grimmer reality. One of Mao's *bons mots* was that a revolution is not a dinner party. Yanan illustrated his point. Suppression and coercion were not merely adjuncts but central features of Chinese Communism as developed there under him.

It is again important to place Mao's authoritarianism in context. In the decade following the creation of the Red base at Yanan in the mid-1930s, the CCP had grown twenty-fold in membership. To keep control over such a rapidly swollen party, it was essential that conformity and discipline be rigorously imposed from the top. It became even more pressing to maintain the principle of democratic centralism. The fiat of the CCP leaders had to be absolute.

Another consideration is that with the end of the united front in 1938 the Guomindang had renewed its campaigns against the Reds, and that Japanese attacks had intensified in the same period. Hounded by the GMD and battered by the Japanese, the Reds had to survive by their wits and their resolution. This was, after all, a warlord era. The sense of peril shared by the Reds made adherence to the party line an act of prudence as well as of duty. By the same token, those members deemed to be jeopardising the party's existence by opposition in a time of crisis could expect no forgiveness from the loyal mainstream. In such a climate, individualism had no place. Mao put it in these terms:

> Some comrades see only the interests of the part and not the whole.
> . . . They do not understand the Party's system of democratic
> centralism; they do not understand that the Communist Party not only

needs democracy but needs centralization even more . . . the Party's interests are above personal or sectional interests.[31]

However Mao's authoritarianism is judged, it is difficult to see how the Chinese Communists, continually hunted as they were for twenty years after 1927, could have survived, let alone triumphed, except by adhering to a strong central command. Having overcome all rival claimants, Mao himself took command. The paradox was that his dictatorial actions, even the most extreme of them, were genuinely directed towards the liberation of China. But it was liberation in its Chinese sense – a collective not an individual freedom. Again, a religious parallel helps towards an understanding of this. A powerful tradition in the world's great monotheistic faiths – Judaism, Christianity, and Islam – has been the belief that the individual can find true liberty only through surrender and obedience to the divine will. Maoism, viewed as a secular religion, carried the same essential message: only by total acceptance of the dictates of the CCP, as expressed in the thought of Chairman Mao, could members be liberated into true enlightenment and class consciousness.

5

FROM PARTY LEADER TO LEADER OF THE NATION, 1943–50

The Chinese Communist Party takes Mao Zedong's thought – the thought that unites Marxist-Leninist theory and the practice of the Chinese revolution – as the guide for all its work, and opposes all dogmatic and empiricist deviations.

Statement issued at the Seventh Congress
of the CCP, June 1945

MAO'S MASTERY OF THE CCP

Mao's crushing of opposition by means of the rectification movement was followed immediately by a rush in the party to acknowledge his leadership. Considering the low ebb in his fortunes in the early 1930s at Jiangxi, Mao's rise to dominance in little more than a decade was a remarkable achievement. In his own assessment of his elevation, which he presented objectively as an account of the 'inner-party struggles' of the CCP, Mao highlighted the Zunyi conference and the rectification campaign as the key stages in the CCP's movement towards correct thinking.[1] Yet his success was not simply a matter of his influential teachings or his successful military and political record, important though these were. A critical factor was that Mao had gained control of the essential component in the party machine – the Secretariat, the body responsible for administration.

In March 1943, a number of key developments had occurred when, in the midst of the rectification movement, the CCP, under Mao's promptings, had restructured itself. Under the terms of the Politburo's 'Decision on the Readjustment and Simplification of the Central Organs', Mao became chairman of both the Politburo and its Secretariat. It was formally declared that the Secretariat was entitled to govern the party when the Politburo was not sitting. Still more significantly, Mao was given the authority to have the final say in any dispute within the Secretariat. Four months later, Wang Jiaxiang in an article, 'The Communist Party of China and the Chinese Nation's Road to Liberation', formalised the concept of 'Mao Zedong Thought', as the CCP's unerring guide. This confirmed that all issues within the party were to be decided by reference to Mao's writings and sayings. An official CCP history appeared in 1944 in which his path to power was presented as a seamless story of insight and wisdom triumphing over a succession of right and left errors until the whole party had come to accept the truth of Mao Zedong's thought.

The climax to Mao's elevation came in April 1945, when the Seventh CCP Congress adopted the 'Resolution on Certain Questions in the History of Our Party'. Its principal assertion was that, in order to achieve ultimate revolutionary success, the party must take Mao Zedong as their teacher and his thought as an infallible text. Members now vied with each other to find adequate eulogies for him. 'Great Leader', 'Supreme Teacher', 'Inspirer of the Masses', 'Great Saviour', and 'Great Helmsman' were among the epithets that poured forth. Enlarged photographs and paintings of Mao began to appear on walls and in public buildings. Toadying to the leader, a phenomenon not entirely unknown in Western politics, had a special meaning in China. To sing the praises of the leader conferred virtue on the singer as well as upon the praised. It was as if by lauding the thoughts of Mao Zedong one proved the correctness of one's own thinking.

By 1945 his authority was supreme; his was now the voice of Marxism-Leninism in Asia. He had been aided in this by a diplomatic twist that had occurred two years earlier. In May 1943, Stalin, in a gesture of goodwill towards his Western wartime allies, had ordered the dismantling of the Comintern which, despite being notably unsuccessful in its efforts to spread international revolution, had nevertheless soured relations between the USSR and the Western nations. The consequence for China of the Comintern's demise was that the CCP was no longer subject to the interference of Moscow's agents in its planning of revolution. In truth, the Comintern had ceased to exercise any real influence over the CCP since Mao's defeat of Wang Ming and the 'Returned Students', but its formal abolition gave strength to Mao's claim that the CCP represented a legitimate and sustainable alternative to Soviet Communism. There was perhaps a touch of smugness about Mao's epitaph on the Comintern's passing. In a speech in Yanan, he observed that:

> correct leadership should be based upon careful, detailed study of local conditions which can only be done by each of the Communist parties in its own country. The Comintern, far away from the actual struggle, can no longer provide proper leadership.[2]

MAO'S MARXISM

In keeping with his neo-imperial status, Mao began to hold court at Yanan. His meetings with government and party officials began to take on the character of formal audiences. Visitors struggled to gain a sight of the great man and hear his words of wisdom. He seldom walked anywhere now; with bodyguards in tow, he travelled by car or American jeep, an upgrade of the practice begun in the late 1930s when he had commandeered the one vehicle available to the Reds in Yanan, a battered Chevrolet van sent to the Red base as a gift from the New York Chinese Laundrymen's Association.

The adulation Mao received raises the fascinating question of why Marxism, a movement based on the primacy of the collective, should almost invariably have become associated with the notion of the great leader. Alongside Mao, one thinks of Lenin, Stalin, Castro, Ho Chi Minh, Pol Pot, and Kim Il Sung. Whether through charisma or terror, these Marxist leaders gave an indelibly personal character to the Communist systems they created. Soviet Communism was Stalinism. Chinese Communism became Maoism. In so many areas, the twentieth century was an age of authoritarianism. Scholars continue to debate the proposition that the major coercive movements of the last century, whether of the extreme left or the extreme right, operated in the same absolutist way because they came from the same stock; they were branches of the same tree. To vary the metaphor, they were mirror images. Communism and fascism, despite their detestation of each other, shared something that was far more significant than anything that divided them – an abiding hatred of liberal values. With this invariably went an intense nationalism.

Here a paradox intrudes. Marxism in its theoretical form was an ideology of internationalism. It spoke of class solidarity and looked forward to the collapse of the nation state when the workers of the world would unite in the overthrow of existing national governments. Yet the history of the twentieth century shows that, in practice, where Communism established itself successfully it did so by becoming the representative of national aspiration. Stalin deliberately and methodically pursued a policy of 'socialism in one country', which meant subordinating the interests of international Communism to securing, first, the survival of the Soviet Union and, then, its consolidation as a world power. Mao Zedong was no less committed to the salvation and regeneration of China. His consistent refusal during the 1930s and 1940s to permit the Bolshevisation of the Chinese Communist Party and his frequent ignoring of instructions from Stalin and the Comintern were examples of this. Later he would enter into a bitter dispute with Stalin's successor, Nikita Khrushchev, whose policy of detente with the West Mao regarded as a direct threat to the existence of the People's Republic of China.

Yet, when all this has been said, there is still the puzzle as to why the CCP, largely composed as it was of hard men who had endured extreme privation in their struggle to preserve and build the party, should have been willing to subordinate themselves wholly to Mao. Part of the answer lies in the loyalty of members to the party he led. As in Soviet Russia with the Bolsheviks, so in Red China with the CCP, the bond between the members of the party was a brotherhood. It had something very akin to a religious quality – the idea of dedication to a supreme cause, the notion of the party's infallibility. Harrison Salisbury has captured the essence of this:

> Mao's men had won their spurs in battle. . . . Some had started life as mercenaries in warlord armies and then had joined Mao's Red army. They were the backbone of the Communist movement. They lived in a military world and they followed military rules. An order was an order. It had to be obeyed precisely and instantly. . . . They were bound by an oath of secrecy. . . . Their oath was holy, and it admitted them to the sanctum sanctorum of the order. The word of the Party was supreme and Mao was its oracle.[3]

Not to belong to the party, or, worse still, to be expelled from it, was to suffer political death. Such concepts did not forbid internal discussions, but once the party had made a decision, the individual had no authority to go against it. That was why it was critically important for the Reds to get things right. Correctness was not an option it was a requirement. As Mao put it, 'Not to have a correct political view is like having no soul.'[4] Truth was not many-sided. When it came to ideology, there were no small issues. Every question became a test of revolutionary validity. There was no deeper pain a party member could suffer than to be classified as a deviationist.

A distinctive characteristic of all Marxist parties has been their claim to be based on scientific truth. It is this that justifies their existence and gives their members their utter conviction that they are right. Incorrect thinking is not permissible. That is why Communist parties have been so severe in crushing internal dissent; violent suppression of error has been viewed not as an excess but as a duty. Mao was a beneficiary of such un-questioning party loyalty. Once he had become the undisputed leader of the CCP, he was regarded by members not simply as a political figure but as the embodiment of revolutionary truth.

The notion of the will of the party superseding individual judgement is not wholly alien to Western understanding. A distinguished British historian and unrepentant Marxist, Eric Hobsbawm, has described the spell that Communist parties cast over their adherents. Recalling his days as a British Communist, he writes:

> The Party had the first, or more precisely the only real claim on our lives. Its demands had absolute priority. We accepted its discipline and hierarchy. We accepted the absolute obligation to follow 'the lines' it proposed to us, even when we disagreed with it. . . . We did what it ordered us to do. . . . Whatever it had ordered, we would have obeyed. . . . If the Party ordered you to abandon your lover or your spouse, you did so.[5]

CIVIL WAR AND WORLD WAR, 1938–45

The rise in Mao's status in the CCP during the Yanan years had been matched by his growing reputation as a leader of the Chinese resistance to the Japanese occupiers. The united front between Nationalists and Communists, which had formally began to operate again in September

1937, did not last. Both sides broke the agreement when it suited them. Chiang Kai-shek's hope remained that the Reds would exhaust themselves against the Japanese, while Mao had no compunction about undermining the GMD's position in the regions which the Communists infiltrated. Red control was spread beyond the areas originally agreed. Each side accused the other of bad faith. There was constant friction, and clashes often occurred when they met each other in the field. In effect, from 1938 onwards a civil war raged in China concurrently with the struggle against Japan. In that struggle the Communists continued to have greater success than the Nationalists. The 'Hundred Regiments' campaign' which Mao organised in 1940 was the nearest the Japanese came to suffering a major defeat in China since 1931.

Despite Chinese pleas for help against Japan, the foreign powers had been reluctant to become directly involved. This dramatically changed in December 1941 with the Japanese attack upon Pearl Harbor, which extended the Second World War into the Far East. The USA and Britain now became China's allies in the struggle against Japan. Yet this did not bring China any immediate advantage. For three years after Pearl Harbor, the Western Allies were preoccupied with the Japanese campaigns elsewhere in Asia. This meant that the conflict in northern China tended to become 'the forgotten war', a factor which intensified the Chinese Communists' sense of isolation and their feeling that what they had achieved had been solely by their own efforts. Moreover, the Western Allies' contacts were invariably with Chiang Kai-shek and the Nationalists. Chiang and his glamorous wife, Soong Meiling, received front-page attention in the Western press, which presented him as the heroic defender of his nation. Publicity was given to his book *China's Destiny*, published in March 1943, in which he claimed the moral high ground by presenting his vision of the nation moving towards prosperity and freedom under the leadership of the Guomindang.

In contrast, Mao and the Reds appeared very much as fringe figures to the outside world. There were dissenting voices among those Westerners who had first-hand knowledge of the situation in northern China. General Joseph Stilwell, a US liaison officer, known for his acerbity as 'Vinegar Joe', tried to correct what he judged as mistaken Western impressions by giving a vivid depiction of Nationalist weaknesses and Red strengths.[6] But the holders of such views were few and largely disregarded. It was understandable in the circumstances of war that the Allies chose to work with Chiang, who was, after all, the leader of the legitimate government of the Chinese Republic. That was why when the Americans, in all good faith, sought to further China's anti-Japanese war effort they liaised first with the Nationalists and accepted their characterisation of the Communists as merely rural bandits. It was something that cut very deep with Mao and explains why, quite apart from questions of conflicting ideology, he never trusted the USA.

Yet there was a moment in the later stages of the Second World War when genuine understanding, if not amity, might have been created. In 1944, the USA, anxious to see an end to CCP–GMD hostility, which was hampering the resistance to Japan, sent the so-called 'Dixie mission' to China. Its leading negotiator was Patrick Hurley, a likeable but tactless soldier and oil baron, given to enlivening the talks he attended by suddenly letting out Southern whoops and yells. Behind his apparent levity, however, there was a deeply serious purpose. He was anxious not merely to bolster the Chinese war effort but to forestall any moves that the Soviet Union might make in China.

The early signs were that the Communists stood to gain considerably from the American mission; it brought them recognition as major players on the Chinese stage. A team of foreign correspondents accompanied the Dixie mission. This provided Mao and the CCP with their first opportunity to make an impression on international observers. Mao instructed the comrades to adopt a moderate tone in their contacts with the visitors. His aim was to impress the Americans that the Reds were not the bandits of Chiang Kai-shek's description.

The attention given to Mao angered Chiang Kai-shek who, from the beginning, had objected to the Dixie mission's dealing with the Communists. But circumstances obliged Chiang to contain his irritation. He could not afford to upset the USA, which since 1941 had contributed vastly to the GMD in dollars and supplies. Reluctantly, therefore, he entered into three-way discussions with the Reds and the Americans. In the end the talks proved fruitless. Mao put forward proposals that the CCP be fully recognised and that Chiang accept the formation of a coalition government in China in which the Communists would have equal representation with the Guomindang. This Chiang refused to contemplate; he was also quick to reject a compromise offer from the Americans to divide their arms supplies equally between the Reds and the Nationalists. Mao became equally obdurate, losing his temper at one point and shouting that if Chiang were present he would call him 'a bastard' to his face. The Communists, Mao declared, did not want American assistance if the price was the sacrifice of their freedom. 'We are not like Chiang Kai-shek. No nation needs to prop us up. We can stand erect and walk on our own feet like free men.'[7]

Given such bitter exchanges, it was little wonder that by the end of 1944 the Dixie mission had failed. In retrospect, it is clear that Hurley and his team had never fully grasped the internal situation in China. The antipathy between Mao and Chiang, and the incompatibility of the two movements they led, made the chance of their reaching a workable compromise extremely remote. Mao's response was expressed the following April when he told the CCP's Seventh Congress that it was vital the Red Army be expanded against the very strong probability that civil war between the Nationalists and the Communists would be renewed once Japan had finally been defeated. What Mao did not know when he made that statement was that the Japanese defeat would occur within four months. His expectation, like everyone else's, was that the Pacific war would last for at least another two years. When, therefore, the war came to an abrupt end with the surrender of Japan following the atomic bombing of Hiroshima and Nagasaki in August 1945, the situation in China was dramatically and suddenly altered.

MAO, CHIANG, AND THE USA, 1945-46

The ending of the war against Japan came too soon for Chiang Kai-shek. It is true that by 1945 he was seen by the outside world as the Chinese leader who had carried his nation to victory after fourteen years of occupation. Moreover, its defeat of the Japanese had raised China to the level of a world power, one consequence of which was that it became a permanent member of the new UN Security Council. But the prize Chiang most cherished – the defeat of Mao and the Communists – still eluded him. He had anticipated that the Pacific war would climax with the landing of huge numbers of American troops in China who would then drive the Japanese into the sea. In the process the Americans, as Chiang's allies, would also crush the Chinese Communists, leaving him in total control of China. But events had not happened that way. Not only had the Americans not stationed their forces on mainland China in mass numbers, but the military dispositions in China when the war came to its sudden end in August 1945 meant that it was the Reds not the GMD to whom the Japanese armies in northern China subsequently surrendered.

What also dismayed Chiang was that Russian armies now occupied Manchuria. This was the consequence of a secret agreement Stalin had made with the Allies at the Yalta conference in February 1945 in which he had promised that the USSR would join the struggle against Japan at some point after the conflict in Europe had ended. The Soviet Union duly honoured that commitment by declaring war on Japan the day after the Nagasaki bombing. The Nationalist writ had never really run in northern China. The warlords, the Communists, and the Japanese in their different ways had prevented that. It was now clearer than ever that this part of China was beyond Chiang's control.

Yet Mao was little happier than Chiang. His initial satisfaction with the way things had swung the CCP's way turned to frustration when Stalin, immediately on learning of Japan's surrender, had rushed to sign a friendship treaty with Chiang's Nationalist government. Stalin's motive was to achieve a temporary easing of his strained relations with the USA by showing favour to America's far-eastern ally. Unbeknown to Mao, he had already agreed with the Americans not to assist the Communists should the GMD–CCD struggle be resumed. So, after a brief period in which they were allowed by the Soviet forces in Manchuria to amass a stockpile of captured Japanese weapons, the Reds were ordered to leave the cities and areas they had seized in northern China. When they were slow to comply, Soviet commanders threatened to crush them with tanks. Peng Zheng, one of Mao's regional officers, exclaimed angrily but impotently, 'The army of one Communist party using tanks to drive out the army of another!'[8]

The news did not improve Mao's state of health. He had again fallen into one of his bouts of depression and nervous exhaustion. It is intriguing that, having achieved near god-like status within his own party, Mao should still have been subject to this crippling malady. Dr Li, his personal physician after 1949, diagnosed Mao's problem as neurasthenia. Without irony, Li described this condition, one unrecognised in Western psychiatry, as 'a peculiarly communist disease, the result of being trapped in a system with no escape'. In Li's analysis, his patient's depression was worsened by chronic insomnia. Mao once declared, 'for me there are only two hundred days [in the year], because I get so little sleep'.[9] Li further judged that what intensified Mao's neurasthenia to the point of being physically incapacitating was his refusal, common among the Chinese, to acknowledge his condition, since this would be to admit to something shameful.

It was his anger with Stalin that helped persuade Mao to listen again to the Americans and agree to further talks with Chiang Kai-shek. In late August 1945, ill though he was, Mao, accompanied by Patrick Hurley, flew in a US plane from Yanan to the Nationalist capital, Chongqing. Six weeks of negotiations followed. Zhou Enlai, who was the chief CCP spokesman, attended nearly all the talks. Mao was present less often, but he did meet Chiang personally on at least four occasions. Their relations were cold and formal. In light of the ferocity of the CCP–GMD struggle that had intervened since they had last set eyes on each other in Guangzhou in 1926, this came as no surprise.

Superficially the talks made progress; the two sides agreed to recognize each other's regions of control, to unite their forces in a national army, and to move towards forming a joint government of China. Yet the evident tension made it clear that neither side was fully committed to the agreement. Late in 1945, President Truman, informed that matters were in the balance, sent General George Marshall to Chongqing as his special representative to see whether a genuine CCP–GMD settlement could be salvaged. The American fear was that a prolonged stalemate between the Communists and the Nationalists would enable the Soviet Union to spread its influence in China. But despite Marshall's best efforts, his mission was no more successful than Hurley's had been. The waters of bitterness had flown too long for there to be any real hope of reconciliation between Communists and Nationalists in China. As events had shown, when Mao and Chiang entered into negotiation it was out of expediency rather than an honest desire for compromise.

By the time Marshall had arrived in December 1945, Mao was in a sorry state. His Chinese interpreter recorded:

> All through November we saw him day by day, prostrate on his bed, his body trembling. His hands and legs twitched convulsively, and he was bathed in sweat. . . . He asked us for cold towels to put on his forehead, but it didn't help. The doctors could do nothing.[10]

The symptoms suggest that his malaria had returned. Zhou Enlai and Liu Shaoqi stood in for him at the key meetings. They kept to Mao's line of being moderate in their dealings with the USA, playing down the CCP's political aims by suggesting that they were essentially agrarian reformers. Acting on Mao's instruction, Zhou told the Americans that the door to an agreement with the GMD was still open. For a brief period early in 1946 it even seemed that Chiang might listen to the more moderate voices in his party and honour his promise to form a joint government with the CCP. This coincided with Mao's recovery from depression; he was uplifted by the thought that the CCP was about to be accepted politically by the Americans and the Guomindang.

But he was to be disappointed. Whatever concessions both sides might have appeared to make, there was no chance of an accommodation. Chiang ordered Nationalist troops to begin moving back into Red-held areas, telling Marshall that unless this was done the whole of northern China would fall to aggressive Communism. His assertion was given added credibility by news from the north of violent land seizures and murders of landlords by peasants, outrages that the Communists had condoned if not organised. By May 1946, Mao had given up all hope of a satisfactory diplomatic outcome. He declared that not only had the Marshall mission failed but that the USA was actively supporting the Guomindang.

It was certainly the case that, after the collapse of Marshall's mission, the Americans continued to recognise Chiang as the leader of China. In addition to airlifting Chiang's forces to the northern cities, the USA in June concluded a Lend-Lease agreement with the GMD, which provided for the transfer to the Nationalists of arms and equipment worth $1.7 billion. The American reputation in CCP eyes was further damaged by the report around this time of the rape of a Chinese woman by two US soldiers in Beijing. Isolated though the incident was, it led to mass student demonstrations and was held up by the Communists as an example of the new brand of Western imperialism that the US presence in China represented.

In the summer of 1946, Mao informed his party that the failure of the peace negotiations meant they must organise for full-scale war against the Guomindang. The Communists were the aggrieved party, he declared. They had done all they could to bring about peace, only to be betrayed by Chiang's perfidy and America's imperialist meddling. But the comrades could take heart. Their eventual victory over internal and foreign enemies was assured. In one of most celebrated statements he declared:

All reactionaries are paper tigers. In appearance the reactionaries are terrifying, but in reality they are not so powerful. From a long-term point of view, it is not the reactionaries but the people who are really powerful. . . . We have only millet plus rifles to rely on, but history will prove that our millet plus rifles is more powerful than Chiang Kai-shek's aeroplanes plus tanks. . . . The reason is simply this: the reactionaries represent reaction, we represent progress.[11]

Mao was to use the term 'paper tigers' frequently thereafter as a way of dismissing the supposed threat that came from nations and forces that outweighed China in military strength. He applied it directly to the atomic bomb. In his public statements, he refused to be impressed by the United States' use of nuclear weapons in 1945. Yet he was aware of the immense significance of what had happened at Hiroshima and Nagasaki. He knew it had changed the world. As soon as it was in a position to do so, two decades later, the People's Republic of China under his direction turned itself into a superpower by successfully detonating its own atomic bomb in 1964 and its own hydrogen bomb in 1967.

Despite Mao's powerful rallying call, the truth was that he had not provided inspired leadership during the months of negotiation that followed the Japanese surrender in August 1945. A combination of illness and uncertain judgement suggested that he had begun to flounder politically. What prevented this from damaging him to any significant extent was the quality of those who stood in for him, principally Zhou Enlai and Liu Shaoqi. Moreover, such was his control of the CCP by 1945, that whatever doubts there may have been among some members these were not expressed publicly. There was never a likelihood of a serious challenge to him.

VICTORY OVER CHIANG AND THE GMD, 1946–49

Once Mao had returned fully to the fray, he showed that his temporary lapses had not lessened his powers. His leadership of the CCP during the three-year struggle against the Nationalists that began in June 1946 proved inspirational. Under his direction, the Red Army, renamed the People's Liberation Army (PLA) in 1949, although heavily outnumbered at the beginning of the war in 1946, was ultimately to triumph over

Chiang's forces. In an exhortation of July 1946, Mao spelled out the strategy that was to take the Communist forces to victory:

> For defeating Chiang Kai-shek the general method of fighting is mobile warfare. Therefore the abandonment of certain places or cities is not only unavoidable but also necessary . . . we must co-operate closely with the masses of the people and win over all who can be won over.[12]

In this apparently simple formula, Mao was expressing the essence of the strategy the Reds would pursue successfully for the remainder of the civil war. Nor was it a matter merely of military dispositions. Mao showed that he had grasped an abiding central weakness of the Guomindang that made their defeat in a protracted war against the Communists unavoidable:

> Although Chiang Kai-shek has US aid, the feelings of the people are against him, the morale of his troops is low, and his economy is in difficulty. As for us, although we have no foreign aid, the feelings of the people are for us, the morale of our troops is high, and we can handle our economy.[13]

Events were to prove Mao's analysis to have been fundamentally correct. Despite the superiority in resources that Chiang initially enjoyed, he was never able to match the Reds in the propaganda war that was as significant as the military struggle it accompanied. Save for a few elite corps, the great majority of the Guomindang troops were conscripts, dragged from their villages by press gangs and obliged to fight under threat of savage reprisals against them or their families if they deserted. But desert they still did. GMD commanders came to expect that, every month, quite apart from the casualties suffered in fighting the Reds, they would regularly lose between 6 and 10 per cent of their troops through desertion. Those who stayed did so from terror, not loyalty. It was not unknown for GMD officers to hobble their men so that they could not run away. Whole units marched and slept roped together. The men were permitted to relieve themselves only collectively and at set times. Each soldier was held responsible for the next man in the line of march; if his neighbour made off, he was beaten or denied rations for not preventing it. The rank and file lived constantly on the edge of starvation. This was partly because of the poorly organised

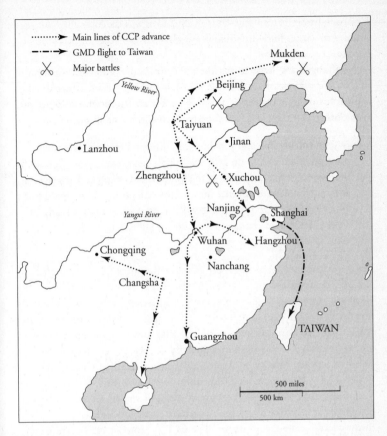

Map 5 The civil war, 1946–49

GMD supply system, and partly because many officers auctioned off their troops' food rations to civilian hucksters.

Such practices were representative of the venality that characterised Nationalist China. By 1945, the GMD had been running China for well over a decade. Its record was unimpressive. A few Chinese had enriched themselves at the expense of the many. The mass of the people had derived no tangible benefit from Chiang Kai-shek's regime. It was not that Chiang was personally corrupt – an avowed Methodist, he was legitimately renowned for the frugality and restraint of his life-style – but he presided over corruption. Nationalist China under him was the Shanghai gangster world writ large. Its hallmarks were graft and racketeering, leavened by terror and assassination.

Mao taught the Reds to exploit the Chinese people's consciousness of all this. He also encouraged the CCP's agents and agitators to modify their approach in the countryside so as to enlist all those who had become disenchanted by the GMD's failure to address the land question:

> [W]hen solving the land problem, rely firmly on the farm labourers and poor peasants and unite with the middle peasants. . . . We should be more strict in our treatment of the traitors, bad gentry and local tyrants, and more lenient in our treatment of the rich peasants and middle and small landlords. In places where the land problem has already been solved, we should change to a moderate attitude towards the landlord class as a whole.[14]

Mao's instructions were an aspect of his willingness to adapt to circumstance. The situation after 1945 suggested that a softer line towards the landlords, resulting in fewer violent expropriations, might win the Reds more adherents in the country areas. The adjustment did not betoken any real change of heart. Communist brutality towards the landlords had not gone away; it had been temporarily suspended in the interests of public relations. Mao's aim was to blacken the name of Chiang and the GMD. His opponents helped him immeasurably in this. Vastly superior in numbers and *matériel* at the start of the civil war in 1946, and backed financially and militarily by the Americans, the Nationalists contrived to throw away all their advantages. The CCP's record of spirited resistance to the Japanese, its readiness to forego aid from imperialist America, and its sensitivity to the needs of ordinary Chinese contrasted markedly with the failure of the Guomindang to represent Chinese aspirations. Mao urged the CCP to capitalise on this on as broad a front as possible.

> Unite workers, peasants, soldiers, intellectuals and business men, all oppressed classes, all people's organizations, democratic parties, minority nationalities, overseas Chinese and other patriots; form a national united front; overthrow the dictatorial Chiang Kai-shek.[15]

The Guomindang's political failings might not have proved fatal had they been able to maintain their military supremacy over the Reds. But they were outfought and suffered a continual haemorrhaging of manpower and morale. When the civil war restarted in 1946, Chiang's primary aim was to assert Nationalist authority in the northern provinces, including Manchuria, by driving the Reds from the areas they had liberated from the Japanese. Hoping to overwhelm the Communists with the GMD's greater resources, he ordered a series of large-scale assaults on Red positions. This played into Mao's hands. He responded by adapting the tactics employed by the GMD themselves during the anti-Japanese struggle – the principle of selling space to buy time. That was the logic behind Mao's willingness to abandon apparently key positions, including even Yanan, to Chiang's forces; he wanted to leave them only empty victories. He told his commanders: 'We should not try to stop them. . . . Chiang thinks when he has seized the devils' lair, he will win. In fact, he will lose everything. . . . We will give Chiang Yan'an. He will give us China.'[16]

Mao's readiness to sacrifice what had been the Reds' main base for over a decade may seem odd. Yanan's practical achievements as a Red republic and its symbolic value as the heart of resistance to Japan and the Guomindang, might be thought to have made its defence a priority. But Mao was not looking for another Stalingrad. True, he wanted to wear down the GMD, but not at the expense of his own men. The more appropriate historical parallel for him was Moscow in 1812, when Napoleon's Grand Army had walked into a city the Russians had already burned and deserted. Chiang's taking of Yanan in 1947 was an equally hollow victory. The Reds had packed and left weeks before to create a new base around Yangjiagou in northern Shaanxi. It was from there that Mao directed the next stage of the strategy, which was aimed at exhausting the Nationalist armies. The pattern was to draw the GMD forces into a chase and then disperse and disappear before they could engage. It was a hazardous business and involved great personal risk to Mao. In the gripping description given by Sidney Rittenberg, an American Communist and dedicated Maoist who accompanied the Red columns at this time, Mao played 'a sardonic cat and mouse game'. Knowing how desperately the GMD longed to take him alive, he continually offered himself as a target for capture:

> [Mao] deliberately telegraphed his moves, and . . . made it a point never to be more than one day's march ahead of the GMD. . . . At every encampment he would wait until the scouts brought him news that the

> enemy was only an hour's march away before he would methodically
> put on his coat, mount his horse and lead his little headquarters
> column off down the trail. . . . [W]hen the GMD troops were exhausted,
> Peng Dehuai selected the most vulnerable cul-de-sac . . . and hurled
> [his troops] against them.[17]

It was only when the Reds had massed superior numbers that Mao faced
the GMD in pitched battles, and then only on fields of his choosing. He
was able to do this because the Reds could rely on support in the
countryside in ways that Chiang never could. To be sure, the Communists
were prepared to coerce unco-operative areas, but this was usually a matter
of last resort. In the GMD's case, terror was standard practice. The
Guomindang troops, who were themselves brutally treated, showed the
same savagery towards those who fell into their clutches. Massacre, looting
and rape invariably followed in their wake.

The Nationalists achieved some military gains during the first twelve
months of the renewed hostilities, but these did not amount to substantial
victories. By avoiding direct confrontation until they were ready, the
Reds nullified the Nationalists' numerical superiority. Mao was right in
his estimation that the longer the struggle went on, the more difficult
it would become for Chiang's forces. This was borne out by the shift in
the relative strength of the two sides. In the autumn of 1945 the GMD
army amounted to nearly 4 million troops. By the end of 1948 that number had more than halved. Measured at the same points in time, the PLA
had grown from 300,000 to 1.5 million. It was the same story in
armaments. By 1948 the Red armies matched the GMD in the number
of field and heavy guns, around 20,000 for each side. Although the Reds
did manufacture some of their own weapons, the greater number were
American-made arms captured from the Guomindang.

Even more serious for Chiang than the shrinking size of his armies was
the plummeting morale that accompanied it. Not only the conscripted
rank and file, but officers and commanders were losing heart. Protests and
mutinies multiplied. Chiang's only response was still more severe repression. Intended as deliberate acts of terror, the arrest and public execution
of demonstrators became common events in Guomindang areas. In July
1947, a General Mobilisation Bill was issued giving the GMD unrestricted
call-up powers throughout China. While such measures succeeded in their
immediate aim of cowing the population, they weakened Chiang's moral

claim to the leadership of the Chinese people. Serious divisions emerged within the GMD. Breakaway groups, such as the Revolutionary Alliance and the Democratic League, formed themselves in opposition to the GMD.

Chiang's problems did not end there. Arguably, his greatest burden was economic. This had been Mao's perception at the beginning of the civil war when he had forecast that the Nationalists would be unable to handle the economy. The factor that proved Mao right was hyper-inflation. It so happened that the areas occupied by Japan after 1937 had been China's previously most productive provinces. Once these had fallen under Japanese control, the Nationalist government suffered a severe drop in revenue. To compensate for this, it took out large foreign loans and printed large amounts of paper money, unsupported by financial reserves. High loans and unbacked currency were a lethal combination. The Chinese currency plunged in value and prices rocketed. The price index rose from 100 in 1937 to 287,700,000 by 1948. The Chinese yuan (equivalent to 10 pence at pre-war exchange rates) became worthless. 'In 1940, 100 yuan bought a pig; in 1943, a chicken; in 1945, a fish; in 1946, an egg; and in 1947, one-third of a box of matches.'[18] Nationalist China had collapsed financially.

Such developments disheartened Chiang's previous supporters at home and abroad and were both cause and effect of the GMD's increasing military reverses. In the last two years of the civil war it proved incapable of achieving a single major victory. The catalogue of Nationalist defeats at Red hands continued to grow. In 1948 Mao was able to declare that, having achieved the first objective of weakening the GMD, the Communists would now alter their strategy so as to take on the enemy in pitched battle. Lin Biao, Peng Dehui, and Deng Xiaoping distinguished themselves in carrying out Mao's instructions. The first decisive success for the Reds occurred at Mukden in November 1948, a victory which left them in control of Manchuria and the northern regions of China above Beijing.

This was followed a few weeks later by the taking of Xuzhou, the high point of the Reds' Huaihai campaign, which involved nearly a million troops fighting in four provinces. Xuzhou was a vital railway junction, whose fall meant that the GMD had lost central China north of the Yangxi. The climax of the civil war came in January 1949 when the Communist advance forced Chiang's forces to abandon Beijing. Although fighting would drag on for another year, the outcome of the struggle had been decided. The Guomindang was about to lose mainland China.

In the hope of salvaging something, Chiang Kai-shek had suggested late in 1948 that GMD–CCP peace talks be reopened with a view to forming a coalition government. He appealed to both the USA and the Soviet Union to act as mediators. Mao would have none of it. Knowing that Chiang's move had been made out of desperation, Mao would settle for nothing less than complete victory over the enemy he had fought for nearly two decades. He rejected Stalin's suggestion that the Guomindang's offer should at least be considered. In an exchange of telegrams, the Soviet leader put it to Mao that there might be advantages for the Reds in accepting Chiang's proposal. Reading between the lines, it seems that Stalin saw in the possibility of the USSR's being a mediator a chance for him to regain an influence over the Chinese Communists. But Mao was immovable. Some days before receiving Stalin's first telegram, he had made a 1949 New Year's Day Declaration in which he had described Chiang and the GMD as 'snakelike scoundrels' towards whom 'no pity' should be shown. He thanked Stalin for his interest but put him firmly in his place:

> We think that if we now start peace negotiations . . . with these people, that would be the exact fulfilment of the US government's wishes . . . we are inclined towards rejecting the peace deception by the Guomindang with full righteousness, because now as the balance of class forces in China has already changed irreversibly and the international opinion is also unfavourable to the Nanjing government, the PLA will be able to cross the Yangzi this summer and start the offensive towards Nanjing.[19]

Events later in 1949 showed the significance of Mao's reference to crossing the Yangxi. As the PLA prepared to make this move, Stalin warned Mao that if the Reds did cross the river and then tried to link northern and southern China, it would prove too much for the Americans. They would not tolerate a unified China under Communist rule. Better therefore, Stalin urged, for China to remain divided with Chiang nominally in control in the South and the Reds consolidated in the north. Again, Mao ignored Stalin's advice, judging that it was aimed not at thwarting the USA but at preventing a united Communist China from rivalling the Soviet Union. He did not accuse Stalin of this at the time but he later said:

> Even in 1949 when we were about to cross the Yangtze River, [Stalin] still wanted to prevent us. According to him we should under no circumstances cross the Yangtze. If we did so America would send troops to China and become directly involved in China's Civil War and the South and North dynasties would reappear in China. I did not listen to what [he] said. We crossed the Yangtze. America did not send troops and there were no South and North dynasties.[20]

By June 1949, the GMD had lost Shanghai and Nanjing while Guangzhou was on the verge of collapse. This convinced Chiang Kai-shek that he could no longer hold China south of the Yangxi. Leaving some divisions to fight a delaying action, he led the GMD to the offshore island of Taiwan with as many troops and as much bullion as could be conveyed. Once in Taiwan, Chiang re-established what he claimed was still the legitimate government of the Chinese republic. He promised his supporters that one day the Guomindang would return to retake the mainland from the Communist usurpers. Mao Zedong reciprocated by pledging to seize Taiwan, which he regarded as part of the sovereign territory of Communist China, at the earliest opportunity. Taiwan had entered Chinese and international politics as an intractable problem.

With the turn of the tide against the Nationalists in 1947, Mao had left Shaanxi province and for the next eighteen months was constantly on the move, usually on pony or horseback, conducting operations. His wife, Jiang Qing, occasionally travelled with him, but more often than not she stayed behind. Late in 1948 he moved to the outskirts of Beijing to an area rejoicing in the name of the Fragrant Hills. It was here that he waited even after Red troops took Beijing in January 1949. He decided not to make a formal entry into the city until victory over Chiang Kai-shek was complete. This was achieved in September 1949 when Chiang finally fled from the mainland. The CCP promptly appointed Mao as chairman of the People's Republic of China. In his first address as chairman, Mao declared that after a century of 'exploitation by foreign imperialism and domestic reactionary governments' a new Chinese nation had come into being:

We have united and have overthrown both domestic and foreign oppressors through the People's War of Liberation and the great people's revolution, and now proclaim the founding of the People's Republic of China. . . . Our nation will never again be a nation insulted by others. We have stood up.[21]

On 1 October 1949, Mao, flanked by his victorious generals, stood on a balcony of the Tiananmen Gate in Beijing's ancient Forbidden City, to review a march-past of the PLA. At his signal, the five-star red flag of the new nation was hoisted high. Over loud speakers he announced to the 300,000-strong crowd: 'The Central People's Government of the People's Republic of China is founded today.'[22] His words were carried by radio across the land. The fifty-five-year-old Mao Zedong was now the ruler of one quarter of humanity.

MAO AND STALIN

Very soon after the establishment of the PRC in 1949, Mao visited the USSR, the first time he had ever ventured out of China. He had been invited by Stalin over a year before but had delayed until victory over the GMD was assured. His reasons for going now were simple. The new China needed resources and the Soviet Union was the only country that could provide them. During the ten-day train journey from Beijing to Moscow, which began in mid-December, Mao enjoyed the changing scenery of provinces and lands he had never seen before. But his neurasthenia returned. He was confined to bed with bouts of shivering and fierce headaches. Apprehension about his meeting with the Soviet leader may well have contributed to his illness.

Mao had good reason to be anxious. In Western eyes, his official visit to the USSR was a meeting of the two great Communist dictators, intent on forging a monolithic Red bloc stretching across two continents. But this was not the reality. Despite Mao's being accorded full diplomatic honours on his arrival in Moscow in late December, relations between the two leaders were wary and uncertain. In their formal speeches and communiqués, they expressed profound respect for each but there was no meeting of minds, let alone real friendship. Their difficult relationship up to 1950 prevented that.

It is arguable that Stalin never understood Chinese Communism as represented by Mao Zedong. As a young member of the CCP in the 1920s, Mao had initially followed the Kremlin line but he had come rapidly to the judgement that the Comintern's advice was founded on an unrealistic grasp of the situation in China. The instruction that the CCP should maintain its front with the Guomindang in the face of Chiang Kai-shek's White Terror confirmed Mao's doubts. During the Jiangxi years, as he tried to construct a Chinese soviet, he had been accused by the Comintern of deviationism for pursuing an independent path and resisting the Bolshevisation of the CCP. Mao believed that the Soviet advisers who were sent to China came not assist but to control their brother Communists. The Long March was opposed throughout by the Comintern, whose anger was increased when Mao was elected chairman of the CCP in 1935 in place of their nominee, Wang Ming. In the war against Japan between 1931 and 1945, Stalin continued to support Chiang and the Nationalists rather than Mao's Communists.

Similarly, throughout the intermittent Chinese civil war, which lasted until the victory of the Reds in 1949, Stalin had shown his disregard for the CCP by subordinating its interests to those of the Guomindang. His appeal to Mao not to allow the PLA to cross the Yangxi into southern China was an illustration of this. Soviet supplies had invariably gone first to the Nationalists, the PLA receiving only the leftovers. With the Soviet occupation of Manchuria at the end of the Pacific war in August 1945, Mao had expected that his forces would be invited in by Stalin. The opposite happened. The Reds were debarred entry and then obliged to watch as American planes flew in Chiang Kai-shek's armies to seize the cities and accept the Japanese surrender. In the process the Guomindang recovered much of the weaponry that they had previously lost to both the Japanese and the Reds.

Stalin in the end had to accept the fact of the Red triumph of 1949, but he did so with scant grace. Behind the formal Soviet paeans celebrating Mao's success, Stalin was less than enthusiastic. The USSR now had a neighbour, the PRC, possessed of a strength and unity that China had not known for centuries. Stalin also feared that Mao would begin to rival him personally as leader of the Communist world. Looking back in 1962, Mao reflected that Stalin in 1949 'suspected China of being a Yugoslavia, and that I would become another Tito'.[23] Mao's reference was to Marshal Tito, the Communist leader of Yugoslavia, who, by successfully maintaining his country's independence of the Soviet bloc, had been a constant reproach to Stalin.

A fascinating perspective has been provided by Dmitri Volkogonov, a leading Soviet historian who worked under Stalin. Commenting on the 1950 meeting between Stalin and Mao, the two great leaders of world socialism, Volkogonov mused:

> The situation must also have been somewhat unusual for Mao, who had never been outside China, had not participated in the work of the Comintern and whose links with other Communist parties were minimal. The two men sitting opposite each other at the conference table also thought differently, had different scales of values, represented different civilisations. Even their Marxism gave them little in common, since Mao was fond of mixing his with Confucianism, while Stalin generally confined himself to quoting his own works. They were, however, both pragmatists.[24]

Mao had not enjoyed his journey to Moscow, nor did he enjoy his ten-week stay there. Beneath the formal courtesies, a conflict of wills was going on. This was evident in a dispute over a seemingly minor piece of protocol. Mao insisted that Zhou Enlai, the PRC's foreign secretary, be present at the talks. This was his way of testing whether Stalin was prepared to break the Soviet links with Chiang Kai-shek. Mao wanted the existing Sino-Soviet Treaty, which the USSR had signed with the Guomindang in 1945, to be revoked. Only by accepting the request that Zhou be invited to Russia to sign a new Treaty, could Stalin prove that the Soviet Union was willing to abandon all connection with the GMD. For some days the Soviet leader declined to respond, a sign, in Chinese eyes, that he had been angered by the request.

Mao thought that this explained why he and his delegation did not receive the hospitality they had expected. The *dachas* in which they were housed were hardly sumptuous. Little thought had gone into catering for Mao's recreational needs or personal comforts. There was no heated pool for him to indulge in his second favourite physical activity, swimming. The programme of visits drawn up for him by his hosts was unusually tedious, even by Communist standards. Apart from the official meetings and visits to a succession of factories and model farms, nothing had been laid on to lighten his time. It was as if Stalin wanted to bore him. Mao complained to Yan Mingfu, his Russian interpreter, 'I have nothing to do but eat and shit.'[25] In retaliation, Mao reacted with studied indifference to many of the things he was shown. Taken on a short visit to Leningrad, he cast only perfunctory glances at the treasures housed in the Hermitage museum and declined to be impressed by the monuments commemorating the great wartime siege of the city; China, too, he told his hosts, had its war memorials.

Despite such skirmishing, Stalin eventually agreed to Mao's demand that Zhou Enlai be recognised as the chief Chinese negotiator. It was Zhou who was co-signatory with Andrei Vyshinsky, his Soviet counterpart, when, in the presence of Mao and Stalin, the Sino-Soviet Treaty of Alliance was signed on 14 February 1950. Stalin had been initially reluctant to enter into a binding treaty. He told Mao that the 1945 treaty with the GMD had been signed by the Soviet Union in keeping with a commitment made to the Western Allies at Yalta and that to abandon it now would be to provoke them unnecessarily. However, on learning that Britain was preparing to give diplomatic recognition to the PRC, he acknowledged that the question of provocation no longer applied. He now accepted Mao's argument that a new treaty was appropriate. In response to Stalin's question as to what the PRC wanted from the treaty, Mao produced a list whose main items were 'a credit agreement for 300,000,000 dollars', supplies of industrial goods, and 'your assistance in creating a naval force'.[26] Stalin agreed on the major points and these were incorporated into the treaty.

When Mao left Moscow, he had reason to think he had accomplished his mission. At his last stop on Soviet soil he sent a telegram to Stalin expressing his 'deep gratitude' and his 'best wishes for the continuous strengthening and prospering of the Soviet Union'.[27] On his arrival back in Beijing, Mao was given a hero's welcome. It soon became apparent, however, that he had bought the Sino-Soviet agreement at a high price. The small print of the treaty was not in China's favour.

The aid that the USSR had agreed to advance was not a brotherly grant from one Marxist state eager to help another. Stalin had treated it as a business deal. As security for the $300 million credit, the PRC had to hand over a large part of its bullion stocks to the Soviet Union. In addition, it had to pay in full the salaries and upkeep of the 10,000 economic advisers who were sent to China. Of the money advanced by the Russians, barely 5 per cent took the form of genuine investment; the bulk of the capital came as loans that were to be repaid with interest. Nikita Khrushchev later admitted that the treaty had been 'an insult to the Chinese people'; he said it had marked the point where the USSR had taken over from the old imperialist powers in the exploitation of China.[28]

The USSR's influence over China in the 1950s was pervasive. It was oppressively visible in the public buildings that were erected under Soviet advice at this time. Beijing, Shanghai, and Chongqing were disfigured by new government office blocks and 'halls of culture', built in the heavy architectural style described by some foreign observers as 'Russian brutal'. To make way for the new structures, large areas of the cities had to be cleared, a process which saw the demolition of many classical Chinese buildings. Mao was unmoved by such sacrilege. The new China needed money and development. For these, he was prepared to tolerate temporary Soviet dominance and the loss of some of the trappings of China's heritage.

6

MAO THE NEW EMPEROR,
1950–62

First and foremost, things are determined by people's hearts and minds. It has always been like that in history. In history, the weak have always beaten the strong.

Mao Zedong, 1957

During the first months of existence of the People's Republic of China Mao adopted what in retrospect appear relatively restrained domestic policies. Although he ordered private property to be confiscated, he also promised indemnity and compensation to former property owners and shareholders, provided they were prepared to work for the 'socialist-agrarian-industrial society' that was being planned in the new China. A similar offer was made to all those who had served as officials or civil servants under the GMD governments. Mao's aim was to ease the CCP's task of moving towards Communism by preserving continuity in administration. How long Mao would have remained patient and accommodating is difficult to judge, but the question became academic once China became involved in war. Less than a year after its creation, the People's Republic of China (PRC) found itself embroiled in the Korea peninsula in the first open conflict of the Cold War. The demands of a ferocious military struggle destroyed all thought of tolerant economic and political policies.

THE KOREAN WAR, 1950–53

Oddly, in view of what was soon to follow, Mao and Stalin had not discussed the Korean question in their 1950 Moscow meetings. The Russian leader had encouraged Mao to prepare to seize Tibet and Taiwan, but he had not mentioned Korea. Stalin's silence adds weight to the suggestion that he was deliberately planning to manoeuvre the PRC into the Korean imbroglio.

The close of the war in the Far East in 1945 had ended the Japanese occupation of Korea. The peninsula had then been partitioned along the 38th parallel, leaving a Communist north, led by Kim Il Sung and supported by the USSR, facing a non-Communist south which looked to the USA for protection. In June 1950, Kim created an international crisis when he sent his North Korean forces across the parallel with the aim of taking the whole country by force. The Americans, who were still in shock from two events that had occurred the year before, the Soviet Union's development of the atomic bomb and the victory of Mao's Reds in China, interpreted the invasion as a joint move by the newly-formed Sino-Soviet unholy alliance.

The American reaction was understandable in the circumstances, but mistaken. The evidence now available from Soviet and Chinese sources indicates that Mao had played no part in the planning of the initial North Korean invasion.[1] Up to that point, the PRC's military preparations and expenditure had been concerned exclusively with China's internal provinces and Taiwan. The Korean conflict was engineered by Stalin, who wanted a war that would draw in both the USA and the PRC, but would not directly involve the USSR in the fighting. To this end, without consulting Mao, he urged Kim Il Sung to invade South Korea. Stalin led Kim to believe that Soviet forces would join the war should the North Koreans meet sustained resistance, although at no time did he make that a formal commitment. Stalin had banked on two probabilities: that the North Koreans would prove capable of a prolonged campaign that would tie down the Americans should they enter the struggle, and that the PRC's strategic interests would oblige it to come into the war on the North Korean side.

His judgement proved astute on both counts. The war became a prolonged conflict and Mao felt compelled to commit the PRC to it. However, when Stalin first suggested that China should ally with the

North Koreans, Mao hung back. He could see the enormous risk to which the young PRC was exposing itself; the cost in resources and men was likely to be fearful. The effort of bringing himself to make the decision left him sleepless for seventy-two hours, despite his downing a range of sedatives. Since he could not sleep, he sustained himself by chain-smoking and non-stop infusions of coffee. As Stalin had calculated, what eventually led Mao to commit China to the war was the fear was that if the Americans gained mastery over Korea they would have every opportunity to complete their underlying aim of invading China itself. It was an anxiety that conditioned Mao's approach to international affairs until at least 1972 when his personal meeting with President Nixon went some way to assuage his terrors. In 1950, Mao judged that the new China was being put to a test of its resolve. It could not remain detached. He explained as much to Stalin when taking the final decision to enter the war:

> The Korean revolutionary force will meet with a fundamental defeat, and the American aggressors will rampage unchecked once they occupy the whole of Korea. This will be unfavourable to the entire East. . . . [W]e must be prepared for a declaration of war by the United States and for the subsequent use of the US air force to bomb many of China's main cities.[2]

In the event, the USA did not need to declare war. It entered the struggle as the major component of a United Nations liberation army. Even that twist in the story was largely Stalin's doing. At the meeting of the five-member UN Security Council called in June 1950 to discuss the Korean emergency, it was expected that the USSR in its customary fashion would veto any resolution by the other four states (the USA, UK, France, and Nationalist China) to involve the UN in the war. However, at a critical point in the meeting, the Soviet delegation, acting on Stalin's orders, boycotted the proceedings, ostensibly in protest at the UN's continued refusal to recognise the PRC. The Soviet Union's absence allowed the four pro-Western members to vote unanimously for the despatch of a UN force to Korea. But what appeared to be a blunder by the USSR was in fact a subterfuge. The Soviet walkout had produced the very result Stalin had intended. According to a later explanation by Andrei Gromyko, the Soviet foreign minister in 1950, Stalin had calculated that had the USA unilaterally declared war on North Korea, Mao could then, at any time after

China had become an ally of the North Koreans, have invoked Article 1 of the Sino-Soviet Treaty which required the Soviet Union 'to immediately render military and other assistance' to the PRC should it be attacked by the USA.[3] But, since it was as part of a UN force that the Americans fought for the South Koreans, the Soviet Union was not obligated. Stalin had achieved his primary objective – to entice the USA into a struggle from which the Soviet Union could stand aloof, but which the PRC would now have to join. Mao had been duped.

Mao's initial reluctance to enter the war had been shared by his military commanders. Gao Gang, the governor of Manchuria, and Lin Biao told Mao that they feared the PRC was not yet strong enough to undertake what was likely to be a prolonged conflict. It needed all its resources in order to take Taiwan, and impose its authority over Tibet and Xinjiang. It was thus with some difficulty that Mao persuaded his generals that China must fight in Korea. What finally convinced them were the reverses suffered by Kim Il Sung's forces in the first months of the fighting. Fearing that the North Koreans were about to suffer a humiliating defeat, which would leave the Americans poised to attack China, they accepted Mao's argument that the PRC had no choice.

Although it did not formally enter the struggle until October 1950, Mao's China had been sending 'volunteers' to fight alongside the North Koreans since June. In the intervening months an intense propaganda campaign organised by Zhou Enlai prepared the Chinese people for war by portraying it as a gallant crusade against American imperialism. When, in October 1950, US forces crossed the 38th parallel into North Korea, China had its pretext for war.

In the course of the three-year conflict that followed, millions of Chinese troops fought in Korea, the majority of them conscripts, although the PRC continued to hail them as 'volunteers'. It was a bitter struggle, involving the deaths of a half a million Chinese and perhaps the same number again in wounded. Among the dead was the twenty-eight-year-old Mao Anying, the first-born son of Mao Zedong and his second wife, Yang Kaihui. Of all Mao's children, Anying was the one to whom he felt closest, despite seeing him only rarely. Mao confided to his bodyguard, Li Yinqiao: 'My son and I see each other only once every five years. Even when we're not separated, we don't see each other more than a handful of times a year.'[4] Father and son had had their differences; Mao on one occasion had reduced Anying to tears by forcing him to delay his marriage. Nevertheless, Mao took a greater interest in him than in any of his other children. Parted from his parents at the age of nine, Anying had lived a precarious life on the streets of Shanghai, before being reunited with Mao in the 1930s. He had then gone to the Soviet Union to study. It was at his father's prompting that Anying volunteered to serve in Korea in 1950. He went as an interpreter working for Marshal Peng Dehuai. He had been in Korea barely five weeks when he was burned to death during an American incendiary raid on Peng's headquarters. Peng, who survived the attack, telegraphed Mao's secretary, Ye Zilong, with the news of Anying's fate. After consulting Jiang Qing and Zhou Enlai, Ye decided not to inform the chairman immediately. It was some three months before Anying's death was eventually reported to Mao. His bodyguard described the scene:

> His initial reaction was one of shock. He didn't say anything; he just looked at Jiang and Ye. The two hung their heads in silence; they knew better than repeat the news to him or offer him sympathy.
>
> Mao then blinked, slowly turning his eyes away from them towards a pack of cigarettes on the tea table. He picked up the pack and tried to take out a cigarette but he couldn't do it; he tried again, and again he failed. I hurried over and lighted it for him.
>
> The room was silent, except for the hissing sound which Mao made as he exhaled the cigarette smoke between his teeth. Then I noticed his eyes had suddenly turned red and moist around the rims, caused perhaps by some stray cigarette smoke, or by memories flooding his mind.[5]

It has been suggested that with Anying's death 'the one remaining human bond capable of evoking in Mao a deep personal loyalty was severed.'[6] It was certainly one of those incidents that combined to have a deadening effect on Mao. It was if by a strange inverse ratio the more powerful he became as a public figure the more distanced he was from ordinary feelings and emotions. He became impervious to the suffering of his people, a process which enabled him to pursue ends no matter how costly the means.

The Korean war gave an indelible character to the PRC. Whatever plans Mao and the party had had for the young China had to be subordinated to the needs of war. The hardening of Mao's character was matched by a steeling of the PRC. An interesting historical parallel presents itself. Thirty years earlier, revolutionary Russia had taken its shape not in accordance with the original plans of Lenin and the Bolsheviks but in response to a bitter civil war into which Russia was plunged from 1918 to 1920. The Soviet Union was born in violent conflict. So, too, was the People's Republic of China. The Korean war demanded sacrifice and commitment. The effort left no opportunity for a smooth transition from the old China to the new. The PRC was obliged to prove itself in war before it had had time to establish itself in peace.

It did so to considerable effect. Although Kim Il Sung's original aim of taking the whole of Korea was not achieved – the truce of 1953 left the peninsula still divided at the 38th parallel – the PRC's forces had faced the might of the USA and held it at bay for three years. But this had come at a high international and domestic cost. The Korean conflict deepened the hostility between China and the USA and led to a generation of Sino-Western tension. The Bamboo Curtain was as powerful a barrier to international understanding as the Iron Curtain. One particular outcome of the war in Korea was that the USA pledged itself to the defence of Taiwan. This effectively ruled out any possibility of the PRC's reclaiming the GMD stronghold in the foreseeable future. Nor was the deterioration in China's relations with the USA balanced by an improvement in Sino-Soviet understanding. Mao's feeling that Stalin had deliberately misled him was intensified by the Soviet leader's consistent refusal to involve the USSR directly in Korea. In the first contest of the Cold War it had been Chinese not Soviet comrades who had died in the cause of international Communism.

The loss of a million young men in casualties was not the end of the PRC's tribulations. The national economy had to be redirected to meet the war effort. Such was the disruption that the domestic growth that might have been expected in peacetime was delayed by over a decade. The financial burdens were especially heavy. Wartime production costs increased China's debts. Mao remarked that China had to pay down to the last rifle and bullet for the Soviet supplies it received during the conflict.

REPRESSION IN THE PRC

During the course of the Korean war China became a militarised society. The basis for this had already been laid by the initial structuring of the new nation after 1949. To cope with governing an area as vast as the People's Republic of China, the country had been divided into six administrative regions, known as bureaux, all under the ultimate authority of the Central People's Government Council led by Mao Zedong. Each bureau was administered by four chief officials – chairman, party secretary, military commander, and political commissar – the last two of whom belonged to the PLA. It was this arrangement that had helped in the running of the PLA's 'reunification' campaigns for bringing Tibet and Xinjiang under PRC control and for ridding China of the million 'bandits' who were said to be roaming the land in the early 1950s.

Martial law did not need to be officially imposed on China. Conformity and obedience became part of the fabric of a society at war. By providing the justification for extreme measures, the Korean conflict had pushed Mao and China further down the road of political repression. The programme of control was soon under way. The year 1951 saw the introduction of 'the three Anti-Movement', an attack upon administrative corruption, followed a year later by 'the five Anti-Movement', aimed at increasing efficiency in the workplace by rooting out industrial saboteurs such as those who purloined state property or committed fraud. Significantly, Mao declared that the anti-movements were an attack on 'the bureaucratic capitalist class', his term for those who were reluctant or slow to accept the new order of things. Clearly, the honeymoon period for those who had stayed on to serve the new regime was over. Mao spelt out the position in uncompromising terms. His aim was to rid China of all hostile elements: 'Those reactionary capitalists guilty of the worst crimes will be isolated, and the state will be in a strong position to mete out due punishment, such as fines, arrest, imprisonment or execution.'[7]

The purpose of the anti-campaigns was not merely to expose and punish real or supposed enemies of the people. They were intended to frighten the masses into line. Mao promised 'leniency for the majority and severity for the minority, leniency for those who make a clean breast of their wrongdoings and severity for those who resist.'[8] The message was clear: confess or be denounced. People soon learned that the best way to avoid being implicated was to denounce others. Playing on this, party apparatchiks invited workers to inform on their fellows workers, neighbours to report on neighbours, and children to betray parents. The professional classes were among the most eager informers. Knowing that their non-revolutionary background made them suspect, they sought to

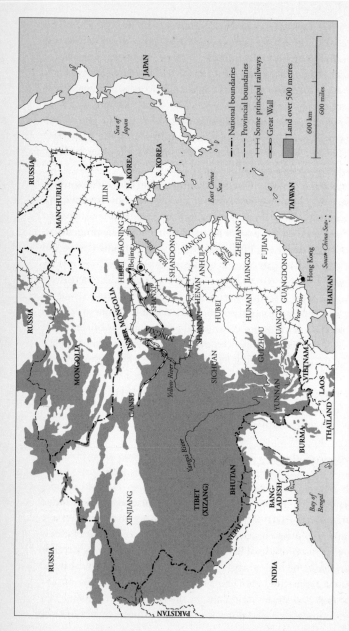

Map 6 China, including the outlying provinces

divert attention away from themselves by accusing others. The labels were readily available: 'bourgeois backslider, 'imperialist lackey', 'counter-revolutionary', 'capitalist roader'. Such terms have a comical naivety in translation, but they were deadly weapons in their Chinese setting. To be so labelled was to be found guilty. Since the charges implicit in the epithets were so imprecise, it was impossible for the accused to defend themselves convincingly. In imperial China, public ridicule had always been a powerful means of condemning unorthodox behaviour or deviant thinking. That tradition was maintained and intensified in Mao's China. The party drew up *dangans* on all Chinese who came to their attention.

These were dossiers containing detailed personal information. A whole army of party clerks was employed on a daily basis in collecting and up-dating the material. The *dangans* were a mechanism of political and social control. Whether a person gained employment, housing, or a pension was determined by the record in his dossier. The CCP-controlled press and radio were filled with daily denunciations of persons and institutions considered to be dangerous to the new state. Religious bodies, particularly those associated with foreign missionaries, came under fierce assault, a prelude to the closing down of Christian churches and the deportation of priests and nuns. China's own religions were not spared; Confucianism and Buddhism were condemned as corrupting superstitions that held the people in subjection. Propaganda became a constant accompaniment to everyday life. China's communal tradition was exploited. Slogans, written on wall posters and chanted over crackling loud speakers, enjoined the people to throw off the decadent past and rejoice in the new Communist society that was being constructed.

COLLECTIVISATION AND THE FIVE-YEAR PLAN, 1952–56

The conformity enforced by Mao's repressive policies proved valuable in China's early efforts to develop its economy. For all Mao's renown as a leader of rural revolution, it needs to be stressed that as leader of the new China his plan was for the PRC to become an industrial power. He accepted that if China was to develop as a major nation it would have to create a strong industrial base. The forging of a peasant revolution had been his response to the situation as it actually had been before 1949. Circumstances had meant that urban proletarian revolution had had to be delayed. That explains Mao's running battle with Stalin and the Comintern over the direction the Chinese revolution should take. In defiance of Soviet orders, Mao had put his faith in the peasants. But that did not mean he wished to keep China permanently as a peasant society. Once the CCP had achieved power, Mao's aim was to modernise China through urbanisation and industrialisation.

For a brief period after the creation of the PRC, Mao had encouraged the peasants to seize the land. They had been quick to respond. Landlords and their families had been attacked in an orgy of retribution; deaths numbered around the million mark. But Mao did not intend the peasants to become private proprietors. He wanted China to be a communal society. Stilling protests from a number of his colleagues, most notably Deng Zihui, whose objection was not so much to the policy itself but to the pace of it, Mao demanded that communes be created throughout China to take the place of private farming. Squads of party cadres were sent to the countryside. Their task was to organise the local people into peasant associations which, under CCP direction, then introduced collectivisation. Mutual Aid Teams supervised the pooling of land, tools and resources and the creation of rural communes and co-operatives.

The speed of the change was staggering. By the beginning of 1957, practically the whole of the Chinese peasantry had been collectivised; barely 3 per cent of farms remained in private hands. Mao had stood the revolution on its head. Under his direction, 'the revolutionary state, having established its legitimacy by freeing the peasant from landlordism . . . had become the ultimate landlord.'[9] His own comment on this remarkable achievement in centralised control was: 'The peasants want freedom but we want socialism.'[10] Like Stalin, he believed that the peasants were instinctively reactionary; this required that they be controlled and directed. The official line, however, was that collectivisation had been introduced in response to the wishes of the peasantry; that was why it had been achieved so swiftly. In the summer of 1958 the CCP's Central Committee claimed on Mao's behalf that China's 500 million peasants, having had their political consciousness raised, had freely embraced 'the collective life'.[11]

In keeping with the Stalinist model in the USSR, Mao decided that the PRC's economic growth was to be directed from the top. A National Resources Committee was established to organise large-scale migration from the countryside to the towns. The committee was also made responsible for directing financial investment into urban and industrial concerns. The result was that between 1949 and 1957 China's urban population rose from 57 million to 100 million. This provided some of the human and financial resources that enabled Mao to embark on a Five-Year Plan (1952–56). A factor that helped greatly here was the PRC's undoubted success in bringing inflation under control, an achievement that had notably eluded the Nationalists in government. A tight restriction on public spending, combined with high taxation and the introduction of a new currency, meant that by 1951 the PRC's inflation rate was running at a manageable 15 per cent.

The results of the Five-Year Plan, though modest by international standards, were impressive in Chinese terms and compared well with the Soviet industrial record of the 1930s. Between 1953 and 1957 the PRC achieved an annual industrial growth rate of 9 per cent, the most significant increases being in the output of coal, steel, and petro-chemicals. The Korean war, which had ended in 1953, had been used to justify a tightening of political control. The same reasoning was attached to the Five-Year Plan. The public was made constantly aware that the effort to modernise China required that backsliders and saboteurs be exposed and shamed. Party cadres were sent into the factories to oversee the workers and report on 'bad practices and bad attitudes'.

Mao exploited the atmosphere, in which anything short of total acceptance of the plan was deemed counter-revolutionary, to remove possible political rivals. In 1954, he authorised the humbling of two of the PRC's highest-ranking officials. Rao Shushi and Gao Gang, the respective CCP secretaries in Shandong and Manchuria, were charged with financial corruption and factionalism. Rao was denounced and expelled from the party. It was intended that Gao, who was a bigger fish and an admirer of Stalin, be subjected to a public show trial at which he would be accused of treason for having attempted to turn Manchuria into his own private fiefdom. However, Gao, in despair at his coming humiliation, committed suicide before the hearing could begin. The CCP claimed that there had been a 'Rao-Gao clique' intent on preventing the progress of the PRC. Mao moralised that their overthrow had been a lesson in 'learning from past mistakes to avoid future ones and curing sickness to save the patient.'[12] His private comment on the affair was less high-toned. He told his doctor how he marvelled at the virility of Gao Gang, who was rumoured to have had over a hundred lovers. 'He had sex twice on the very night he committed suicide. Can you imagine such lust?' Mao did add, however, that Gao's escapades would have been of little real importance had he not made serious political errors.[13]

Mao's vendetta against those he thought might harbour doubts about his policies was extended to include intellectual and literary figures. In keeping with the attacks he had made during the rectification campaigns in the Yanan years, he insisted that conformity to socialist values was the only valid base for artistic expression in Communist China. Works which failed to uplift the people had no place in the People's Republic. He made a virulent attack upon Liang Shuming, a professor of philosophy and writer, who had dared describe the hard conditions under which the great majority of the peasants were still living. Mao intervened at a public meeting to denounce Liang. In the peasant, colloquial style that he invariably reverted to when angry, he snatched up the microphone and shouted at Liang that he was a stinking bag of bones. In a word play on the maxim that the pen is mightier than the sword, Mao accused the professor of killing far more peasants by his writing than GMD troops had with their guns.[14]

The disgracing of Liang Shuming was followed shortly after by an attack on another prominent writer, Hu Feng, for having disputed the right of the CCP to be the sole arbiter of artistic worth. Hu was accused of being a counter-revolutionary. Despite making an abject confession, he was arrested and imprisoned. Hu's incarceration proved to be the prelude to a *sufan*, an organised assault on the Chinese intelligentsia generally. The CCP's mouthpiece, the *People's Daily*, claimed that 10 per cent of the party were suspect and needed to be purged. In 1955 around 100,000 members were arrested and interrogated, with thousands being imprisoned or expelled from the party.[15]

THE 'HUNDRED FLOWERS' CAMPAIGN, 1956–57

It might have been thought that by 1956, with the real if limited success of the Five-Year Plan, Mao would ease his grip on China. But the reverse happened. He intensified his control, albeit in a manner which initially suggested that he was becoming more liberal. Despite the hard line that he publicly maintained, Mao, in his private conversation and when addressing party gatherings, often appeared to encourage open criticism. In a keynote address in April 1956, he declared: 'It would not work to have no discipline, but if the discipline is too rigid, initiative will be stifled.'[16] In a formulation that became the basis of a vast political campaign, Mao called on the CCP to 'let a hundred flowers bloom and a hundred schools of thought contend.' This appeal did not come out of the blue. It was a considered response not only to the political situation in China but to the problems created by de-Stalinisation in the Soviet Union.

In an extraordinary 'secret speech' in Moscow in February 1956, Nikita Khrushchev, the Soviet leader, had delivered a withering exposé of 'the crimes against the party' which Joseph Stalin had committed during the quarter of a century he had ruled the USSR down to his death in 1953. The most telling of Khrushchev's charges was that Stalin had used his power to indulge in a 'cult of personality' and, so, place himself above the Soviet Communist Party. Mao's reaction was to read this as a scarcely veiled attack upon his own leadership of the CCP and China. His apparent call for greater liberalising may be interpreted, therefore, as an attempt to suggest that there was a real difference between his authority and Stalin's.

His desire to distance himself from the Soviet Union was increased by the developments that followed in the wake of Khrushchev's attack upon Stalin's record. In the Eastern bloc satellites there occurred a series of popular nationalist risings against the Soviet-dominated Communist governments, the most serious being in Hungary in October 1956. Although these were firmly crushed by the authorities, Mao blamed their outbreak on the relaxing of government control over the counter-revolutionaries in the countries concerned. This left him in an odd position. If he was truly disturbed by the disruptive effects of the liberalising implied in de-Stalinisation, then it would have made no sense for him to have pursued a similar policy in China. It is this that suggests that the Hundred Flowers initiative had an ulterior motive. It was not the soft line than it initially appeared. Nevertheless, he persisted with his appeal to the comrades to be openly critical.

He pressed this idea at the Eighth CCP Congress held in November 1956, only to be irritated by what then developed. Although the congress applauded him lustily, a formal resolution confirmed that the government of the PRC was a collective not an individual affair. In itself, this was not especially important since the PRC had been founded in 1949 on the principle of collective leadership. More significant, perhaps, was congress's acceptance of a proposal, put forward by Peng Dehuai, that it should omit the standard reference to Mao Zedong's thought as the inspiration of the party and nation. Mao took the omission badly. He felt that his fellow collective leaders, Liu Shaoqi, Zhou Enlai, and Deng Xiaoping, did not fully share his ideas of progress and that the CCP was sliding towards deviationism. Mao appears to have believed that Peng Dehuai's proposal showed that were elements in the party willing to challenge his authority.

It was shortly after the congress that Mao succumbed to his recurrent depression and withdrew for three months. However, when he returned he immediately took up his earlier theme. In a major speech in February 1957, he repeated his call for a hundred schools to contend within the party. He told the comrades that such contention would be a means of resolving the 'various contradictions [that] continue to exist in socialist society.'[17] The free discussion and competition of ideas would promote the development of art and science and thus contribute to China's current economic drive. 'Marxism is a scientific truth and fears no criticism. . . . Marxists should not be afraid of being criticised by anyone.'[18] Reading between the lines, it is reasonable to conclude that, given his distaste for what had happened at the Eighth Congress, Mao saw in the Hundred Flowers campaign a ready means of exposing the enemies he believed to be lurking in the party.

Members were slow to respond to Mao's appeal for open expressions of opinion. They sensed that there was something dubious about the invitation. After all, it was in the same Hundred Flowers speech that Mao had stressed that certain patterns of thought would not be tolerated. He had singled out 'bourgeois reasoning, dogmatism, revisionism and opportunism' and had emphasised the continuing need to 'eliminate counter-revolutionaries'.[19] It was difficult for conscientious members to judge where the line was between the types of thinking of which Mao approved and those which he rejected. What was acceptable as legitimate criticism on one day might be condemned as revisionism on another.

Unhappy with the initial diffidence of the party, Mao, in the spring of 1957, threw himself into a campaign to promote the Hundred Flowers. Deng Tuo, the editor of the *People's Daily*, was summoned to Zhong-nanhai, Mao's official government residence in Beijing, where the chairman berated him in foul language, and ordered him to give the movement priority coverage in his newspaper. Mao then set off on an extensive tour of China in his special train, which had been converted into a travelling government centre. He claimed that this put him in touch with the people and allowed him to meet party members in their own localities. However, the truth was that such meetings were stage-managed affairs. They provided copy and photo opportunities for the government-controlled press to portray Mao as the leader who understood the people because he was one of them. But in reality the peasants and workers he met were hand-picked individuals and groups who had been trained to say nothing that he did not want to hear. Nevertheless, the apparent warmth that greeted him further convinced Mao that the time was ripe for gathering suggestions as to how best the nation and party could construct the new society.

Under his promptings the members began to put forward their ideas. These began as a trickle, but, as the comrades gained confidence, they became a spate. It was as if suppressed frustrations were being released. As the criticisms increased in number, they turned sharper in tone. Mild suggestions for the improvement of the party were overtaken by increasingly shrill denunciations of individuals and policies. Doubts were even cast on whether the CCP had the sole right to govern China. The climax came with direct attacks on Mao himself. One university professor went so far as to refer to the 'arbitrary and reckless' character of the chairman's authority.[20] This would have been unthinkable even a few months before. Mao declared himself appalled and took to his bed again.

Yet it is doubtful that he was genuinely surprised by the reaction he had provoked. Certainly, the speed with which he then acted suggests that he was prepared for what had happened. He confided to his doctor: 'We want to coax the snakes out of their holes. Then we will strike. My strategy is to let the poisonous weeds grow first and then destroy them one by one.'[21]

Having shaken off his depression, Mao proceeded to invert the Hundred Flowers movement. It was transformed into another deadly rectification campaign, an assault on those who had dared to say the unsayable. In May and June 1957, he rounded on the intellectuals who had taken him at his word and offered criticism. In a series of addresses and articles, he branded them as 'Rightists' who were bent on betraying the revolution:

> They attempt to seize this opportunity to overthrow the Communist Party and the working class, and to topple the great cause of socialism. They want to drag history back to a bourgeois dictatorship . . . and to resubjugate the Chinese people to the reactionary rule of imperialism and its running dogs.[22]

Mao described the campaign against them as 'squeezing the pus out of an abscess'.[23] Those who had co-operated by helping a hundred schools of thought contend were now made to confess their 'evil thoughts' and purge themselves through 're-education' in remote labour camps. Some were to languish in such places for twenty years. Estimates of the number of victims vary between half and three-quarters of a million party members.[24] What had begun as a call for free expression had ended as a programme of thought control.

The fierce policies that Mao introduced in the 1950s had a profound significance for China. Their imposition meant that the opportunity for the PRC to advance a genuinely alternative form of Marxism had been lost. Maoism, like Stalinism, was revealed as essentially a system of repression. China became a society of informers and conformists willing at Mao's urging to impose a rigid uniformity of thought upon the young nation.

THE GREAT LEAP FORWARD, 1957–62

Mao's success in redirecting the Hundred Flowers campaign into a popular movement to defeat his rightist critics helped prepare the way for the next stage of his economic programme. A conformist society would provide the means of achieving growth. He was moving towards the belief that China could achieve industrialisation by a great act of collective endeavour. This marked a significant change in Mao's thinking. Earlier in the 1950s he had told the party that it was unrealistic to expect the PRC to achieve parity with the world's advanced nations in less than twenty years. Now, however, he judged that by an effort of national will China would be capable of matching the Soviet Union and the leading Western countries within a decade. The peasants, who formed China's great spine on which the revolution had been built, could be drawn into a concerted and integrated effort to provide the human resources that industry needed.

It is hard to determine how exactly Mao arrived at this conclusion. One of his characteristics was that he seldom allowed himself to be burdened by detail. This did not prevent him from being meticulous in his own writings; his major political and social analyses were many-layered in description and argument. However, when developing grand ideas he employed assertions. He had convinced himself that great things could be achieved by sheer will-power. What inspired him would also inspire the people. If it involved suffering and sacrifice, so be it; these were prices worth paying for the regeneration of China.

Also influencing Mao's thinking were recent developments in the USSR. He had been impressed, as had the world, by the Soviet Union's achievement in launching two 'sputnik' satellites into space in the autumn of 1957. Mao was convinced that China could attain similar success. But he was not greatly concerned with the science of it all. He admitted he was no expert: 'I only understand social sciences but not natural sciences.'[25] Nonetheless, he felt able to lay down broad directions. The crucial factor was the participation of the people. Through collective enterprise, individual efforts would be utilised to their best effect. This was possible, he claimed, because China's socialist revolution had ended for ever 'the contradiction between individualism and collectivism'.[26] Each person would now find ultimate fulfilment in mass endeavour. That was the reason he laid great stress on manual work. For him, the development of machines and devices that saved time and effort was not a priority. The sophistication of the production process was not the goal. The aim was the direct involvement of the people in their nation's regeneration.

> In order to build socialism and communism in China, we must depend on the creative power of the working class and the millions of labouring people under the leadership of their vanguard. As for an individual, he is no more than a small screw in the revolutionary works. . . . [A]ll achievement is the result of the strength of the collective, and an individual without the party to lead him or an organisation and the masses to support him, cannot accomplish anything.[27]

In a speech in November 1957, Mao surveyed what the CCP under his leadership had achieved. His theme was that at every key point it had been strength of will that had carried the party through against overwhelming odds. The defeat of the Japanese and the GMD had been gained not by superior numbers or resources but by superior will. In that respect, the achievement of the Chinese Communists matched that of the Russian Bolsheviks. He had no doubt that in the clash between East and West, history was on China's side:

> [T]he imperialists are like the sun at 5 o'clock in the afternoon, while we are like the sun at six o'clock in the morning. . . . The east wind is bound to prevail over the West wind, because we are powerful and strong.

The problem is that you just cannot decide things with the quantity of steel and iron; rather, first and foremost, things are determined by people's hearts and minds. It has always been like that in history. In history, the weak have always beaten the strong; those without guns [have] always defeated those who were fully armed.[28]

Significantly, Mao delivered this speech in Moscow in 1957 during his second and last visit to the USSR, which also proved to be the last time he left China. He had flown to the Soviet capital at Nikita Khrushchev's request to participate in a gathering of international Marxist parties. Khrushchev's aim was to quell the doubts that had developed in the Communist world in the wake of de-Stalinisation. Mao was not impressed by the proceedings. He had not wanted to go in the first place, and was finally persuaded only by the thought that he would meet Tito. At the gathering (which Tito did not attend), Mao formally acknowledged the Soviet Union's primacy as a socialist nation, but he let it be known that he was unhappy with Khrushchev's policy of co-existence with the West. It was during the discussions on that issue that Mao had declared China's readiness to undergo nuclear attack in the cause of international revolution. He added that the Soviet Union's attempt to reach *détente* with the Western powers was an act of revisionism. Peace was not an absolute good if it meant betraying socialism. Mao astounded Khrushchev by telling him that, if it came to a war with the West, he was willing to contemplate the loss of half of China's 600 million population in a nuclear attack. China had so many people, he informed his host, that it could soon make up the loss.[29]

Mao returned from the USSR even more determined to drive the PRC towards modernisation. But he no longer intended to do it by slavishly following the Soviet Union's methods. The disaffection from his hosts that he had felt in Moscow confirmed his growing conviction that the Soviet model was no longer suitable for China. This marked a distinct break from the policy followed since 1949. Mao now chose to lead his people along 'a Chinese road'. Some years later, he explained why he had changed course. In the early days of the PRC:

the situation was such that, since we had no experience in economic construction, we had no alternative but to copy the Soviet Union. In the field of heavy industry especially, we copied almost everything from the

Soviet Union. . . . At that time it was absolutely necessary to act thus, but at the same time it was a weakness – a lack of creativity and lack of ability to stand on our own feet. Naturally this could not be our long-term strategy. From 1958 we decided to make self-reliance our major policy.[30]

Mao had thus created a paradox: China was to modernise without using modern methods. Not technology, but the physical exertion of the people would create the conditions for rapid economic growth. The striking example of this was his insistence on the development of backyard furnaces. Aware that steel was the essential to industrialisation, he called upon the whole people to engage directly in its production:

The Soviet Union progressed from having only about four million tons of steel at the end of 1918 to only eighteen million tons in twenty years' time. We [on the other hand, aim at] attaining twenty million tons of steel in three five-year plans. . . . This demonstrates that we are capable of doing things a bit faster. I propose that there is advantage in opening up more small steel factories from now on.[31]

Mao's notion of small included very small. Let the people produce the steel not only in the great foundries but in individual furnaces which each family could build and tend. Peasants as well as urban workers could all contribute. Indeed, by mobilising the peasantry as steel producers, China could overcome its lack of a trained work force. The applied enthusiasm of the people would circumvent the need for experts and planners. The disarming simplicity of Mao's scheme swept aside all objections. Marshalled by eager officials, the Chinese rushed to do Mao's bidding. It required either bravery or foolhardiness not to join in the vast enterprise. The furnaces changed the landscape of China. Smoke and flames filled the air in every town and village and at night the sky glowed red. It was a piece of theatre produced by Mao, the grand impresario, and directed by thousands of officials who vied with each to carry out his instructions. At Zhongnanhai, Mao could look out at night across the government compound at the light from hundreds of tiny furnaces dutifully erected by government officials to produce their quota of steel. To keep the furnaces fuelled with wood, large areas in a number of provinces were deforested, an ecological blunder from which China has still not fully recovered.[32]

Mass endeavour was not limited to steel production. Roads, canals, irrigation networks, bridges, and dams were built by communal labour. A major prestige project, intended to impress foreigners and Chinese alike, was the construction of Tiananmen Square, a huge hundred-acre paved site facing the ancient Forbidden City in the centre of Beijing. Mao took great personal interest in the building of the square, which he insisted had to be grander than Moscow's Red Square. Mao frequently visited such sites to show solidarity with the workers. On one occasion in 1958, he joined in the digging of the Ming Tombs Reservoir to the north of Beijing, wielding a shovel for half an hour. This, according to his doctor, was 'the only time in the twenty-two years I worked for him that Mao engaged in hard labour'.[33]

The Great Leap Forward was both magnificent and absurd. As a piece of applied populism, with hundreds of millions of Chinese working for the same goal, it was breathtaking. Foreign observers testified to the extraordinary efforts and enthusiasm that Mao had wrought from his people. Roderick MacFarquar, a British scholar resident in the PRC, wrote of China being gripped by 'seething, clattering frenzy'. He described a typical village scene: 'People carried baskets of ore, people stoked, people goaded buffalo carts, people tipped cauldrons of white-hot metal, people stood on rickety ladders and peered into furnaces, people wheeled barrows of crude steel.'[34]

Its absurdity lay in its divergence from economic reality. Mao had convinced himself that through a massive voluntary effort, backed by state terror waged against the doubters, China could bypass the need for integration and planning. It was as if he resented being in thrall to experts and specialists. The Great Leap Forward did have its highly visible successes; impressive buildings and structures did arise. But these were not manifestations of planned economic progress. It was all too haphazard. The political regimentation that made the Great Leap Forward possible as a grand project was not matched by a comparable control of the productive process itself. So much was left to local initiative that it would be wrong to speak of China's operating a national plan. Officials issued admonitions and threats aplenty, but hardly any detailed instructions as to how things were to be done.

The result was that effective organisation and quality control became difficult to achieve and impossible to sustain. Nowhere was this more evident than in relation to the outstanding symbol of the Great Leap Forward,

steel production. The fact was that the only steel of value came fr
large foundries. What was produced in Mao's beloved backyard f
proved worthless. Smelted from the low-grade material to be found in such
domestic items as pots, pans, and bicycles, the peasant's steel was unusable.
The authorities soon learned this, but went on encouraging its production
so as not to give the game away. The steel was regularly collected, taken to
large secret dumps and never used again. What was true of steel applied
equally to the economy overall. The initial upsurge could not be sustained.
A severe recession set in. The economic falsifications and imposed political
correctness that characterised Mao's transformation of the PRC were about
to reap a deadly reward – the worst famine in China's history.

CHINA'S GREAT FAMINE, 1958–62

China's bitterest tragedy, the great hunger of 1958–62, began with collectivisation. As Mao saw it, the key to Chinese growth was the production
of grain and steel. These were the two 'generals' who would modernise
China. He worked to a simple formula. The Great Leap Forward would
produce the steel; collectivisation of the land would produce the grain.
But this vast piece of social engineering wrought disruption and insta-
bility in the countryside. The peasants were made not merely to live
communally but to farm collectively – and produce steel. They were
confused and disorientated. It was here that Mao's supposed understanding of the peasantry betrayed him. His plans ran counter to Chinese
rural practice. The peasants were subsistence farmers. By tradition,
they grew just enough food for the immediate needs of their families. They
were not equipped suddenly to increase food yields. Their response to
collectivisation was to produce not more but less.

Even in those few areas where greater output was achieved, this did
little to improve things. The reality was that China's transport and com-
munication systems were inadequate to cope with the scale of the problem.
Surpluses in one area could not compensate for shortages in another. What
is remarkable is that at no time did Mao actually define the way in which
the communes should be run. He seemed to believe that the ending of
private ownership would of itself create efficiency and increase production.
He privately admitted that he had no idea of how collectivisation operated
in practice. 'There are lots of things we don't know. How is this people's
commune organized? How does it work?'[35]

Mao's blind faith in the communes was matched by his adherence to false science. He gave his imprimatur to the ideas of Trofim Lysenko, a Soviet agronomist and protégé of Stalin, who claimed to have discovered ways of developing 'super-crops', which would grow in any soil in any season and provide a yield anything up to sixteen times greater than the harvests produced by traditional methods. Mao accepted all this, declaring 'in company grain grows fast; seeds are happiest when growing together.'[36] He had convinced himself that there was such a thing as 'socialist science', which could be used to reshape nature and produce abundance. In his attack on the intellectuals during the Hundred Flowers campaign he had demanded the dismissal of those scholars who still clung to the bourgeois notion that scientific research was a matter of objective observation rather than socialist enlightenment. He seemed not to appreciate that this demand contradicted his earlier and oft-repeated admonition that the comrades should 'seek truth from facts'.

In 1958, Mao gave instructions that Lysenkoism was to be strictly followed in the planning of agriculture. An eight-point programme modelled on Lysenko's theories and covering all aspects of crop production was made mandatory in the countryside. There was one small flaw in Mao's plans: Lysenko was a charlatan and his science wholly bogus. Indeed, his worthless theories had contributed to the famines in the USSR in the 1930s. But protected by Stalin, who had regarded him as an oracle, Lysenko had become unchallengeable, which left him free to spread his absurdities.[37] Mao learned too late that the ideas which he had imposed on Chinese agriculture were not the findings of a genius but the concoctions of a quack. Had the consequences not been so deadly it would all have been highly comic. But what began as farce ended as tragedy. Lysenkoism did not multiply China's harvests, it destroyed them. At the very time when a bewildered peasantry were struggling to come to terms with the disruption of collectivisation they were made victims of an imposed pseudo-science that caused their crops to wither in the field.

Mao's pursuit of socialist ways of increasing food supplies was at its most irrational in his plan for what amounted to the destruction of China's bird life. Responding to party instructions, villagers across China came out of their houses at prescribed times and sundered the air with shrieking, the banging of drums, and the beating of pots and pans. The purpose of this collective cacophony was to confuse and terrify the birds until they fell exhausted to the ground. The rationale for such madness was that this vast cull would save China's grain stocks from being eaten by the birds. But the outcome was the reverse of that intended. Rather than protecting the stocks, the policy of 'sparrowcide' allowed the insects and pests, who would have normally been eaten by the birds to feast unmolested on the grain. Safe now from their natural predators, vermin devoured the stored harvests.

Mao was selective in his reading of the reports that he received from the provinces. He wanted to hear good news. Yet so many accounts of distress accumulated that he eventually acknowledged there were pockets of hunger. However, he was not prepared to accept that these constituted a major famine or that the problems were caused by his communal policies. According to his doctor, if Mao had fully grasped what was happening he would have halted the disaster: 'But the truth had to come to him on his own terms. . . . He could not accept it when it included criticism of him.'[38] So Mao variously attributed the difficulties to grain hoarding, mistakes by local officials, and poor weather. In regard to the last point, it is true that in 1958 a combination of flooding and drought did damage the harvest in a number of central provinces, but in the following two years the weather was exceptionally benign. Whatever Mao and his officials might claim, the famine could not simply be attributed to climatic conditions.

Chinese sources now show that at least 50 million Chinese died from hunger in the period 1958–62. Few provinces escaped the famine entirely, but the greatest number of deaths occurred in a great arc of misery that swept from east to west through central China: Shandong – 7.5 million, Anhui – 8 million, Henan – 7.8 million, Sichuan – 9 million, Qinghai – 0.9 million, Tibet – 1 million. In proportional terms, it was Tibet that suffered most, losing an estimated 25 per cent of its population of 4 million.[39] The most distressing feature of this was that the PRC deliberately increased the severity of the famine there as part of the campaign it had waged since 1950 to destroy Tibetan culture and identity. In 1962, following a secret tour of Tibet, the Panchen Lama sent Mao a 90,000-word report accusing the PRC authorities of having engaged in genocide. Mao ordered that the report be suppressed and the writer imprisoned.[40]

The strain that the grim consequences of the Great Leap Forward created within the party hierarchy was revealed by Mao's decision in December 1958 to relinquish his position as chairman of the PRC. This was not as self-effacing as it might appear. Mao did it out of irritation, not humility. It was a tactical retreat which left him free to pass on the blame should any criticism come his way. In any case, his withdrawal did not weaken his position; he remained chairman of the party and, as the formal acceptance of his decision indicated, he could resume his full authority whenever he chose: 'Comrade Mao Zedong will remain the leader of the entire people. . . . If some special situation arises in the future which should require him to take up this work again, he can still be nominated again to assume the duties of the Chairman of the state.'[41] The reality was that Mao's deification within the party and the nation, a process that had gone on since the rectification campaigns of the 1940s, rendered his authority absolute regardless of any formal title he held. As Mao grew older, he became increasingly determined to keep his personal power. For him, it was the only guarantee that the revolution whose progenitor he was would not be betrayed. His determination was to lead to the second greatest disaster that befell China under his leadership – the Cultural Revolution.

THE LUSHAN MEETING, 1959

How little Mao had been damaged by giving up the PRC chairmanship was clear from the Lushan conference of the CCP in July 1959. The official party line was that the Lushan gathering had been convened to discuss the progress of the PRC under the Great Leap Forward, but there was little doubt that its real purpose was to consider why the programme had gone wrong. Mao expected trouble and had prepared himself against it. He even called in his wife Jiang Qing to aid him. She flew in to Lushan to help direct attacks on his likely critics. In the event, although there were anti-Mao mutterings behind the scenes, only one of the CCP leaders, Defence Minister Peng Dehuai, had the courage to challenge him openly. Peng had toured a number of areas in 1958–59, including Mao's own province of Hunan. He had been appalled by the extent of the suffering he witnessed.

A tough, abrasive veteran of the Long March and the Korean war, Peng refused to be overawed by Mao at Lushan. He stood his ground and traded insults with him in the foulest of language. Peng's most telling point was that the CCP had borne thirty years of struggle and sacrifice in order to liberate the people of China; but now those people were being destroyed by a famine created by the party. The tragedy made nonsense of all that Chinese Communism claimed to represent. Mao responded by branding

Peng a 'rightist', a catch-all term the CCP applied to anyone who challenged its policies. Peng was accused of hatching a plot 'to sabotage the dictatorship of the proletariat' by creating an opposition clique within the party.[42]

Peng Dehuai's stand against Mao provided a cue for all those CCP and government officials who knew the truth of the Great Leap Forward to condemn it for the giant failure it was and to expose the reality of the horrors it had created. But in one of the great betrayals of modern Chinese history, the self-proclaimed leaders of the people rallied to Mao and turned against Peng. Deng Xiaoping and Liu Shaoqi developed diplomatic illnesses that excused them from attendance, while Zhou Enlai, ashamed by his failure to support Peng, withdrew to his room and drank himself into a stupor. Their inaction condemned millions to agonising death. Mao's victory over Peng Dehuai was a victory for falsehood; it was now impossible to deal with a famine that officially did not exist. To keep up appearances, grain continued to be exported abroad even from provinces where the death toll was mounting daily. Mao did not want the Soviet Union to know China's real plight. In an especially unworthy move, he blamed the shortages on those peasants who had hoarded their crops. It was a fiction but it became official policy. Squads of party thugs were sent into the countryside to punish the putative hoarders; those who were not publicly beaten or shot were dragged away to swell the numbers languishing in the labour camps of the *laogai*, China's equivalent of the Soviet gulag prison system.[43]

There were three defining political battles in the Chinese Communist Party in Mao's time. One was in 1930 over the Li Lisan line, the second was over strategy at the Zunyi meeting in 1935, and the third was the Lushan meeting of 1959. Mao was successful in all of them. His victory at Lushan had fearful consequences for the Chinese people since it rendered his agrarian policies unchallengeable.

The result was a study in fraudulence, sycophancy, and terror. From the provincial leaders to the lowest functionaries, all sang Mao's praises even as they rigged the crop-production figures. Since every official in every province pretended he was witnessing huge increases in the grain harvest, no one dared isolate himself by telling the truth. Photographs appeared in the newspapers purporting to show that the crops in the field were so luxuriant that children could play on the leaves without falling through. To maintain the appearance of plenty, some provinces, such as Anhui, which in fact had suffered particularly severe shortages, actually exported their 'surplus' grain. As Mao made his way around selected regions, the peasants, under orders from local officials, filled the fields that he was likely to inspect with plants lifted from the fields he would not see. When Mao's entourage had moved on, the spurious crops were returned to their original sparse surroundings.

Any peasant foolish enough to tell the truth about the famine and the horrors it had produced, which included cannibalism, could expect little mercy from the authorities. The labour camps rapidly filled with starving wretches whose only crime had been to describe the conditions in the countryside as they actually were. Some 10 million were incarcerated in the *laogai*, most of whom were worked and starved to death.

An unavoidable conclusion is that the world's worst famine was man-made. It was a product of Mao's intransigence and the cowardice of his colleagues, who failed to challenge his policies even though they knew them to be lethal. There is an old Chinese saying that a fish starts to decay at the head. It was Mao Zedong who was ultimately responsible for the tragedy that beset his people. Errors were certainly made lower down the chain of command but he created the policies and gave the orders. Through collectivisation, corrupt science, and a refusal to acknowledge the truth, he set in motion a process that culminated in the horrific deaths of millions of his countrymen.[44]

MAO AND KHRUSHCHEV

Mao's anxiety to keep the truth of the famine from the Kremlin arose from his fear that the Soviet Union would use it to humiliate China. The Sino-Soviet estrangement had steadily widened since 1958, when Khrushchev had paid a return visit to Beijing following Mao's trip to Moscow the previous year. The Russian leader had hoped that he might be able to patch up the differences between the two great socialist powers. But Mao had been unaccommodating – literally so. Khrushchev believed that his hosts had deliberately set out to discomfit him by housing the Soviet delegation in a hotel without air-conditioning during Beijing's hottest and most humid season. He had been particularly embarrassed by the Chinese insistence that one of the meetings be held in Mao's private pool in Zhongnanhai. Khrushchev, who could not swim, and who, when undressed gave a passable impression of the Michelin man, had to suffer the indignity of splashing helplessly while wearing baggy borrowed trunks and a rubber ring. In retaliation, he had gone back to Moscow after only three days rather than the week which the visit had been originally scheduled to last.

Beneath this game-playing lay personal dislike. Mao did not get on with Khrushchev any more than he had with Stalin. Khrushchev bitingly observed, 'Mao thought of himself as a man brought by God to do God's bidding. In fact, Mao probably thought God did Mao's bidding.'[45] But there were reasons deeper than mere personal antipathy to explain Sino-Soviet disharmony. The PRC and the USSR were neighbours whose common frontier stretched thousands of miles across Asia; border disputes were frequent. They were also great powers, representing alternative and conflicting forms of Communism. It was very short odds that they would fall out. In retrospect, the observer can see that the division between them had been there from the beginning; it was implicit in Mao's insistence on the primacy of the Chinese way. Mao distrusted Khrushchev's pursuit of better relations with the West. He viewed it as a plot by the Soviet Union to ingratiate itself with the USA and leave China internationally isolated. He was offended by Soviet reluctance to give the PRC diplomatic or military support in its long-running wrangle with the USA over Taiwan. The Soviet Union was sternly criticised by Deng Xiaoping, whom Mao assigned to be the PRC's chief ideologue, for its 'great power chauvinism' in assuming that it led the Communist world as the true voice of Marxism-Leninism.[46]

Khrushchev countered by describing Mao as a Trotskyist whose distorted vision blinded him to the realities of a world in which the Communist and capitalist blocs possessed the nuclear weaponry to destroy each other. It was only Mao's arrogance that would not let him see that some form of accommodation with the West was necessary if the world was not to be blown to bits. Mao was accused of irresponsibility in risking war with the USA over Taiwan without consulting the USSR. A dramatic development came in 1959, when the Soviet Union, claiming that its representatives had been driven out by Chinese animosity, withdrew its engineers and economic advisers from the PRC. Mao pronounced good riddance on them, claiming that all along they had acted not as fraternal helpmates but Soviet spies. Mao's anger was intensified by his belief that the USSR was relishing the news passed on by Peng Dehuai of the failures of the Great Leap Forward and the accompanying famine in China.

Diplomatic relations between the two Communist giants were finally broken off in 1961 following a staged walk-out by the Chinese delegation, led by Zhou Enlai, from the Congress of the Communist Party of the Soviet Union, held in Moscow. The Chinese protest was against Khrushchev's declaration that the PRC had put the brotherhood of the Communist world at risk by recognising rogue Marxist states, such as Albania, which had broken away from the Eastern Bloc.

Once diplomatic relations had been severed, there were no restrictions on the insults the Chinese and Soviet leaders could fire at each other. Khrushchev called Mao an Asian Hitler and 'a living corpse', while Mao described his adversary as a worn-out boot, fit only to thrown into a corner. These exchanges may have been less than profound as pieces of political analysis, but they provided rich copy for the international correspondents, many of whom was eager to present the Sino-Soviet dispute as a personal duel between the circus clowns of Communism. Yet there was nothing comic about Mao's bitter resentment when, in 1962, the USSR supplied MiG fighters to India to assist it in its Tibetan border war with the PRC.

1962 also witnessed arguably the most dangerous moment in the whole of the Cold War. It was in that year that the USSR began secretly installing rockets equipped with nuclear warheads in Fidel Castro's Cuba. When US aerial reconnaissance spotted them, President Kennedy demanded their immediate removal under pain of direct American military retaliation. After a tense stand-off between Khrushchev and Kennedy, the Soviet leader backed down and ordered the missiles to be withdrawn. The Chinese saw this as a total defeat for the Soviet Union. What the West lauded as Khrushchev's great act of statesmanship in stepping back from the brink of war was ridiculed by Mao as 'capitulationism'. Chinese newspapers mocked the USSR's inability to stand up to the American threats. How could it claim to be the world's leading socialist state and the model for the world's struggling peoples when it bowed the knee to Communism's greatest enemy?

7

THE CULT OF MAO AND THE CULTURAL REVOLUTION, 1962–76

Great chaos will lead to great order. Everything is turning upside down.
I love great upheavals.

Mao Zedong, 1966

In 1966 Mao launched one of the most remarkable campaigns in Chinese history, arguably in world history. Aware that old age was overtaking him, he set out to perpetuate his domination of China by imposing upon it an immutable character. To this end he resolved to destroy China's past.

THE CULT OF MAO ZEDONG

Between 1962 and 1966 Mao chose to limit his direct involvement in affairs of state. He left others to deal with the calamitous consequences of the Great Leap Forward. His withdrawal from the limelight was not an act of contrition. He had no intention of relinquishing his power. Indeed, it was during this period that the cult of Mao attained its apogee. The principal agent in this was Lin Biao, who had replaced Peng Dehuai as the PRC's minister of defence in 1959. Working with Chen Boda, the party's leading intellectual, Lin became, in effect, Mao's minister of propaganda. He made it his task to inculcate the notion that Mao Zedong was a unique being whose successful leadership of the Chinese Revolution since the 1920s was proof of his faultless judgement. Mao was projected as the outstanding interpreter of class struggle, the last and the greatest in the line of prophets of revolution that stretched from Marx, by way of Lenin and Stalin, to reach its culmination in him. Lin's aim was to elevate Mao above ordinary politics and put him beyond criticism as the embodiment of wisdom.

Lin chose to popularise this concept in ways that proved brilliantly successful. The outstanding example was the printing of millions of copies of the 'little red book', a collection of short extracts drawn mainly from the volumes of Mao's writings and speeches already published by the CCP.[1] Bound in red plastic and printed in handy pocket size, *Quotations from Chairman Mao Tse-tung* was presented as a distillation of Mao's sagacity. Lin's preface admonished the reader: 'Study Chairman Mao's writings, follow his teachings and act according to his instructions.' The little red book, which first appeared in 1964, is best understood as China's secular bible. It was Revelation in plastic covers. By 1968 over 740 million copies had been distributed. Under Lin's direction, it became a prescribed text for schools and universities. Classes and lectures began and ended with readings from it. It became *de rigueur* for everyone to carry a copy. In factories, the workers were uplifted by continual loudspeaker broadcasts of Mao's words. The sayings of Confucius had once been invoked to settle legal and social disputes. It was now the thoughts of Chairman Mao that were the ultimate reference.

For Mao, the vital feature of all this was the swift adoption of the little red book by the People's Liberation Army as their inspiration and guide. Lin Biao, as a marshal of the PLA and head of the armed services, insisted that the troops make it their basic training manual. Since the 1920s Mao had consistently defined the role of the Red Army, and its successor the PLA, as a political one. 'The Chinese Red Army is an armed force for carrying out the political tasks of the revolution.'[2] Having been the instrument by which the Chinese Communist revolution had been achieved, its historical role was now that of guarantor of continuing revolution. 'Without a people's army the people have nothing.'[3]

Since 1962, the PLA had attracted many of its new recruits from the Socialist Education Movement, which had been set up that year with Mao's approval to act as a ginger group to keep party members focused on revolution.[4] Such developments confirmed that under Lin Biao the PLA was a force on whose loyalty Chairman Mao Zedong could fully rely. Mao reciprocated by urging the Chinese people to 'learn from the PLA' as the model of revolutionary spirit and integrity. The special relationship between the chairman and the politicised armed services was to be of vital importance in the development of the Cultural Revolution.

The Chinese were soon given added reason to venerate Chairman Mao. In 1964 the PRC strengthened its claim to equal status with the USSR by exploding its own atomic bomb; three years later it successfully detonated a hydrogen bomb. China, under Mao, had become a superpower. Exulting in having achieved this by their own independent efforts, the Chinese called their nuclear programme 59/6, a pointed allusion to the year and month when Khrushchev had announced that the Soviet Union would no longer provide assistance to the Chinese in developing their nuclear programme.[5] Mao remarked sarcastically that Khrushchev could not have done the PRC a greater favour and deserved to be rewarded with a large Chinese medal.

PRELUDE TO REVOLUTION

Despite these domestic and international successes, Mao brooded. The unbounded adulation did not bring him peace of mind. He suspected those around him of disloyalty; he doubted that they shared his commitment to revolution. Paradoxically, his suspicions had been aroused by the efforts of Liu Shaoqi and Deng Xiaoping to repair any damage that his reputation might have suffered as a result of the great famine. In 1962, Mao had asked Liu and Deng to undertake the task of restoring China's food supplies. They had gone about this with a will. Using the ideas of Chen Yun, the leading economist of the First Year Plan and one of the few critics of the Great Leap Forward, they set out to restore stability on the land by allowing the peasants to farm individually and to sell surplus produce. They hoped that such incentives would encourage the growth of markets and stimulate food distribution. The strategy was largely successful; agriculture began to recover and hunger lessened.

Yet this very achievement made Mao uneasy. The return to individual farming was tantamount to admitting that the previous communal policies had not worked. Developments in certain provinces in the early 1960s increased Mao's worries. Taking their lead from the policies introduced by Liu and Deng, a number of local governments in Gansu and Qinghai, areas which had suffered particularly badly during the famine, began to dismantle the communes. This was not provincial revolt; the local leaders did not openly challenge Mao and the CCP. But Mao chose to put the worst interpretation on events. He judged that his detachment from the centre of things had allowed opposition within the party to emerge.

Mao's special resentment was directed towards Liu Shaoqi who, he believed, had been behind the criticisms of the Great Leap Forward voiced at the '7,000 Cadres' conference in 1962. He believed that Liu's adverse comments on policy had encouraged the conference to be critical. Mao had complained at the time that the delegates were losing sight of true socialist values: 'they eat three meals a day – and fart. That's what Marxism-Leninism means to them.'[6] When Liu Shaoqi was later diagnosed with tuberculosis in 1964 Mao chose to be vindictive. Denying that Liu's high rank entitled him to special care, Mao ordered the closing down of the Central Bureau of Health, the body responsible for organising treatment for party and government officials. Behind such pettiness he was girding himself for a far greater act of retribution on his enemies.

THE CULTURAL REVOLUTION BEGINS

It must be seldom that an obscure piece of theatre has started a revolution. But this is what seemed to happen in China in 1965. The beginnings of the Cultural Revolution can be traced to the reaction to *The Dismissal of Hai Rui from Office*, written by Wu Han. Set in the Song court of the eleventh century AD, the play told the story of an honest official who rebelled against government corruption only to be dismissed in disgrace by the despotic ruler. The play was an allegory, the oblique form of criticism traditional in China. For those with eyes to see there was an obvious parallel between the fate of Hai Rui and that of Marshal Peng Dehuai, who had been removed from office for daring to tell the truth about the famine. Initially the play, which had first been produced in 1961, aroused little response but by the autumn of 1965 Mao had been alerted to its hidden meaning. He turned on the playwright, Wu Han, accusing him of belonging to an anti-government clique.

The charge had some substance. Wu was known to belong to a circle, which included Peng Zhen and Deng Xiaoping, that had been critical of the Great Leap Forward. It was Peng, who, as editor of an influential Shanghai literary journal, had published an article which in an elliptical way had drawn attention to the message implicit in *The Dismissal of Hai Rui*. The article was reprinted in a number of Beijing newspapers. In

February 1966, Mao summoned Peng to his presence and demanded an explanation. Claiming to have been totally unaware of the play's double meaning, the trembling Peng agreed to publish a denunciation of Wu Han's work. This was the cue for Mao to launch his assault; Wu and his supporters were fiercely attacked for their temerity in criticising the chairman and for undermining Marxist-Leninist-Maoist thought. Two years later Wu was to commit suicide rather then face further persecution.

The anger over *The Dismissal of Hai Rui* was contrived. There is little doubt that in 1965 Mao and his supporters used the play, which had barely caused a ripple during its very brief run four years earlier, as a pretext for exposing their opponents and exciting a confrontation. In that sense it recalls Mao's tactics over the Hundred Flowers campaign. Its effects were certainly very similar. It exposed the factions at the top of the party and the government and it provided a pretext for Mao to rid himself of the nominal restrictions on his authority. At the Party Congress of the CCP in 1956, resolutions, proposed by Liu Shaoqi and Deng Xiaoping, had been passed condemning 'the cult of personality' and declaring that collective leadership was the only proper form of government for the PRC. These principles had never been formally rescinded. While they had not seriously limited Mao's authority, they had continued to irk him. He now used the *Hai Rui* affair as the occasion to remove them as official party policy and at the same time undermine Liu and Deng, their original proponents. The Cultural Revolution began, therefore, as another stage in the long-running power struggle within the Chinese Communist Party.

Mao now set in motion a full-scale purge of the CCP. At a specially summoned meeting of the Politburo in May 1966, he denounced the growth within the party of 'bourgeois intellectualism' and 'revisionism'. In the '16 May Circular', he called on the party 'to hold high the banner of the proletarian cultural revolution'. It was the duty of members 'to repudiate those representatives of the bourgeoisie who have sneaked into the Party, the government, the army and all spheres of culture.'[7] To combat these mounting evils, Mao announced the creation of a Central Cultural Revolution Group whose task would be to expose and remove the bourgeois enemies within the CCP itself. Mao was declaring open war on officialdom in the party and in the government. His real or imagined opponents were now under fire.

The leading members of the Group were named as Kang Sheng, Lin Biao, Chen Boda, and Jiang Qing. Also included were three others

– Zhang Chunqiao, Yao Wenyuan, and Wang Hongwen – who, together with Jiang, made up what Mao later described as the 'Gang of Four'. What was particularly significant was that the Gang represented the powerful Shanghai element in the CCP. The three men had made their name as party workers in that city and had become members of the Politburo. Shanghai was often a counterweight, if not a rival, to the power of Beijing. Playing on China's traditional regional jealousies, Mao now used the Central Cultural Revolution Group with its Shanghai associations to undermine the influence of the Beijing branch of the party led by Peng Zhen. The attack upon Peng had an added purpose. He was known to be a moderate. As mayor of Beijing he belonged to a set of prominent officials who preferred conciliation to confrontation and who wished to see the divisions in the CCP narrow, not widen. Lin Biao and Jiang Qing had a deep dislike of Peng. They abused him and his colleagues by screaming that in this time of great danger to Mao and the party moderation was little short of treason and betrayal.

The extremism that Jiang called for was personified in the ruthless character of her three associates in the Gang of Four. In Shanghai they had been prepared to use the secret society and triad networks that had survived from the Guomindang era to advance their cause. Zhang Chunqiao had exploited his contacts with Shanghai's gangster underworld to destroy his personal and political enemies. It had been the equally ruthless Yao Wenyuan who had recently come to national prominence by launching the attack on *The Dismissal of Hai Rui from Office*. Wang Hongwen was a young protégé of Zhang. He had made the textile union which he led in Shanghai into a formidable radical force. His name became a terror during the Cultural Revolution, when he was responsible for the persecution and death of thousands in Shanghai.

Another of Mao's major allies was Kang Sheng, the man who had run the deadly rectification campaign in Yanan. The head now of the PRC's secret police, Kang was deeply feared since his closeness to Mao made him unassailable. His success in catering to the chairman's sexual needs by providing a string of nubile young women gave him entrée to Mao's court. It was unwise to fall foul of Kang, as Luo Ruiqing discovered. Luo had risen to a high position in the security forces, a promotion which brought him into personal rivalry with Kang. In the infighting which followed in the wake of the *Hai Rui* episode, Kang worked with Jiang Qing and Lin Biao to destroy Luo. Hauled before a specially convened meeting of the

Central Committee, Luo was forced to confess to treason. Soon after he threw himself from a high window. This may have been from guilt or shame or he may have been tossed out. He survived, but only as a cripple; during the Cultural Revolution he was periodically put on public show for ridicule as an enemy of the people who had tried to 'suicide' himself.

THE RED TERROR

The literal and figurative fall of Luo Ruiqing in 1966 raised the purge another notch. It was announced that a plot against Mao had been uncovered. A number of high-ranking party officials, including Lu Dingyi, a Long March veteran, and Tian Jiaying, one of Mao's private secretaries, were arrested and tortured. Liu Shaoqi and Deng Xiaoping joined in protesting against such treatment. But their protests merely served to show how isolated these formerly dominant figures had become. Mao's bitterness towards them gravely weakened them at this juncture. The power now lay with the Central Cultural Revolution Group, who were intent on violent upheaval. How much their extremism reflected Mao's own wishes is not clear. What is certain is that Mao, having created the Group, made no clear move to limit their activities.

Such was the momentum of the purge that by the summer of 1966 it had widened into a campaign for the reform of all those institutions and systems that had ceased to serve their true revolutionary role. Mao defined the enemy as the 'four olds' – old thoughts, old culture, old customs, old habits. These were protean categories that could be stretched to cover all the institutions and personnel which met the disapproval of those engaged in the cultural purification of China. Mao's attack on the old was complemented by his selecting the youth of China to be the instrument for carrying through the Cultural Revolution. Mao believed that he had a special affinity with the young. It was they who had helped organise the various 'anti' campaigns in the 1950s, and who had been most prominent in responding to his call for a Great Leap Forward. Since the late 1950s it had been young people who had followed the party's instruction to take to the streets to protest against the revisionist, pro-Western policies of the Soviet Union. Mao felt it was the young who best understand China's pressing need to regenerate itself as a nation by following a truly proletarian path. He judged that they had a particular energy which, when harnessed and directed from above, would prove unstoppable. For him, youthful naivety and ignorance were positive virtues. 'We have to depend on them to start a rebellion, a revolution', he said, 'otherwise we may not be able to overthrow the demons and monsters.' Mao had developed this strategy in discussions with Kang Sheng and the Gang of Four in Shanghai in the winter of 1965–66. He remarked 'we must liberate the little devils. We need more monkeys to disrupt the palace.'[8]

Kang responded immediately by organising a mass recruitment of idealistic students, who were instructed to carry Mao's message forward into the schools and universities. Taking the name Red Guards, which betokened their total loyalty to Mao, they adopted military-style dress and wore distinctive armbands. In the name of Mao and the Revolution, they led pupils and students in denouncing their teachers as reactionaries and disrupting the everyday running of classes. They then moved from the classroom into society at large to hunt down and publicly savage the decadent and reactionary elements that were preventing China from achieving its revolutionary destiny. Their fanaticism made the Red Guards a brutal force. Freed from the shackles of the customary Chinese respect for age and wisdom by Mao's dicta that rebellion was virtuous, and chaos better than order, they rampaged through towns and cities, intent on terrifying those people, no matter how venerable, and destroying those artefacts, no matter how precious, that they deemed to represent China's corrupt past. Callow youths of sixteen abused scholars with a lifetime of learning, and took hammers to smash the treasures of Chinese antiquity.

So fearfully successful were the Red Guards in carrying out Mao's injunctions that Chinese education was soon in chaos. In an attempt to limit the disorder, Deng Xiaoping and Liu Shaoqi sent special 'peace teams' into the universities. Zhou Enlai also appealed to the CCP to encourage the students to moderate their campaign. Such efforts were unavailing for two reasons. The disruption was so widespread that it proved impossible to control. Still more significant, Mao expressly ordered Deng and Liu to disband their teams and publicly confess that they had been wrong to attempt to stop the revolutionary process.

Mao's stern intervention coincided with an episode that added a touch of light relief to the drama that was unfolding. In July 1966, the Chinese media exploded with rapture. Every newspaper, television programme and cinema newsreel gave itself over entirely to the celebration of a seventy-three-year-old man swimming in a river. The aged one was Chairman Mao himself. Accompanied by teams of beaming supporters, Mao was shown bobbing along in the Yangxi River at Wuhan. The great helmsman had returned. His physical presence back among the people had a powerful impact on the Chinese. They understood the symbolism. By swimming in China's greatest river, Mao represented a life force. By reappearing at Wuhan, the scene of the 1911 rising that overthrew the Qing, he emphasised his role as the inheritor of the revolution and the maker of modern China. What to Westerners seemed an amusing public-relations exercise, to the Chinese represented a national reawakening. Mao had shown that he was still in control and leading China onward to its historic goal. Millions of Chinese openly wept for joy at his reappearance.

The Wuhan episode gave impetus to the expanding student movement. By the late summer of 1966, it was a common throughout China to see groups of chanting Red Guards aggressively extolling the virtues of Chairman Mao and threatening those who did not join in worshipping him. A high point came in Beijing on 18 August 1966, with the largest of a series of rallies that took place that month in Tiananmen Square. A million young people gathered. It was an extraordinary scene. Periodically between dawn and midday Mao came out onto the Tiananmen balcony overlooking the square to receive the acclamation of the vast throng below. At each appearance the noise became more thunderous as the students, all dressed in identical Mao uniforms, chanted 'Long live Chairman Mao Zedong' and sang 'The East is Red'. The ecstasy on their faces as in unison they waved their little red books has become one of the enduring images of China in the twentieth century.

Although Mao went down to the front of the crowd to meet a selection of the students, he did not formally address the gathering. That honour was conferred on Lin Biao, an indication of his current eminence. Lin's speech lionised Mao Zedong as the outstanding revolutionary genius of the age, who was 'remoulding the souls of the people'. In Mao's name, Lin called on the young to make the 'four olds' their enemy. Also present on the balcony were Liu Shaoqi, Deng Xiaoping, and Zhou Enlai. But they wore civilian clothes, as previously instructed to by Mao. This contrasted pointedly with the military uniform in which he and Lin appeared. The trio were also positioned some distance from Mao. Such things were not accidental. They were the visible signs, not lost on those schooled in Chinese ways, that the three had been demoted in the party's hierarchy.

The excitement aroused by Mao's spectacular return to public view strengthened his political control. It was against the backdrop of the great

August rallies that he summoned another special meeting of the Central Committee of the CCP, during which he repeated his attack on the reformism creeping into the party. This was the prelude to his announcement that Lin Biao had been elevated above Liu Shaoqi in the party ranking. Chen Boda then took up the attack by indicting Liu and Deng Xiaoping as 'spearheads of the erroneous line'. Wall posters appeared accusing them of dishonouring the thoughts of Chairman Mao. A Red Guard demonstration was organised with the sole purpose of execrating the names of Liu and Deng. This proved to be the prelude to their removal from party and government. The official explanation was that they had pursued 'a bourgeois reactionary line'. Mao, however, hinted at what was undoubtedly the real reason when he complained that Deng and Liu had recently taken to disregarding him in official matters, treating him, he said, like a corpse at a funeral.

Once they had been removed from office, they were subjected to direct physical assault. Liu Shaoqi was first softened up by Red Guards who camped outside his official residence and kept him sleepless for days by bathing his windows with lamplights and maintaining a constant loudspeaker din. He and his wife, Wang Guangmei, were then dragged out and badly beaten in front of their weeping children. They were both subjected to a series of brutal 'struggle sessions' during which they were forced to incriminate themselves. Liu was subsequently imprisoned in conditions which were calculated to break his health. He eventually died in November 1969 in solitary confinement, emaciated, lice-ridden, and deprived of the insulin his diabetes needed. Right to the end, Liu expected Mao to intervene to save him, but the chairman made no move. He did, however, show clemency towards Wang Guangmei. In April 1969, when Lin Biao showed him a list of 'bad elements' who had been condemned to death, Mao took a pen and crossed off Wang's name. Deng Xiaoping's family were victimised. His son, Pufang, was thrown from an upstairs window by Red Guards, an act that left him permanently paralysed. Deng himself escaped physical ill-treatment, but he was publicly denounced before a baying crowd of three thousand before being exiled to Jiangxi province to perform 'corrective labour'.

As the rumours and charges spread, an atmosphere of terror prevailed. Jiang Qing was prominent in creating this. Jiang, who hated easily, had a special loathing for Zhou Enlai. Since she could not openly attack him as long as he retained Mao's favour, she made it one of her main tasks to ruin his reputation. For Jiang, part the attraction of the Cultural Revolution was the opportunity it provided for pursuing personal vendettas. She took undisguised delight in the humiliation of Liu Shaoqi's wife, Wang Guangmei, whose beauty and sophistication Jiang had long resented. She also frequently led Red Guard teams round to the various gates of the government compound where they whipped the crowd into a frenzy, demanding vengeance on Mao's enemies.

Zhou Enlai often followed her and after the Red Guards had moved on he sought to calm the crowds. He made no attempt to defend those who had been denounced but appealed in broad terms for moderation and good order. That indeed was the role Zhou chose to play throughout the disturbances. At no time did he attack the Cultural Revolution itself. His aim was to limit the damage and lessen the extremism. He had little success. His rationality was out of joint with the crazed times; his appeal for responsible behaviour made him suspect in the eyes of the Maoists who screamed that the crisis required not effete moderation but violent commitment.

Many of the accused party members turned to Mao himself for protection. He did respond but in an arbitrary way. If he liked a particular individual he might intervene on his behalf but there was no reliable pattern to his behaviour. Throughout the period of the Cultural Revolution people came to Mao whenever he was available, begging for special audiences so that they could put their case to him. His influence was enough. If Mao gave support then the petitioner was safeguarded. It was not a question of justice but of the great man's whim.

Once he had set the Cultural Revolution in motion, Mao played only an intermittent part in its development. He left Beijing for long periods, taking the opportunity to go on tours of the countryside, and staying at places of which he was fond, such as Hangzhou, Wuhan, and Shanghai. His absence left affairs in the hands of Jiang Qing and her adherents. He said to his doctor: 'Let others stay busy with politics. Let them handle the problem of the movement by themselves.'[9]

When Mao did return to Beijing he did not find it easy to relax. He insisted on frequently changing his location within the city so as to make it more difficult for his enemies to plot his death. He would often change his living quarters within his various official residences. Sometimes he resided in the government compound in Zhongnanhai; at other times he moved into the Great Hall of the People, a huge building looking on to Tiananmen Square and containing myriad apartments where he could hide himself away. These frequent changes were invariably announced at the shortest of notices. Nobody quite knew where he would be at any given time. Attendants had to stand by at the ready. Mao also stayed for periods aboard his special train whose mobility he regarded as his most effective form of security. He ordered his chief bodyguard, Wang Dongxing, to increase the extensive protection that already surrounded him. He even gave up his women for a time in the belief that they might try to poison him.

Mao's frequent detachment from the political centre meant that while he broadly approved of the policies that were pursued in his name, he was seldom responsible for the details. The individual acts of brutality were not his. The Cultural Revolution was perhaps pushed further than Mao had intended. Jiang Qing and the Gang of Four were arguably more Maoist than Mao himself. This does not, of course, absolve him from responsibility for what occurred. Everything was done in his name. The Cultural Revolution would not have taken place without him. It had been Mao who, in August 1966, had presented the students of Qinghua University with a banner inscribed in his own hand, 'Bombard the Headquarters.'[10] By leaving Jiang and the extremists in control, he gave them his authority for what they did to the Chinese people.

THE REASSERTION OF ORDER

By the late 1960s, it was clear even to Mao that for economic and social, if not political, reasons the disruption should be halted. When students stop studying it is barely noticeable, but when workers stop working production plummets. China by 1970 was in industrial crisis. Something had to be done. The first move was to bring an end to the Red Guard nonsense. It was announced that the revolutionary tasks of the Red Guards would be carried on by the PLA. This was code for saying that the youngsters had to give up their activities and leave the physical defence of the revolution to real soldiers.

In a major act of social containment, Mao then urged the young idealists to disband their Red Guard units and direct their energies into a new campaign – 'to go up to the mountains and down to the villages'. This was a grand plan for the young people to live and work among the peasants in the countryside. In doing this they would benefit their hosts by providing unpaid work, while they themselves would gain a true understanding of the lives of the people and so learn the dignity of labour. It is difficult not to think that Mao was being grimly humorous.

He knew how arduous peasant life was, and therefore, how hard a time the youngsters would have of it. In any case, the real purpose of the campaign was not idealistic but practical. It was a convenient way of removing from the towns and cities the hordes of ill-disciplined youngsters who, having been initially encouraged by Mao to rebel, had now become a social menace. Notwithstanding its doubtful motivation, the campaign was a major success. By 1972 nearly 13 million young people had gone into the countryside. There the great majority went through an experience so unremittingly bleak that it drained them of the idealism that had first inspired them. Those who spoke about it after Mao's death said that they felt they had been used. They resolved in post-Maoist China to work for material gains.

Although local conditions and personal rivalries make the infighting over the Cultural Revolution appear complex, the broad divisions are discernible. There were two main competing factions: the 'rightists' and the 'leftists'. The former were those who considered that the Chinese Revolution, while not perfect, had largely fulfilled its objectives in creating a socialist society. They were concerned that an unnatural attempt to increase the pace of change threatened to destroy what had been achieved. The leftists, however, started from the conviction that the revolution was on the verge of collapse. Too many party and government officials had become comfortable and self-satisfied and were now indistinguishable from the bourgeoisie they had originally overthrown. They followed Mao in believing that unless the government was purged of these reactionaries the revolution would be betrayed. In the hysteria generated by the Cultural Revolution, moderates such as Zhou Enlai remained largely ineffectual. Along with the rightists they were swamped by the tidal wave of the left.

When the situation threatened to get out of hand Mao called on the PLA to support the leftists. Some 2 million troops backed them; against such forces the rightists had nothing to offer. Military might rather than ideological purity was the deciding factor. Since from the beginning Mao and the Central Cultural Revolution Group had been able to rely on the loyalty and support of the police and armed services, his victory over the counter-revolutionaries was never in doubt.

It was the success of the left that enabled a mad woman to embark on what was arguably the most radical and the most frightening feature of the reformation that Mao had begun. His wife, Jiang Qing, undertook nothing less than the recreation of Chinese culture. Her work dominated China during the remaining ten year's of her husband's life.

THE PURIFICATION OF CHINESE CULTURE

In July 1966 Mao wrote to Jiang Qing, instructing her to take on the role of cultural purifier of the nation. 'Great chaos will lead to great order. The cycle appears every seven or eight years. The demons and monsters will come out by themselves. Their class character dictates it.'[11] Jiang regarded the letter as her writ for turning Mao's broad attack on China's 'four olds' into a detailed campaign for the reformation of Chinese culture. She began by imposing a severe censorship on all art forms. Works for publication, showing, or performance had to be submitted for vetting by a bureau over which she presided. The first question asked of any work was whether it was truly proletarian in character. Did it further the cause of socialism? Nearly all foreign works were banned, and Chinese submissions were accepted only if they were of contemporary relevance to the revolutionary struggle of the masses. This ruled out classical Chinese opera, which, ironically, had been one of Mao's great loves. The rigidity of her approach meant that in the end there were only some half-dozen operas permitted to be performed, and these she had had specially commissioned. Even then, Jiang turned up at rehearsals to give final instructions to directors and performers. The operas' common theme was the triumph of the virtuous workers and peasants over evil landlords and capitalists. Westerners imprudent enough to accept invitations to the performances were rendered catatonic by works of the utmost banality and tedium. President Nixon's private comment after enduring one such performance in 1972 was that it was 'humorless . . . and single-minded'.[12]

What characterised Jiang's operas typified all the artistic offerings of the period. Writers, painters, sculptors, and musicians had to choose between two courses. They either did the politically correct thing and presented works that conformed to Jiang's tightly restricted definitions of acceptability or they stopped producing altogether. Either way, intellectual freedom was stifled and the spirit of creativity stilled. This was puritanism at its most extreme. The result was dross; nothing of genuine quality was produced. China became an artistically barren land. It had just been through a terrible physical famine; it was now subjected to an equally devastating spiritual deprivation. By the cruellest of ironies, the Cultural Revolution which had been intended to reform Chinese culture ended by destroying it.

Depressing though all this was in the eyes of Westerners and Chinese traditionalists, Jiang's approach to Chinese culture has to be seen as a logical development of Mao's Yanan thoughts on the purpose of the arts. His central premise had been that culture was not an adjunct of society but a definition of it. It was not to be confused with refinement, still less entertainment. Culture was the pervasive force that held society together. It was a direct expression of the values of the dominating social class. Feudal society had produced a feudal culture, and bourgeois society a bourgeois culture. It followed that in socialist China its culture must be socialist, otherwise it would not be truly representative of the proletarian character of the PRC. Divorced from its social context, artistic value was a meaningless abstraction. In Mao's China, the merit of any work was to be judged solely in terms of how well it served the interests of the masses. That is why Jiang Qing was so resolute in seeking to remove from the PRC all remnants of Western and ancient Chinese culture. These were, in a very precise sense, alien and socially corrupting. They could, therefore, be allowed no place in a proletarian state.

MAO'S MOTIVES

There can be few societies which have called down on themselves such horrors as those suffered by the Chinese during the Cultural Revolution. People were brutalised. The ordinary decencies disappeared. Torture and execution became spectator events. Killings ran into millions. It was reported at the trial of the Gang of Four in 1980 that they had been responsible for the deaths of half a million party officials. Lo Yiren, who had been a Red Guard, later lamented: 'We became beasts. There was not a human being left in China. We were worse than beasts. At least beasts do not slaughter their own kind.'[13] Deng Pufang, the crippled son of Deng Xiaoping, gave a precise definition of the inhumanity to which China had succumbed: 'The Cultural Revolution was not just a disaster for the Party, for the country, but for the whole people. We were all victims, people of several generations. One hundred million people were its victims.'[14] The notion of the Cultural Revolution as China's self-inflicted wound was taken up by Harry Wu, a noted dissident, who spent nineteen years as a political prisoner in the *laogai*, Mao's system of labour camps:

> Everybody in China has suffered, or knows somebody who suffered. When the Red guards were running around like madmen in the middle 1960s it wasn't really a case of us-against-them. It was us-against-us. You could call it a class war, but it was worse. It was Chinese savaging Chinese.[15]

Why, then, did Mao Zedong, the people's hero, allow the people to suffer these barbarities for so long under the Cultural Revolution? Why, when he could have called a halt, did he let Chinese society continue to plumb the depths? One possible explanation relates to his physical and mental condition. Descriptions of Mao's mood and behaviour by those who came into direct contact with him around this time suggest that he frequently appeared confused. The large number of drugs he took did not help; they left him befuddled for long periods. It was not uncommon for him to become so depressed that he took to his bed for days at a time. Significantly, it was during the early stages of the Cultural Revolution that Mao's doctor first noted the symptoms in him of motor neurone disease, an affliction of the central nervous system similar to Parkinson's disease.[16]

Yet even when Mao's distraction has been allowed for, the truth remains that the Cultural Revolution was the product of his rational decisions. Some of the most momentous developments in twentieth-century Chinese history have been expressed in paradoxes. The revolution of 1911 has been described as 'a revolution against the world to join the world'.[17] Similarly, in 1966, Mao claimed that in destroying the revolution he would save it. His stated justification for unleashing the havoc of the Cultural Revolution was that 'great chaos will lead to great order'.

Behind the destructiveness was a calculated attempt to preserve what had been achieved since 1949. Mao aimed to stamp his personal authority indelibly on China by a transformation of society and politics that was so radical it could not be reversed even after his death. To ensure this, he judged it necessary to dismantle the bureaucracy that had developed since 1949. He had become increasingly aware that the structure of the PRC, with its various administrative layers, provided a job market for a privileged elite. Its existence mocked the notion of social equality which he had pursued ideologically since the 1920s. He now intended to pare down the bureaucracy so that there could be a restoration of the purity of the revolutionary ideal. It may be argued that Mao's aim was unrealistic, that he was attempting an impossible task since Chinese Communism was essentially and necessarily bureaucratic. Indeed, it is another striking paradox that it had been Mao himself who had created the bureaucracy as the means of imposing the party's control. He had chosen to rule China through what was, in effect, a new mandarin class of CCP officials.

It may strain credulity to suggest that what Mao had wanted all along was equality, After all, the rectification campaigns, the Great Leap forward, and the Cultural Revolution had been studies in authoritarianism. But here yet another paradox resides. Mao's dilemma was one which faces all revolutionaries. How, in a reactionary society, is authoritarianism to be destroyed except by the exercise of authority? In such a country as China, which historically had only ever known autocracy, the problem was particularly acute. How could egalitarianism be established in a society which was conservative in character and despotic by tradition? Mao's answer was to engage in a great populist act. By enlisting the people in his campaign to destroy party bureaucracy he could claim that the Cultural Revolution was not an imposed policy but a direct expression of the people's will.

Mao's populism was further evident in his desire to preserve the Chinese Revolution as an affair of the peasants. His outstanding achievement as a Marxist had been to turn Communist theory on its head by leading the peasants to victory in China in 1949. Thereafter, the revolution had been largely taken over and run by urban bureaucrats and intellectuals. Mao had initially allowed this to happen but had became disenchanted with the outcome. It was from the towns and from the intellectuals, not from the countryside and the peasants, that the critics of the Great Leap Forward had came. In many respects, of course, Mao could himself be classed as an intellectual; his writings and poems testified to that. But it was as a political organiser and guerrilla fighter that Mao liked to be regarded. He tended to distrust those party members who were purely intellectual and not men of action. This led him to demand that university staff leave their lecture rooms and join with the peasants in the labour of the fields, a requirement that delighted many liberal academics on American and European campuses, though surprisingly few of them rushed to engage in these enriching activities themselves.

Mao was also uncertain about the loyalty of his colleagues. It seems perverse that at the height of his power, when he enjoyed godlike status, he should have had doubts about his position. The thinking that drove the ageing chairman was astutely assessed by Henry Kissinger, the American statesman, who had a number of personal meetings with Mao in the early 1970s: 'he was the unchallenged leader of a revolution which had claimed tens of millions of victims in the name of a historical truth, yet he was assailed by premonitions of the potentially ephemeral nature of his achievements.'[18] The adulation in which Mao was publicly held makes his fear of opposition look like paranoia. As with Stalin, so with Mao – the greater his authority became, the greater grew his suspicion of colleagues. It was such suspicion that had led him to see the restrained criticism voiced by Peng Dehuai at the Lushan conference in 1959 as an outright challenge. He became convinced that there were elements in the CCP out to destroy him. It was a belief that gripped him at Lushan and intensified thereafter. This makes it appropriate to see the Cultural Revolution unleashed seven years later as a reckoning for Lushan. As he said in July 1971, 'The Lushan Affair is not finished, the problem is not at all solved.'[19]

Mao's determination to achieve a root and branch reform of the CCP was deepened by his perception of what had happened in the Soviet Union. He considered that, under both Stalin and Khrushchev, the Soviet Communist Party had squandered Lenin's legacy. Mao believed that the party led by Khrushchev and his successors had engaged in de-Stalinisation not as a means of revitalising Communism but in order to maintain its position as a privileged elite. The Communist Party of the Soviet Union had been corrupted by its own exercise of power into a self-perpetuating oligarchy, detached from the Soviet people and incapable of leading international Communism. Mao was not prepared to allow the same fate to overtake the CCP in China. Convinced that the older revolutionaries who had established the People's Republic had lost their zeal and integrity, he concluded that the only way China and its revolution could be saved was by removing the old guard and letting the new generation of party idealists take over. His understanding of the dialectic told him that these changes would meet fierce resistance from those who stood to lose their privileges. That is why the Cultural Revolution had to be so sweeping and so ruthless.

Since it was necessary to destroy in order to create, even the progressive forces in China had to be removed. Arguably the most serious aspect of this rejection of modernity was its harmful impact on the economy. The disruption of scientific and technical education and the purging of such creative economic planners as Deng Xiaoping made nonsense of Mao's previous promise that China's industrial development would soon match that of the capitalist West. Manifestly, his priorities now lay elsewhere.

LIN BIAO FALLS TO EARTH

By 1970, so sweeping had been the purge of Mao's real or supposed opponents that there was every reason to think that the Cultural Revolution would now peter out. This did indeed begin to happen, but only after one of the most dramatic developments in the whole story. In an astonishing fulfilment of the principle that revolutions devour their own children, Lin Biao fell victim to the very process which he had started. Lin had created the Maoist cult and had been the great executor of Mao's wishes regarding the Cultural Revolution. Mao had even nominated him as his successor, but it had never been his wish that Lin should rival him in his lifetime. Conscious of the reputation that Lin had gained from his leadership of the Cultural Revolution, Mao decided to strike him down before he could use his influence as head of the PLA to mount a challenge. The evidence that Lin was guilty of planning to oust Mao is very thin. The only document of substance was leaked from a group of Lin's supporters, who were led by his son Lin Liguo. A high-ranking air force officer, Liguo had become concerned by the rumours that were beginning to circulate about his father's disloyalty. He called a group of fellow officers together to consider ways of clearing his father's name.

Unwisely, the group kept printed records of their meetings. One passage referred to the tyrannies of B52, a code-name for Mao Zedong: 'Today he uses sweet words and honeyed talk to those whom he entices, and tomorrow he puts them to death for some fabricated crimes. . . . Looking back at the history of the past few decades, is there anyone he supported initially who has not finally been handed a political death sentence?'[20] The irony is that it is unlikely that Lin Biao knew of his son's activities. Nonetheless, once the statement had been leaked it was held to be a direct representation of Lin's own views. His position had become impossible; in distress, he increased his intake of the morphine to which he was addicted. He tried to withdraw into the background. Mao, however, insisted that Lin continue to attend major public functions, at which Mao then studiously and pointedly ignored him. Li Zhisui records that Mao remarked, 'There is somebody who says he wants to support me, elevate me, but what he really has in mind is supporting himself, elevating himself.'[21]

In 1971, Mao's rumour factory went into overtime. Stories circulated that Lin Biao, under cover of preparing China's civil defence system, had built secret getaway tunnels from his own house; this was in case his plan for a coup against Mao, led by renegade officers in the air force, failed. State security officers then announced they had narrowly foiled a plot hatched by Lin to assassinate Mao by blowing up his special train as it went through Shanghai. It is difficult now to separate truth from fabrication but one thing was clear: Lin Biao was finished politically. Events soon doomed him absolutely. On 12 September 1971, in a desperate attempt to escape Mao's retribution, Lin, accompanied by his wife and Liguo, took off from a Beijing airport in a three-engined British-made Trident. His aim was to find sanctuary in the USSR, but early the following morning the plane crashed in Outer Mongolia, killing all on board. There were suspicions that it had been shot down or sabotaged on Mao's orders. But the simplest explanation stills appears the most likely: the plane, which had hurriedly taken off before full flight checks had been completed, had run out of fuel. Mao had expressly turned down Zhou Enlai's suggestion that the aircraft be attacked: 'If we shoot the plane down, how can we explain it to the people of the whole country?' Yet Mao had every reason to relish the outcome. 'This is the most ideal ending', he gloated when he received the news.[22] The crash had removed the man he regarded as his greatest rival.

The CCP waited some months before officially acknowledging Lin Biao's death. It was announced that a 'monstrous conspiracy' against Mao and China had been plotted by Lin whose notoriety would last 'for ten thousand years'.[23] All his works were to be gathered and destroyed. His name was then coupled with Confucius, defined as the great reactionary of Chinese history, in a 'criticise Lin Biao and Confucius' campaign.[24] The major beneficiary of Lin Biao's death and subsequent public disgrace was Zhou Enlai. He had played a major role in unearthing the plot against Mao. It had been to Zhou that Lin's daughter had first leaked the information about her father's intended flight. But Mao had greater reasons than the merely domestic to be grateful to his foreign minister. Zhou was central to one of the major international developments of the Chairman's last years, *détente* between the PRC and the USA.

THE NIXON VISIT, 1972

There had been little diplomatic contact between China and the United States since the Korean war. The long-running dispute over Taiwan had convinced Mao that the USA intended at some stage to attack the PRC. The involvement of the Americans in the Vietnam war in this period had reinforced Mao's conviction that they had hostile designs on Asia. His reaction had been to direct Deng Xiaoping to take over the construction of the Third Line, a vast defensive system, started in the early 1950s at the time of the Korean war, of underground tunnels and bunkers located in a number of inland provinces centred on Sichuan and connected by seven hundred miles of rail. The plan was that, in the event of an aerial attack, there would be a mass migration of government, industry, and workers from the more vulnerable provinces into the Third Line region.[25]

Yet the closest the Third Line complex, which was largely completed by 1970, came to being used was in response to a threat not from the USA but from the USSR. In 1969, Sino-Soviet relations reached their nadir. The tensions created by a series of border skirmishes between Soviet and Chinese troops seemed likely to lead to a full-scale war after Leonid Brezhnev, leader of the USSR in the late 1960s, summoned the leaders of the Communist countries to a conference in Moscow in 1969 with the express purpose of expelling Mao's China from the international Marxist movement. In the event, the Soviet Union, having had its moral case weakened by its invasion of Czechoslovakia in the previous year, was unable to gain unanimous agreement from the conference. But Mao's anxieties were not lessened. His fear was that the 'Brezhnev Doctrine' with its insistence on the right of the Soviet Union to use military force to impose its will on its satellites would be extended beyond Europe in an attempt to break China.

Although an open conflict with the USSR in 1969 was eventually averted by a timely compromise negotiated by Zhou Enlai and Andrei Kosygin, Mao believed that the Soviet threat remained. It was this factor more than any other that explains his desire for a closer relationship with the USA. Such a rapprochement would help nullify the Soviet danger. Mao cared little for notions of international Communist brotherhood; his sole concern was the strength and security of the PRC. Henry Kissinger, the chief US spokesman in the Sino-American preparatory talks that preceded the official visit of President Nixon in February 1972, observed: 'The

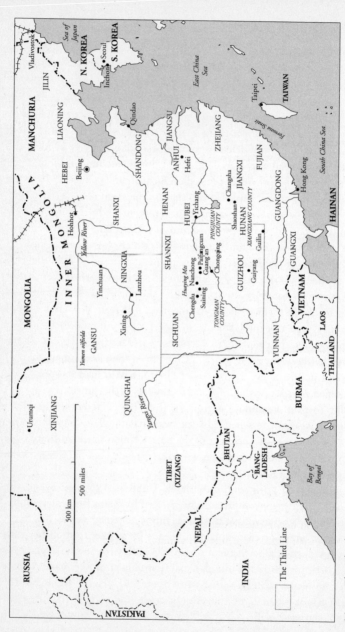

Map 7 The Third Line

Chinese were cold-blooded practitioners of power politics, a far cry from the romantic humanitarians imagined in western intellectual circles.'[26]

Mao played no part in the preliminaries. He left these to Zhou Enlai, who skilfully paved the way by exploiting the mutual good will that had developed following the USA's formal recognition in 1971 of the PRC as a sovereign state with the right to membership of the UN Security Council. The planned visit nearly met disaster when Mao collapsed shortly before the American party set out for China. He developed severe breathing problems which threatened to make it impossible for him to meet Nixon. However, a combination of pounding on his chest, pushing a tube down his throat to suck out the phlegm, and large injections of antibiotics produced the desired effect. He remained shaky but he could stand and was able to shuffle a few steps unaided. This was enough to enable him to play host to the first president of the USA to visit the People's Republic. Mao was genuinely excited by the thought of meeting Nixon. He wanted things to go well. In readiness, he allowed himself, for the first time in six months, to be washed and shaved.

The talks between president and chairman did go well. Mao liked what he regarded as Nixon's plain speaking. When the American leader suggested that after a generation of constant Chinese condemnation of the USA, typified by the daily repetition on radio and television of the cry 'Death to the Americans and all their running dogs', it would be difficult to heal the wounds, Mao remarked wryly that there was no need to take Chinese propaganda too seriously.[27] His teasing illustrated an important diplomatic point. Up to now the Americans had been constantly harangued by Beijing in the bitter vocabulary of the Cold War. The unrestrained language, however, was a cover for the protection of national interests. As long as the USA was perceived as the major threat, the Chinese people were instructed to regard it as the enemy. But by the late 1960s, the USSR had superseded it as the greater menace. This required China to make a strategic adjustment in order meet the danger that the Soviet Union now represented. The logical step was to reach an accommodation with the USA. China was aiming, in effect, at a restoration of the balance of power.

Nixon and his advisers were surprised by how undogmatic Mao was during their talks. He was willing to cover a whole range of issues and seemed to bear no bitterness towards the USA for its support for Chiang Kai-shek. A problem for the American team was Mao's style of speech. He tended to speak elliptically, which occasionally made them struggle to appreciate his exact meaning as conveyed by the translators. This was doubtless deliberate on his part; it left him in control of proceedings without straining to be. Kissinger described Mao's negotiating style:

> [H]e would generally begin with a question, quite often in a needling tone. With deceptive casualness, Mao would then offer a few pithy comments ranging from the philosophical to the sarcastic and gradually expanding the subject matter.[28]

At the conclusion of his visit to Beijing, Nixon claimed that it had 'changed the world'.[29] This was hyperbole, but it was not an entirely inappropriate comment. That the visit had taken place at all gave it its significance The Bamboo Curtain dividing East and West had not been lifted, but it had been parted.

THE STRUGGLE DURING MAO'S LAST YEARS, 1972–76

As Mao grew older it became increasingly difficult for those around him to adjust to his habits. Senility made his quaint ways increasingly unpredictable and irritating. Mao had a peasant's proximate sense of time. He declined to be ruled by the clock. To him there was no difference between night and day in regard to when he worked. This made him unwilling to follow a regimen. He disliked conforming to a regular daily pattern of behaviour. To the frequent consternation of his officials, he followed his own inclinations. If he felt like a party meeting, he called one, regardless of the hour. He seemed to be unaware of the strain this put upon those responsible for trying to organise his formal business. Li Zhisui's experience of Mao's exasperating wilfulness in this regard led him to remark: 'Mao saw schedule and routine, protocol and ritual, as a means to control him, and he refused to be subordinate to them. He revelled in his own unpredictability.'[30] Visiting foreign dignitaries, such as Nixon and Kissinger, were often surprised to find that their meetings with Mao Zedong were not precisely scheduled. They were summoned at short notice when Mao was ready. The message, 'Chairman Mao will see you now', could come at any moment night or day.[31] The time was not negotiable. Such traits in Mao added to the mystique that built up around him and contributed to the idea that he was different from other men and not to be judged by the standards that applied to them.

One important outcome of the parting of the Bamboo Curtain was the strengthening of the position of two key players on the Chinese political stage, Zhou Enlai and Deng Xiaoping. Zhou had been the chief Chinese host and organiser of the American visit. Never had the subtlety and finesse of this urbane and cultured diplomat been better displayed, adding greatly to his reputation at home and abroad. Zhou used his enhanced standing to persuade the party to bring Deng back into the government. Deng's modern ideas were in tune with the more progressive economic approach being adopted by the PRC, as evident in the Sino-American trade talks that had accompanied Nixon's visit. The restoration of Zhou and Deng meant that in Mao's declining years, as his grip on events became more enfeebled, the PRC split into two camps. On one side stood Zhou, the PRC's foreign secretary, alongside Deng, the CCP's general secretary. Against them stood Jiang Qing's Gang of Four. The situation was sufficiently fluid for supporters to change sides. In the Chinese Communist tradition, labels were bandied about in an attempt to define the characteristics of the enemy. 'Dogmatist', 'revisionist', and 'empiricist' were among the most frequent words used as terms of abuse. Insofar as they had meaning, 'dogmatist' referred to the younger members of the CCP, who had joined the party or come to prominence since 1949, while 'empiricist' was applied to the older Long March generation. But in truth the terms were elastic, used as semantic weapons against opponents in much the same way as 'Trotskyite' and 'saboteur' were used in Stalinist Russia.

What was happening was that government and party were engaging in a power struggle in preparation for Mao's death. In his cogent moments, Mao expressed great annoyance with this jockeying for position. He complained of both dogmatism and empiricism and was especially critical of the Gang of Four. He had unleashed the Cultural Revolution to secure the continuation of the China he had created, but as he grew frailer he began to doubt that those he would leave behind in authority would fulfil his dream. He certainly no longer trusted Jiang Qing. This is the possible explanation for his turning to Hua Guofeng, a relative unknown. It may be that he thought Hua was a safer bet than the ambitious but squabbling leaders.

Things appeared to have gone the way of the Gang of Four after Zhou Enlai died in January 1976. Three months later, many thousands of mourners gathered in April in Tiananmen Square to honour his memory and pay tribute to the services he had rendered China. Interpreting this as an implicit attack on those, such as themselves, who had opposed him, Jiang and her associates demanded that crowds be forcibly dispersed before their criticisms developed into an anti-government demonstration. The Beijing authorities duly obliged by sending in riot police; heads and limbs were broken in the ensuing mêlées before the square was cleared.

Browbeaten by Jiang, the Politburo labelled the disturbances the 'Tiananmen Incident', which they ascribed to rightist agitators acting under Deng Xiaoping's influence. The charge was untrue but Deng, judging that the Gang of Four's power would not long outlive Mao's imminent death, chose not to resist. He slipped away from Beijing, believing that his time would soon come again. Events were to prove the shrewdness of Deng's assessment. During the last six months of Mao's ebbing life, the Gang of Four retained the semblance of control. However, the authority they claimed rested wholly on their apparent closeness to Mao. Yet he made no move to hand the succession to Jiang and the leftists. Once he died they would have no automatic right to continue in power. Everything would be thrown into the air.

So it had come to this. After leading the CCP continuously for forty years and the PRC for twenty-seven, Mao left confusion and uncertainty. In one sense this was a tribute to the towering presence he had been in Chinese life. His authority had been so personalised that he had made himself irreplaceable. But it also signified that, new emperor though he may have been, he had not founded a dynasty. When Mao had disarmingly told the American president in 1972 that he had made no permanent contribution to the history of China, he may have spoken more truly than he realised.[32] There was to be no continuity. After he had gone, Mao Zedong's successors were to spend the next thirty years steadily abandoning his policies and pursuing the modernity he had rejected.

8

MAO AND WOMEN

Love is sacred, and cannot absolutely be arranged by others, cannot be forced, cannot be bought.

Mao Zedong, November 1919

Mao's personal physician, Li Zhisui, once remarked that the favourite hobby of men in rural China was sexual intercourse. It was a tradition to which Mao Zedong showed great loyalty and commitment. He came to adore women's company. But it had not been ever thus; as a young man, Mao apparently had no time for women. Until his late teens he eschewed sexual or emotional entanglements.

WEN QIMEI

As with most men, Mao's first relationship was with his mother. Wen Qimei bore seven children, three boys and four daughters. Of these, only the sons, of whom Mao was the oldest, survived beyond infancy. Wen, whose name translates as 'seventh daughter', an indication of the de-personalised way in which female children were often classified, played a quiescent role in the household. This is not surprising; tradition and circumstance made it difficult for any woman in rural China to be dominant. Wen remained illiterate throughout her life. But in Mao's eyes she was a paragon. She was always willing to share what she had; in times of famine, beggars who called at the house seldom went away empty-handed. Her generosity often angered her husband and Mao invariably sided with her in the arguments that followed. However, Wen avoided open rows whenever she could. Mao recorded that she preferred 'a policy of indirect attack' and criticised him for being too open in expressing his emotions and challenging his father. She regarded such action as being out of keeping with 'the Chinese way'.[1]

Mao felt no sense of embarrassment that his mother was a devout Buddhist. Later, under Communism, all religions and metaphysical philosophies were condemned as feudal superstitions, yet Mao himself always remained superstitious, as did most Chinese. Even as a guerrilla leader, he was not above consulting fortune-tellers before deciding on his military moves. A powerful impression of his regard for Wen Qimei can be drawn from the funeral oration which he delivered at her graveside in 1919:

> How deep was mother's kindness in raising us! It was like the sunshine in spring and the morning clouds. When can I ever return her love? Alas mother! You have not died after all! Although the body is gone, your spirit lasts forever. As long as I live, I will return your love; as long as I live, I want to accompany you.[2]

Mao's sorrow was leavened with guilt. At the time his mother first fell seriously ill, in March 1919, he had to choose between staying to look after her or going ahead with a scheduled visit to Shanghai on behalf of the New People's Study Society. He decided on the latter. He was away for a month. By the time he returned to Changsha, his two brothers had already made arrangements for her treatment. Wen appears to have developed a form of lymphatic cancer, which proved incurable. She died in October, aged fifty-two. He wrote to members of his family explaining that as soon as he had learned of the seriousness of Wen Qimei's condition he had 'rushed back home' to be at her side. That was untrue. As he admitted at the time to a friend, absence from home at critical times for the family was one of the drawbacks of radicals such as himself who were always on the move. He later told Edgar Snow, inaccurately, that his mother had died while he was still a student. In his conversations with Snow, Mao was often wrong in his dating of incidents. This may have been simple memory lapse or his deliberate confusing of the order of events to make himself appear less culpable. Three months after Wen Qimei's death, her husband, Rensheng, followed her to the grave, but Mao made no recorded mention of his father's passing.

MAO ON THE STATUS OF WOMEN

During his college years Mao deliberately avoided romantic attachment. The New People's Study Society regarded falling in love as frivolous and did not encourage females to join its ranks. Life was too important to allow thoughts of the flesh to distract members from the task of purifying China and saving the world. Yet Mao was obviously very conscious of the power of sex. When seeking a metaphor to describe the intensity of the inner drive that created heroes, he wrote of 'the irresistible sexual desire for one's lover, a force that will not stop, that cannot be stopped.'[3] Moreover, he was already deeply involved in the question of the relations between the sexes as a social issue. At the age of fourteen Mao had successfully challenged the notion of arranged marriage by refusing to be paired off to a girl of his parents' choosing. He had also began to argue in the abstract for the equality of women.

An incident occurred in Changsha in 1919 which helped define his attitudes. Zhao Wuzhen, a twenty-three-year-old woman of good family, had been betrothed to a wealthy merchant considerably older than herself. This was against her wishes, but out of family loyalty she had appeared to suppress her misgivings. On her wedding day, resplendent in red silk bridal finery, she was carried in a sedan chair the quarter mile from her home to the place of the ceremony. In accordance with custom, the curtains were closed so that during the short journey she could not be seen by the applauding onlookers. When the chair was set down on arrival, the door was opened and the curtains were drawn back. The welcoming shouts of the wedding guests turned to exclamations of horror when she was seen to be slumped in her seat, her mouth hanging open and her eyes filled with pain. Her dress was now stained a darker red. Zhao Wuzhen had sliced her own throat with a jade shard. Desperate efforts were made to staunch the bleeding, but, despite being taken to two hospitals, she finally choked to death on her own blood.

The incident became a cause célèbre in Hunan. Traditionalists berated the dead bride for bringing disgrace upon her family. Romantics lauded her for following the dictates of her heart. Mao was quick to join in the dispute. In the space of twelve days he wrote ten articles on the subject. He defended Zhao's right to kill herself by quoting an apposite Chinese proverb, 'Better to be a shattered vessel of jade than an unbroken piece of pottery.' But Mao was not concerned simply with questions of romance or dishonour. He took the opportunity offered by the controversy to attack China's archaic social conventions. He presented Zhao's death as a tragedy that illustrated 'the rottenness of the marriage system and the darkness of the social system'. He called on young people to reject arranged marriages as 'indirect rape'. One of his articles was provocatively headed 'Smash the Matchmaker System'. Another carried the subtitle 'Smash the Policy of Parental Arrangement'. In these, he denounced the decadent trade of the professional marriage brokers, who were examples of what made China 'a society of dirty tricks'. Mao urged the young to follow their own inclinations when seeking partners. When he wrote the following he may well have been recalling his own rejection of Miss Luo eleven years earlier:

> Dear young men and women throughout China. . . . Having seen such a tragedy of 'blood spattering the city of Changsha', you must be stirred to the depths of your souls. . . . The policy of letting parents arrange everything should absolutely be repudiated. Love is sacred, and cannot absolutely be arranged by others, cannot be forced, cannot be bought.[4]

Mao broadened his attack to include the marriage system itself. He condemned it as an unholy mixture of capitalist exploitation and rural superstition, which turned husbands into 'a rape brigade'. In a powerful plea for female emancipation, he asserted that Chinese women had always been denied 'status in any area of life' and 'relegated to the dark corners of society'. He denounced the Chinese conventions that forced women to be submissive, denied them economic freedom by keeping them illiterate, and made them the chattels of men. Refusing to accept that women were emotionally or psychologically inferior to men, he ascribed their apparently lower physical strength to the effects of foot binding and of childbirth. In a striking passage he summarised the corrupt convention which reduced women in China to peonage:

> A wife is only for doing the slave-work. When a woman is given in marriage, her parents don't say they have chosen a husband for their daughter, but rather that they have selected a happy son-in-law. A 'happy son-in-law' means only that this will make the parents happy. It doesn't matter whether their daughter will be happy or not. And even all the dowry payments are just so that they themselves can eat well. In short, capitalism and love are in conflict with one another.[5]

One effect of the Zhao Wuzhen affair was a relaxation in Mao's attitude towards the direct involvement of women in political action. It is notable that around this time the New People's Study Society and the Cultural Book Society began to admit many more females into their ranks. Mao welcomed them and made arrangements for them to be included in the programme for work-study visits to Russia. Two women of particular note in this regard were Tao Yi and Xiang Jingyu, the companion of Mao's close associate Cai Hesen, the man who helped introduce him to Marxism. Mao described Cai's intimate but unmarried relationship with Xiang as a model union since it was 'based on love'.[6] Xiang worked in both France and Soviet Russia, promoting the interests of women comrades. Having joined the Chinese Communist Party in 1922, she became the first secretary of the Women's Section of the Central Committee. Her young life ended in 1928, when she was killed by the GMD during the White Terror.

Tao Yi was one of the first women to join the New People's Study Society in 1919. She became highly regarded by Mao and the other members for her work in the Hunan independence movement and in the running of the Cultural Book Society. Mao had great respect for her opinions on the best ways of advancing the revolutionary cause. Her work for the Dawn Society, which was founded in 1920 with the aim of raising the political consciousness and status of women, greatly impressed him. In one of his letters to her he described her as 'a very enlightened and purposeful person'.[7] Tao Yi and Mao became close and it is possible that she was the first female with whom he had full sex. However, after Tao declined to join the CCP in the early 1920s, the couple drifted apart politically. They had long ceased to have any contact with each other by the time of Tao's death in 1930.

Struck by the contribution made by female members, Mao came quickly to accept and then to emphasise the vital role that women had to play in the unfolding politics of China. As a party worker in the 1920s, drafting GMD conference and congress agendas, he was insistent on including resolutions advocating women's liberation. He later made it a primary objective of the All-China Peasant Association that it actively seek 'to improve the status of women in the countryside'.[8] A consistent theme in his reports was the importance of women to the revolutionary movement. In a striking passage from 1929 he wrote of the extraordinary political potential of Chinese women:

Women account for half the population. The economic position of working women, and the special exploitation suffered by them, prove not only that women have an urgent need for revolution but also that they are a force that will decide the success or failure of the revolution.[9]

Mao saw in the inequality of women an outstanding example of the feudalism that the CCP was pledged to destroy. He chided those soviets whose slowness to implement CCP requirements was 'hindering women from taking part in the revolution'. Throughout the Jiangxi and Yanan years, he continued to make the furtherance of women's rights an integral part of the CCP's message. Mao's numerous and celebrated studies of the peasant question all showed a sensitivity to the special place and needs of women in the economic and social order and offer a number of fascinating insights into their status and position as he saw it. He commended the special skills of women as propaganda agents. He pressed for their right to hold property on the same terms as men and demanded that this be incorporated into the drafting of constitutions and laws at provincial and national level. 'If women have no property, then attempts by women to solve problems such as those of education, occupation, participation in politics, and marriage are nothing but empty talk.'[10] A theme running through Mao's observations was the appalling conditions in which most farm labourers worked. In a descriptive passage he specified the hardships suffered by rural women:

Although men help out, women are chiefly responsible for hulling [de-husking] grain, polishing grain, watering gardens, transplanting vegetables, cutting wood, mowing grass, making tea, cooking meals, raising pigs and other domestic animals . . . washing and ironing clothes, mending clothes, sweeping floors and doing dishes. Besides these tasks, raising children is also a woman's duty; thus the toil of women is harder than that of men. Women's tasks come one after another, and their work never ends. They are appendages of the male economy.[11]

Mao suggested that the burdens on women could be lifted 'only by raising a women's revolutionary army'.[12] He bemoaned the high levels of female illiteracy and calculated that between 30 and 40 per cent of rural women still had bound feet.[13] Prostitution, which he regarded as a relic of feudalism and an outstanding example of female subjugation, earned his special scorn – on economic not moral grounds. In one town he counted between thirty and forty brothels servicing a town with a population of only 2,700. He made a point of naming 'the best known among the hard-bitten lot of prostitutes' and offered a class analysis of their clientele.[14] Aware of the incidence of rape that invariably followed in the wake of Nationalist and Japanese victories, Mao urged the Red Army forces to remember that the decent treatment of women was not only humanitarian; it had huge propaganda value in the struggle to win over the peasantry to the CCP.

Mao's approach was thus a mixture of idealism and practicality. Since women constituted half the population, they were a potential force that no true revolutionary could ignore. He believed that the CCP faced a major problem that could be met only by recruiting women as active members of the party. With so many male party members at the front fighting the Nationalists and Japanese, it was essential there was a willing clerical army at the rear to take on the everyday but vital tasks of administration. It followed that the soviets must always support the women's movement by implementing laws and regulations in their interest. Criticising those soviets that 'displayed a tendency to slight women', Mao laid down a twenty point programme for the establishing of women's rights in the areas controlled by the CCP. This included reforms guaranteeing the right of working women to vote and to be elected as deputies in the townships, to have full access to education, to hold land on equal terms with men, to reject forced marriage and sue for divorce, and to share fully in the political and cultural life of the soviets. Mao held that such reforms were necessary for a position to be achieved in which 'men and women are absolutely equal under the Soviet Government'.[15] It is notable that soon after its creation in 1949, the PRC formally made the full recognition of women's rights part of its legal and constitutional structure.

But these were official attitudes. Feminists have complained that, in their actual treatment of women, the CCP in its Jiangxi and Yanan days were patriarchal and uncaring. Mao undoubtedly colluded in the torture and humiliation of women in the suppression of the Futian rebellion.[16] Ding Ling, a campaigner for women's rights, found Mao to be hypocritical. She claimed that while he luxuriated at Yanan among his coterie of women, others starved.[17] Another writer, Wang Shiwei, one of those purged during the rectification campaigns of the early 1940s, supported the women's complaints.

YANG KAIHUI AND HE ZICHEN

Mao's formally stated views on the rights of women were strikingly progressive. This makes it fascinating to turn from the public figure to the private man and consider his personal relationships. By 1920, his views on women's status closely corresponded to the ideas of Yang Changji, his most influential college teacher, who, in an article in 1915, had attacked the scandal of arranged marriages. What renders this especially interesting is that by 1919 Mao had fallen for Yang's daughter, Kaihui. The sense of personal conviction which infused Mao's articles of 1919 on marriage thus has an easy explanation: he was in love. Mao had met Kaihui in 1915 when she became a student in Changsha under her father's personal tutelage, but it was in Beijing in 1919, attending to the arrangements for Yang's funeral, that he got to know her well. Mao was drawn to this bright eighteen-year-old, who had inherited her father's lively intelligence and strong radical opinions. Given that Kaihui's progressive views on the freedom of young people to choose their own partners matched Mao's own, marriage between them was the obvious next step. They were regarded by their fellow radicals in Hunan as an ideal couple.[18] Their wedding took place in 1920.

The marriage lasted eight years, during which Kaihui bore three children, before it ended in divorce in 1928. She died two years later. A love poem of Mao's has survived from 1923 in which he likened their relationship to 'two birds flying side by side, soaring high as the clouds'.[19] Yet in his reminiscences, Mao made little reference to her. Such information about her as exists comes principally from one of the earliest biographies of Mao, written by Xiao Yu, the student who had accompanied him on his tour of Hunan in 1917. In his *Mao Tse-tung and I Were Beggars*, Xiao describes Kaihui as a prominent female member of the CCP in the 1920s, who proved a fierce resistance fighter against the warlords and the GMD. Her death in 1930 was a courageous affair. Having been taken prisoner by the Nationalists during the Futian Incident, she was tortured and then killed for refusing to reveal the whereabouts of Mao and other CCP leaders. Her three children were spared, but, bereft of their mother, they were destined for a hard life: the youngest, Anlong, died in 1931 aged six;

Anying and Anqing survived, but did not meet their father again until 1946.

Beyond mentioning that she had been killed along with her sister, Zehung, Mao himself gave no details of how Kaihui came to her end. He made only two other recorded allusions to her. One was in a letter to Li Lisan, a companion and political rival from student days; writing in 1929, Mao remarked that he often felt lonely when parted from Kaihui and the children. The other was in a sentimental poem, 'The Immortals', written in 1955, in which he recalled Kaihui as his 'proud poplar'. His reluctance to say more was presumably because he did not wish to recall his callous treatment of her during the last three years of her life. Despite sharing the uncertainties and dangers of life as hunted revolutionaries, which involved constant changes of location, Kaihui found herself being supplanted in his affections. By 1927, Mao had taken up with another female comrade, He Zichen. It was not the first time he had strayed. In 1919, shortly before he married Kaihui, Mao had had his brief affair with Tao Yi.[20] The jealousy which Kaihui as a young wife had felt at that time burned again when, after her eight years of loyalty in the most exacting circumstances, she came to know of Mao's fresh betrayal. A letter written in Kaihui's hand has survived from 1928. It tells of her mixture of sorrow and outrage at his behaviour and hints that but for the children she would have killed herself.

If there is a defence for Mao, it is that his life as a revolutionary, with its long periods of enforced absence from wife and home, meant that he was often lonely and frustrated. It was natural that as a prominent figure in the CCP he should have become a cynosure and that the women members should have been attracted to him and he to them. Party camaraderie and a common sense of political struggle created the circumstances in which close personal relationships quickly formed. These could be either casual or sincere depending on the attitude of those involved. Revolutionaries bent on radicalising Chinese society were hardly likely to be constrained by traditional morality. An interesting influence in this regard was that of the American Marxists who, as CCP supporters, visited the Jiangxi and Yanan bases in the 1930s. They tended to be sexual libertarians, like the feminist writer Agnes Smedley, who was an eager advocate of free love. Such progressive Western ideas, while at variance with traditional Chinese rural puritanism, had a clear attraction for the hard-pressed CCP. Many members simply dispensed with formal marriage ceremonies and declared that their sleeping partners were now their spouses.

Mao's relationship with He Zichen appears to have followed this course. A lissom eighteen-year-old in 1927, she had begun to share Mao's bed soon after becoming his assistant during his guerrilla years in Jinggangshan. From 1928, Mao and Zichen considered themselves to be partners. During the next six years Zichen produced five children, all born in the most difficult circumstances, and one during the Long March. Under attack and constantly on the move, the CCP was unable to give its female members special protection. The women had to cope as best they could. Zichen suffered at least one miscarriage. So arduous were her travels that she had to abandon three of her children as babies to the care of sympathetic peasants. Neither Mao nor Zichen saw those children again or learned of what became of them.[21]

He Zichen was one of the hundred or so women who survived the Long March of 1934–35, the great odyssey that secured the survival of the CCP. Her efforts were prodigious. Despite giving birth during the March and suffering shrapnel wounds from an exploding shell, she continued to make Mao's health her chief concern. She regularly treated the constipation which troubled him all his life by giving him enemas and easing out his stools with her fingers.[22] Her dedication went unrewarded. It was said that such were the privations of the journey and the sense of triumph felt by those who survived it that the Long Marchers were ever after united by a special bond. But the hardships shared by Mao and Zichen did not bind them together permanently. Within two years of arriving in Yanan their relationship had become increasingly unsettled. Part of the reason was that Mao's eye had strayed to another female party member, newly arrived in 1937 – Jiang Qing.

JIANG QING

Mao's last wife, Jiang Qing, first came to the attention of the West in the 1960s as the hatchet-faced woman who led the ferocious attack on China's writers and artists during the Cultural Revolution. Her grim appearance and policies made it difficult to appreciate that, as a younger woman, she had been notorious for her sexual allure. Edgar Snow, who met her in 1939, described her as 'slender' and 'vivacious'.[23] For Li Yanqiao, Mao's bodyguard, Jiang had a 'casual kind of beauty. . . . Her large eyes shone brightly underneath pleasantly arched brows. She had a straight and elegant nose, and her mouth, although a bit on the wide side, still added beauty to her face when it was closed.'[24] Jiang was born in 1914 into a middle-class family in Shandong province. Her father deserted the home while Jiang was still a child, leaving her mother to struggle to raise her. There were later suggestions that her mother had survived only by turning to prostitution. Jiang, nonetheless, received a basic primary education before enrolling at a theatrical training school. Largely through the influence of a friend, Yu San, a classical opera singer, Jiang gained entrée in the early 1930s to China's young cinema industry based in Shanghai. She did not play leads but she did get herself noticed. She married twice during this period.

MAO'S WIVES AND CHILDREN

Miss Luo – betrothed in 1908 but marriage unconsummated

Yang Kaihui (1901–30) – married Mao in 1920 – divorced 1928 – killed by the Guomindang – 3 children:

Mao Anying (1922–50 – killed in Korea)

Mao Anlong (1927–31 – died of dysentery)

Mao Anqing (b.1923 – institutionalised schizophrenic)

He Zichen (1910–84) – married Mao in 1928 – divorced 1938 – 5 children:

Xiao Mao (1934 lost at 2)

child (1929 abandoned on Long March to care of peasants)

child (1935 similarly abandoned)

Li Min (1936–)

son (1939–40)

Jiang Qing (1914–94) – married Mao in 1938 – died of throat cancer while serving life imprisonment

1 child – Li Na (1940–)

Her friendship with Yu San, whose family were dedicated revolutionaries, and her association with Kang Sheng, who was later to become head of Mao's secret police, led to Jiang's involvement in the CCP's underground organisation in Shanghai. Her activities resulted in her being imprisoned for eight months. With the spreading Japanese occupation of north-eastern China, following the outbreak of war in 1937, many Chinese fled into the interior. Jiang was one of these. She joined an agitprop theatrical touring company which found its way to Yanan in 1937, the year in which she divorced her second husband. Once in Yanan, she was quick to become a student at the party's training school. It was there she first met Mao, who was one of the lecturers. It was said that Jiang made sure he noticed her by sitting at the front of the class and continually asking questions. The strategy worked; Mao became smitten. Within a year of Jiang's arrival in Yanan in 1937, she had become his personal assistant and his wife.

Not all Mao's comrades approved of the match. There was a feeling that he had treated He Zichen badly. A number of uncertainties still attach to the story. One suggestion is that Mao divorced He Zichen so as to be free to wed Jiang. However, some commentators, of whom Edgar Snow is one, claim that Mao's separation from Zichen had occurred before he met Jiang. This version has it that in 1937 Zichen had accused Mao of having an affair with Lily Wu, a party secretary and interpreter. Edgar Snow's wife, Nym Wales, recorded how susceptible Mao was to engaging women. She noted how Lily, who was acting as interpreter to Agnes Smedley, made a hit with him. Smedley herself quickly came to hero-worship Mao, a sign of the attraction that he exercised for women. His aura of power evidently acted as an aphrodisiac.

Mao neatly extricated himself from his marital dilemma by appealing to a special party court to grant him a divorce from He Zichen. The court found in Mao's favour and ordered both He Zichen and Lily Wu to leave Yanan. If, as some believe, Zichen had already decided to break from Mao before the onset of the Jiang affair, then she may well have welcomed the court's ruling. Despite her initial enthusiasm for the revolutionary life, the pleasures of being permanently pregnant and living in a cave had begun to pall. It was in 1938 that Zichen, with child for the fifth time in six years, had gone, with Mao's approval, to the Soviet Union for an abortion. However, once there, she changed her mind and decided to have the baby. It was while she was in Moscow that Mao sent Li Min, their two-year old daughter and only remaining child, to join her mother there. Since the two sons of his second marriage were already in Moscow, this left Mao in Yanan free of all family entanglements. The way was now clear for him to marry Jiang Qing, whom Zichen referred to witheringly as 'that low class artist'.[25] It would be unreasonable to suggest that Mao had planned all this, but things had certainly worked to his advantage.

No such advantage came Zichen's way. If her decision to give birth was meant to be the start of a new life for herself as well as her baby, she was soon disillusioned. Within a few months of his birth, the baby son died of pneumonia. Zichen fell into a depression from which she never wholly recovered. She stayed for ten years in the USSR as a patient in a variety of mental hospitals, and, even after returning to China in 1947 with Mao's encouragement, she needed psychiatric help for the rest of her unhappy life. Mao helped pay for her care and sent her money and American cigarettes. She died in 1984 in her seventy-fifth year. The couple did meet on one last occasion. That was in 1961 after Mao had received a crazed letter from her in which she warned of plots in the CCP against him. Mao arranged to call on her at a house in Lushan. Mao's doctor recorded that the scene was both touching and embarrassing. The couple embraced and held hands. Zichen seemed genuinely elated as Mao enquired of her health and spoke of their children. But her speech soon became rambling and her eyes glazed over vacantly. Mao said farewell and promised that they would meet again, but they never did. After she had gone, Mao remarked how old and ill she looked. He chain-smoked meditatively and asked Dr Li about Zichen's mental state. Li explained she was suffering from schizophrenia, the same condition that afflicted his son, Mao Anqing.[26]

The ill-feeling among some CCP members at Yanan towards Jiang Qing did not derive solely from her having ensnared Mao and snatched him from He Zichen. There were also doubts about her revolutionary credentials; it was whispered that she had been a GMD double-agent. Mao refused to countenance such stories and defended her stoutly. He claimed that, before being accepted into the party, Jiang had been fully vetted by his security chief, Kang Sheng. Nevertheless, Mao was careful not to antagonise the doubting members further. He did not give her an official position and asked her to keep in the background. Jiang did not take easily to this. She resented the attitude of the party officials towards her. In one outburst she referred to them as 'mother fuckers'.[27] Yet with the lower rank comrades Jiang was more affable. She organised concert parties for them, taught them how to sew and weave and trimmed the men's hair.

One particular attribute for which she was greatly admired was her beau-
tiful curling calligraphy. Mao loved to show this off to visitors to Yanan.
Jiang was also an accomplished rider who loved breaking in wild horses
and challenging the comrades to race. It was on one such chase that her
horse collided with Zhou Enlai's mount. Zhou was thrown off and broke
his arm. Some party members did not regard it as an accident; they
held that such was the antipathy between Jiang and Zhou that she had
deliberately set out to injure him. It was certainly the case that the two
never trusted each other, a fact which conditioned their relationship right
through to Zhou's death in 1976.

The first two years of Mao's marriage to Jiang Qing went well. In 1940
she gave birth to a daughter, Mao's ninth acknowledged child. However,
Jiang then let it be known that one child was enough for her. Proud of
her figure, she was not prepared simply to become a reproductive machine.
She aborted a second child and then had herself sterilised. It rapidly
became clear that her marriage to Mao was not a match made in heaven.
Tensions soon developed. For all his professed commitment to the cause
of female emancipation, Mao did not want an equal for a wife. He found
Jiang's independence of thought and readiness to speak her mind of
limited appeal. She found his insomnia and unwillingness to keep regular
hours especially trying. Fierce disagreements between them became common. Intriguingly, Mao seldom fell out with Jiang during their days of
hardship and danger. Fighting for survival against Nationalist or Japanese
attack seemed to stimulate their affection. The excitement of battle drew
them together. It was in quieter times, when they could relax, that their
personalities and temperaments came into conflict. Their quarrels were
verbally violent. He bawled at her; she screeched at him. In 1942 they
had a particularly angry row during which they exchanged volleys of
abuse. Mao accused Jiang of being a bourgeois egotist who would never
lose 'the mentality of the exploiting class'.[28] It is striking that when Mao
really wanted to humiliate his wife he resorted to challenging her revolutionary integrity. It was Jiang's most sensitive spot. She continually
sought reassurance from Mao on this, asking him to scotch the rumours
which continued to circulate in the CCP that she was a mere time-server.
A detail that especially riled her was that official party records gave her
year of joining as 1935, which post-dated the Long March and the creation
of the Yanan base, whereas she claimed she had become a member selflessly
in 1932 at the time the party was in desperate need.

Although passion could still occasionally ignite between them, everyday proximity became too great a strain. On the pretext that Jiang might have contracted tuberculosis, Mao insisted in 1942 that she sleep apart from him in another cave. Some members took it upon themselves to attempt to bring about a reconciliation, but whatever it was that had first drawn Mao and Jiang together had been lost and was never to be recovered. Mao let it be known that he longed to be free of Jiang, and that had she been merely a secretary he would not have tolerated her. Mao explained his inability to break from Jiang in these terms:

> If Jiang weren't my wife but one of my attendants, I would have sent her away a long time ago. I married her in too great haste. What can I do now? In my position I can't divorce her. She hasn't done anything bad enough to deserve that; a divorce would be viewed unfavourably by the comrades and would give rise to all sorts of rumours.[29]

This explanation, which dates from 1947, is interesting but unconvincing. At the time Mao offered it, he had established a near absolute hold on the party as a result of the rectification campaigns. It would have been remarkable that, with this achieved, he should still have felt so insecure as not to risk giving offence over marital affairs. After all, he had already abandoned three wives, a fact that had hardly retarded his rise in the party. The real explanation for the survival of Mao's marriage to Jiang may lie in the nature of their relationship. They were the type of couple that cannot live together but cannot survive apart.

With the turn of the tide against the Nationalists in 1947, Mao left Shaanxi province and for the following two years was constantly on the move, usually on pony or horseback. Jiang sometimes travelled with him, but for long periods they were apart. As the CCP gained the upper hand in the civil war, Mao moved to Xibaipo and then to the outskirts of Beijing itself. Jiang did not accompany him, and was not with him when he made his triumphal entry into the capital in the autumn of 1949. The reason was that in March of that year she had gone to a Soviet resort in Yalta for treatment for tuberculosis. There is some confusion about whether Jiang, a hypochondriac, was truly ill or whether she was made to go to the Soviet Union simply because Mao wanted her out of the way. By the late 1940s it had become common for CCP members or their wives to accept Stalin's offer of medical treatment in Soviet clinics. This provided obvious opportunities for spiriting away unwanted people at embarrassing times.

Mao's anxiety to have Jiang removed from the scene, even if only temporarily, may have derived from his wish for greater freedom to enjoy the company of young women. This took its most obvious form in the dance parties which were especially arranged for Mao in Zhongnanhai, his official Beijing residence from 1949 until his death in 1976.

Zhongnanhai, a walled complex of buildings, lakes and gardens, formed part of the Forbidden City, one of the few areas to have survived the programmed destruction of the old city of Beijing that the new Communist government had ordered. With the establishment of the PRC, Zhongnanhai became home to a number of CCP leaders, besides Mao. They lived in apartments in what had previously been a series of palaces, which continued to carry their original mellifluous imperial names. Mao's quarters were in the Hall of Longevity, one wing of which contained his formal work room – the Study of Chrysanthemum Fragrance. The reception area for visiting guests was in the Hall of Purple Effulgence. Zhou Enlai and Zhu De stayed in a large accommodation block overlooking the Fruitful Garden. In what was to prove a bitter irony, Liu Shaoqi moved into the House of Good Fortune.

The practice of regular dance parties dated from the Yanan period, when, on one or two nights a week, girls would come to Mao's quarters and waltz and fox-trot with him to the accompaniment of a wind-up gramophone playing records of American dance-bands. These parties began as an innocent way of relaxing but it was not unknown for certain of the girls to stay behind and share Mao's bed. Mao often sought solace in numbers. He had a huge bed which was invariably covered in books; these were pushed aside to make space for him to disport with as many girls as took his fancy and the bed could bear. The dance evenings had begun before Jiang Qing arrived in Yanan and initially she seems to have approved of the more innocent side of the entertainment; indeed, she sometimes attended the dance sessions. However, as might be expected, she did not condone the philandering which they encouraged. Kang Sheng, the head of the secret police, acted as chief procurer, by using his contacts to recruit girls suited to Mao's predilections. When Mao became ill, the dancing parties were suspended but began again when he recovered. The company of the young women evidently helped the recovery process even though the remissions in his illnesses become shorter as he grew feebler in old age.

A year after Mao moved into Zhongnanhai, Jiang Qing returned from Moscow to join him. It was now that Mao began what was the first ordered form of family life he had known since boyhood. His two surviving daughters, Li Min and Li Na, had already come to live with him. The irony was that by the time Mao picked up the threads of domestic life he was already estranged from Jiang Qing. Outwardly the marriage continued, but Mao and Jiang had separate living quarters. Much to her annoyance, Jiang was required to make what were, in effect, formal appointments to see her husband. Rumour suggested that this had been imposed following the embarrassment caused by Jiang's unannounced arrival in Mao's rooms before the young women he was entertaining had had time to dress. Mao's doctor noted that sexual relations between Mao and Jiang became less and less frequent in the early 1950s and stopped altogether after 1955. This did not prevent Jiang from openly boasting to anyone who would listen about her erotic couplings with the chairman and his sexual stamina. But the evidence suggests that from the early 1950s on she was relying largely on memory.

After her fall from grace in the period following Mao's death in 1976, Jiang became publicly reviled in China. A common assertion was that she was a nymphomaniac who had slept around in order to gain advancement in the CCP. Tales were told of orgies in her Zhongnanhai apartment and her lusting after young male athletes, such as Zhang Zedong, a champion table tennis player. A scurrilous underground book, *Empress of the Red Capital*, portrayed her as a scheming man-hunter who had built her reputation on 'Three Falses – false hair, false tits and false arse'.[30] Stories circulated that Jiang Qing had used her wiles with the ultimate aim of making herself empress of China on the model of Wu Zetian, the notorious matricidal empress of the Tang dynasty, or at least reaching the eminence of the Dowager Empress Cixi, who had terrorised the court in the last decades of imperial China.[31] The readiness with which such stories were believed was a sign of the long pent-up detestation for Jiang that at last could be expressed once Mao had gone.

However, at the time when Jiang was supposed to have been voraciously devouring her men, little had been heard of it. If she were engaging in such escapades, for others to have revealed them would have been to scandalise the chairman's wife and to risk calling attention to his own adventures. What was commonly known about Jiang was that she was not a well woman. In 1956, she flew to Moscow to receive treatment for suspected cervical cancer. Whether her illness were real or imagined was again uncertain; Chinese and Russian doctors who treated her at various times found her ailments difficult to diagnose. But whatever their findings, the fact was that she frequently took to her bed. Her indisposition for most of the 1950s helps to explain why she made little political impact during the first decade of the PRC. However, that rapidly changed in 1959 when she made a dramatic first entrance into politics at the PRC's Lushan conference. She flew to Lushan by special plane to give her support to Mao in his battle with Peng Dehuai during the final stages of this critical CCP gathering.

It is odd that Mao should finally have allowed Jiang Qing to begin taking a political role at the very time their marriage had become meaningless. One logical inference is that Mao's lifting of the restrictions he had imposed upon her for twenty years was a form of compensation to Jiang for the failure of their personal relations. Another is that Mao no longer felt constrained by the party's dislike of his wife and now judged that she would be a political asset rather than a liability in the intra-party struggles that Lushan had exposed. However, there was one restriction on Jiang that Mao kept in force: he refused to allow her to read the official documents which came to him daily. This rankled with her, but she did not let her annoyance hold her back. Having been quiet since the Yanan days, she now began to make a mark in public affairs. By 1962 she had become a prominent figure, featuring in the national press and being present at Beijing receptions for foreign VIPs.

Abetted by Mao, Jiang took up as her main cause the purification of China's culture. In 1963, on the flimsy grounds that her experience as an actress gave her special insight into artistic matters, she began a wide-ranging assault on Chinese writers, composers and producers for their failure to produce works of revolutionary integrity. The charge was that, instead of serving the needs of the people, they were engaging in 'revisionism' by promoting decadent Western bourgeois values. Her attack was to develop within three years into a major part of the full-blown Cultural Revolution.

However, the reason for Mao's encouragement of Jiang's campaign in the early 1960s was more specific: it provided a very useful means of undermining Liu Shaoqi. Those whom Jiang attacked were invariably those intellectuals who had been appointed to their artistic posts by Liu and were, therefore, his committed supporters. Jiang was thus doing Mao's dirty work for him, preparing the way for the eventual removal of Liu. This was also the reason why Mao sent Jiang to Shanghai in 1965. Her mission there, which she successfully fulfilled, was to use her local knowledge to build up a team of contacts willing to lay the ground for a later attack on Peng Zhen, the local party secretary and a staunch supporter of Liu. The Maoists had chosen Shanghai as the starting point of the Cultural Revolution.

Jiang Qing served Mao loyally throughout the Cultural Revolution. As she put it succinctly and accurately at her trial in 1981, 'I was Mao's dog. Whoever he told me to bite, I bit.'[32] Indeed, she may be regarded as being more Maoist than he was. By the time he died, her fierce radicalism had antagonised so many of those whose support she then needed that she had destroyed any chance of continuing the revolution on her terms. Mao's frequent criticisms of Jiang Qing in the 1970s indicated that he had no intention of entrusting his political legacy to her. In 1975, Mao told Henry Kissinger that he would gladly have dispatched Jiang and all the Chinese women radicals who had made his life a misery, to the USA where, he understood, there was a shortage of females. He twice repeated himself to convince Kissinger that he was not joking.[33] How far Mao felt estranged from his wife he expressed unequivocally in a note to her in 1974, in which he rejected her request that they work more closely together:

> It would be better for us not to see each other. For years I have advised you about many things, but you have ignored most of it. So what use is there for us to see each other? There are Marxist-Leninist books – and books by me – but you won't study them seriously. I am eighty-one years old and seriously ill, but you show hardly any concern. You now enjoy many privileges, but after my death what are you going to do?[34]

ZHANG YUFENG

Callous though Mao's words were after forty years of marriage, his analysis was correct. He could afford to be dismissive of Jiang. He did not need her, while she was nothing without him. This was as true personally as politically. The companion of Mao's last years was not Jiang but Zhang

Yufeng, who doubled as secretary and nurse and on whom he came to depend completely. Zhang had first come to Mao's notice in 1962 when she became one of a number of young girls who achieved the much sought-after position of tea server in the dining car of his special train. She was eighteen, fifty years Mao's junior, and already married when she joined the train. Finding her particularly vivacious, Mao invited her to be an attendant in his sleeping car. This was, in effect, to make her his chief concubine. There were uncorroborated stories that Mao was the father of one of her two children. Zhang was despised by many in the CCP hierarchy, in part because of the obvious scandal that attached to her relationship with Mao, but also because she was an illiterate peasant girl.

It is striking how persistent traditional class prejudices could be in the new egalitarian China. The truth was that Mao had a penchant for young, naive and poorly educated girls. According to his doctor, Mao's taste in women was like his eating habits. When he liked a particular dish he would have it for days on end until he was sated. He would then push it away and try another.

Yet for the young women who serviced Mao's needs there was no greater coup than to have slept with Chairman Mao. It was something they could boast of among their peers. Nor were any of them deterred by his less than perfect bodily hygiene. Mao had a habit of publicly putting his hand down his trousers and hunting for lice in his pubic hair. When he had located the bugs he would withdraw his hand and proceed to crack or squeeze them between his finger and thumb. He never brushed his teeth or used toothpaste: his only form of dental care was to swill his mouth with green tea. It is unlikely that his girls all escaped contracting the sexually transmitted diseases that he carried. Gonorrhoea and genital herpes were among the hazards they risked. But there was no lack of takers to fill his bed.

Zhang Yufeng appeared willing to acquiesce in Mao's need for sex with as many women as possible. She helped to keep Apartment 118 in Zhongnanhai as a designated 'pleasure room' in which Mao relaxed with his women. While officials never openly criticised Mao, they would sometimes express their disapproval of things by tut-tutting about the brazen behaviour of particular girls. On one occasion, a member of Mao's female entourage was accused of being disloyal to the chairman by carrying on an affair with a junior clerk. Zhang was quick to come to the girl's defence, insisting that her relationship with the man was merely one of friendship. From time to time Apartment 118 was closed and the dancing parties suspended. This was usually when Jiang Qing was back in town or when the situation in China at large seemed to call for some concession to propriety.

Yet even at the height of the Cultural Revolution it was common for Mao to withdraw from affairs of state in order to dally with his female companions. It was during the terror that Mao, in one of his rare direct intrusions into the progress of events, responded to a plea from Zhang Yufeng for help. In November 1966, Red Guards had taken control of the Special Transportation Services which technically was the department for which Zhang worked. Fearful for her position and personal safety, she appealed to Mao for protection. Mao not only provided this by threatening to have her boss dismissed, he also extended his protection to two of Zhang's female work colleagues by inviting them to join him in his love nest in Zhongnanhai. In an inverse ratio, the number of girls jointly sharing Mao's bed went up as he grew physically feebler. Voyeurism had become the main attraction. He could not perform, but he could watch.

Zhang Yufeng appears to have helped Kang Sheng select women for Mao's pleasure rooms. Her willingness to play the role of complaisant procuress to the chairman makes it easier to understand why Zhang became the chief partner of the last fourteen years of his life. But it was not a case of his going gentle into that good night. Despite their closeness, Mao's relationship with Zhang was a fraught one. He frequently raged against the dying of the light. Fierce arguments between them occurred regularly and mutual curses rent the air. In this respect it was not unlike his marriage to Jiang Qing. One of the heart attacks that Mao suffered in the last year of his life followed a slanging match with Zhang Yufeng. A special insult Mao used was to accuse Zhang of being a foreign spy, a reference to the rumour that one of her parents was Japanese. But the quarrels did not destroy their intimacy.

The establishment around Mao were angered that Zhang's closeness to him enabled her to exert influence in ways denied to them. Dr Li complained of Zhang's constant interference in the treatments he prescribed. When Mao, who suffered chronic skin irritations, developed a form of blood poisoning as a result of spots on his chest becoming infected. Zhang admitted to Li that she had squeezed the spots with unwashed hands. She had already defied Li; against his express instructions, she had encouraged Mao to sip *mao-tai*, a sorghum-based liquor with the potency and taste of paint stripper. Zhang's defence was that since Mao was so unwell, a little alcohol could hardly matter.

In one extraordinary scene, Zhang Yufeng summoned the doctors who had submitted the report and informed them that Mao did not accept their recommendations. She told them that she proposed to continue with her own special treatment for him, which consisted largely of injections of glucose. Li Zhisui protested at this medical absurdity, but his fellow doctors, frightened by the knowledge that Zhang had Jiang Qing's backing, declined to support him. The eventual outcome was a special meeting of the Politburo, chaired by Deng Xiaoping and attended by Jiang Qing. The meeting reflected the growing divisions in government and party. The medical team, who felt they were on trial, were subjected to a hostile barrage of questions from Jiang. She accused them of disrespect towards the chairman by being too frank in describing his condition. Common sense, however, prevailed. As the meeting closed, Deng expressed his gratitude to the doctors and told them that they should follow their medical judgement.

Zhang Yufeng remained critical of the treatments prescribed for Mao. Despite her lack of formal medical training she overruled his doctors and insisted that he be given regular injections of glucose. She objected to the number of tubes inserted into Mao and encouraged him to pull them out. Zhang also arranged for part of the swimming pool area to be converted into a make-shift cinema in which Mao could daily watch a series of feature films. Even this caused a battle. The medical team were unhappy with the physical exertion that moving to the cinema brought him. Jiang Qing sided with the doctors but Zhang Yufeng again got her way. Doubtless she felt that the sheer uplift brought by such Western offerings as *The Sound of Music* and *Love Story* compensated for any bodily discomfort Mao suffered.

As remarked on by the American party that accompanied President Nixon on his visit to China in 1972, Zhang Yufeng was constantly at Mao's side. During his last two years, as his sight failed, she held the books and papers which were specially printed for him in large typeface. His loss of speech also became increasingly evident in 1974. It was in that year that the Politburo, at Mao's bidding, formally appointed Zhang Yufeng as his private secretary. This left her, the closest companion of his last two years, in a remarkable position. She was the only one able to understand the incoherent sounds he made. The government officials, CCP leaders, and foreign dignitaries whom Mao met depended on Zhang to make sense of his dribbling utterances. She became his interpreter. She also gained access to something which had always eluded Jiang Qing. Mao's physical frailty required that Zhang had to read and deal with the official papers that came to him daily. Everything had to go through her. She it was who decided which papers required a response and which officials should be honoured with a reply. It was an extraordinary power for a former tea-girl to exercise.

Unsurprisingly, Zhang's influence with Mao did not go unchallenged. On the grounds that she had become haughty and impolite in dealing with officials, Wang Dongxing, Mao's chief body guard, who answered directly to the party hierarchy, obtained Mao's permission to call a special meeting to criticise Zhang. She resented this but submitted herself to questioning. In the required act of self-criticism, she acknowledged some minor errors in carrying out her duties but admitted to nothing serious enough to threaten her position. The problem for her would-be accusers was that there was a fine line between attacking her and attacking Mao. So close were Zhang's relations with the chairman that any suggestion that she had been guilty of serious impropriety would necessarily reflect on Mao himself. This afforded her the protection she needed. She survived unscathed. Her only punishment was that she had to kneel before Mao and beg his forgiveness for having been too intimate with a party official. It is difficult to think that either of them took this very seriously.

Jiang never lost her distaste for Zhang Yufeng, but she was careful not to upset unnecessarily someone whom she needed as an ally. The result was a strange, strained relationship between the two women. Ostensibly, they were courteous, even friendly, towards each, but in the nature of things there was little trust between wife and mistress. Zhang Yufeng had a child late in 1972. There were whispers that Mao was the father, but this was extremely unlikely. Dr Li's notebooks showed that the eighty-year-old Mao had long been both infertile and impotent.[35] Nevertheless, it was on Mao's insistence that Zhang during her confinement and delivery received the best hospital treatment available in Beijing. Knowing of Mao's solicitude, Jiang Qing made a point of visiting Zhang, bringing gifts for mother and baby.

Eventually Mao grew so incapacitated that he could do nothing for himself. Constipation so plagued him that bulletins were issued recording his bowel movements. When news came that he had excreted successfully his bodyguards would stamp their feet and shout for joy. Zhang Yufeng had less reason to be elated. She spelled out to Zhou Enlai the details of how she had to hold Mao while he defecated and then mop up after him. She complained of the intolerable strain this put upon her and angrily asked Zhou whether something could be done about it, but an embarrassed Zhou could not think of a satisfactory response. It was an inglorious ending to the tea girl's years with the chairman.

Since the revelations in the 1980s of Mao's sexual habits, there has been a tendency to regard him simply as a lecher. But there is an aspect of his behaviour that should be emphasised. The older Mao grew, the more frequently he sought solace and gratification in the company of young women. The obvious physical satisfaction this brought seems to have been only part of the story; he may have been ruler of a sixth of the world's population but he was a lonely man. The more emperor-like in status he became, the less contact he had with ordinary people. In Zhongnanhai, he became detached from his family.

As with the emperors of old, his associates were all underlings. He had devoted followers but no friends. It is unlikely that the officials at Zhongnanhai ever relaxed sufficiently in his company for them to be less than formal in their conversation with him. They were either too frightened or too awestruck. It is one of the drawbacks of being an emperor or a living god that those who wait on him become sycophants. Mao's attendants were too ready to laugh at his jests and acknowledge his great wisdom. They became versed in saying what they judged he wanted to hear rather than what they genuinely thought. The old colleagues or extended family members from Hunan who were occasionally allowed to see him invariably came as supplicants. There was nobody he could talk to on equal terms. In his later years, the consolation that other men derive from their wives or families was denied him. Jiang Qing and he had grown apart. His daughters, Li Min and Li Da, were brought up in a separate apartment at Zhongnanhai by Jiang and her sister and were then sent away to boarding school. His favourite son had been killed twenty years earlier and another had been confined to a mental home. His isolation as neo-emperor meant that sex was one of the few intimate relationships in which he could engage. His female entourage were there not merely to cater to his libidinous needs, but to lessen his sense of loneliness and isolation.

CONCLUSION

MAO'S PASSING

By mid-1975, the eighty-one-year-old chairman was in a bad state. Blind, deaf, unable to speak, and paralysed down his right side, he began to suffer a series of increasingly serious heart attacks. Li Zhisui, his doctor, was unwilling to tell Mao that he was terminally ill, but through Zhang Yufeng's intercession Li eventually persuaded him to go to Wuhan for further relieving treatment. It was in Wuhan that, against doctor's orders, Mao insisted on swimming in the pool. His wasted muscles were simply not strong enough: he floundered and nearly drowned before being pulled out by his bodyguards. Nevertheless, it was publicly announced that the chairman had resumed his lifelong passion for swimming.

Part of the problem for Mao was that the cocktail of drugs he had taken over the years had made his body resistant to them. Sleeping pills and pain-killers needed to be consumed in ever-greater quantities to have any effect. Mao was a chronic insomniac and this tended to compound his medical problems. He was also particularly stubborn in refusing to submit to surgery. This had consequences beyond his own health. His prejudice against operations meant that he seldom gave permission for other leading Communists to be given this type of treatment. Kang Sheng, who died from stomach cancer in 1972, had not been allowed to have an operation.

Zhou Enlai, who died in January 1976, was similarly denied surgery for his lung cancer. Mao's terminal illness coincided with Zhou Enlai's, but, whereas Mao was bedridden, Zhou performed his public duties to the last.

Eventually, in 1975, Mao did accept treatment to remove the cataracts that were causing his blindness. Before he was operated on, it was decided to make a practical test to determine what form of surgery might best suit him. Some forty geriatrics in a Beijing old-people's home were used, without their knowledge, as guinea pigs. They were divided into two groups. One set received the simpler treatment, in which their cataracts were merely pushed to one side; the other group underwent the full Western-style operation in which their cataracts were wholly removed. The results were then passed on to Mao for him to make the final decision. He opted for the simpler Chinese operation, which in the event proved partially successful. He recovered the sight in one eye sufficient for him to read large-print documents when wearing spectacles. The operation on his other eye was never carried out since, from October 1975, his general condition made it too risky for him to undergo even minor surgery.

Dr Li tried to gather a team of specialists to deal with each of the many symptoms that Mao had begun to manifest. This was in part the expected solicitude of doctor for patient, but Li was also very aware that when Mao's death came he would inevitably be accused of not having done enough to save the chairman. Mao did eventually submit to a full examination. After four days of tests early in 1976, the diagnosis could not have been worse. Mao was suffering from:

> cataracts, amyotrophic lateral sclerosis [motor neurone disease], coronary heart disease, pulmonary heart disease, an infection in the lower half of both lungs, three bullae in his left lung, bedsores on his left hip, and a shortage of oxygen in his blood.[1]

During the last months of his life, a team of sixteen doctors and twenty-four nurses worked in shifts to look after him. In his last days, Mao had to be fed through a tube passed directly into his stomach. Before it reached that stage, Zhang Yufeng had fed him by spooning liquids, usually chicken broth, into his mouth. This became impossible once he lost the power to swallow and began to choke on the soup. His left lung finally collapsed and he had to lie on his side to be able to breathe. Finally he became dependent on a respirator.

Mao's physical deterioration was accompanied by increasing paranoia. He interpreted the scratching noises made by a pair of lynxes that had found their way into the roofing at Zhongnanhai as a proof that he was being spied upon. In his final months the only political companion he would allow near him was Hua Guofeng, a colourless party official but one who was totally loyal to Mao. Hua's podgy cheeks and corpulent frame also gave him a passing resemblance to the chairman. It was on Hua that Mao, with his last recorded intelligible words, conferred the succession: 'With you in charge my heart is at ease.'[2]

On 28 July 1976 a huge earthquake devastated the city of Tangshan in the northern province of Hebei. Those many Chinese traditionalists who believed that the earth's release of such elemental force presaged some great event in the state did not have to wait long for the portent to be fulfilled. On 2 September Mao suffered his final heart attack. Although he held on for another seven days, he was past recovery. Twelve minutes after midnight on 9 September the cardiograph to which he was wired recorded his last pulse. Mao, the Red emperor, the saviour and destroyer of his people, was dead.

MAO ZEDONG: AN EVALUATION

The adulation Mao received during his lifetime and the outpouring of national grief evoked by his death may have appeared excessive, but they were not wholly irrational. The Chinese people had good reason to look upon him with awe. At home, he had led a vast social revolution, had resisted the Japanese invader, had defeated Chiang Kai-shek and the Nationalists, and had destroyed the vestiges of European imperialism in China. On a wider front, he had transformed his country into a world power and taken it into the nuclear age, had challenged the Soviet Union for the leadership of international socialism, and had made China a model and inspiration for emerging nations still engaged in anti-colonial struggle. By any measure, these were towering achievements.

Yet beside them have to be set failures that were equally monumental. Mao's attempt to revolutionise the Chinese economy in the Great Leap Forward of the late 1950s ended in the death from starvation of 50 million people. Further millions died or suffered during the Cultural Revolution when Mao tried during the last ten years of his life to impose a binding political correctness not only on his contemporaries but on China perpetually. It has been said that Hitler killed people for what they were, Stalin for what they did, and Mao for what they thought. The charge against Mao is not that he willed those deaths but that he allowed them to happen, that he did not balance the risks, and finally acquiesced in losses that were avoidable.

The People's Republic of China under Mao exhibited the oppressive tendencies that were discernible in all the major absolutist regimes of the twentieth century. There are obvious parallels between Mao's China, Nazi Germany, and Soviet Russia. Each of these regimes witnessed deliberately ordered mass 'cleansing' and extermination. However, it is doubtful whether anything elsewhere matched the Chinese experience. Taken together, the Great Leap Forward and the Cultural Revolution resulted in the deaths of at least 50 million people and possibly 100 million. The scale was so staggering that for a long time neither Chinese nor Western scholars could bring themselves to accept it. The question that presses for an answer is why Mao Zedong allowed the movement he had created to reach such destructive political, social, and economic proportions.

To understand Mao's extremism one must necessarily appreciate the character of the China into which Mao was born. Here was a country whose people after two millennia of independence had been forced by fifty years of subjection to the foreigner to realise that in all respects that mattered they were subordinate to the West. They tried desperately to recover, but were unable to do so because the nation was led by an effete imperial ruling system that collaborated with the Western occupiers more often than it resisted them. When the Qing dynasty finally collapsed in 1911, there was an attempt to introduce the electoral system, but the republic soon proved a disappointment. Genuine popular participatory politics did not take hold. The weakness of central government allowed the warlords to impose a new form of authoritarianism. Lacking the institutions necessary for structuring an ordered civil society, China reverted to factional and regional conflict. In such turmoil, it was the common perception of all those who yearned for the regeneration of China, whether they were republicans, nationalists or, communists, that the only means to achieve this lay in the forcible removal of all those who barred the path to recovery, whether they were reactionaries, warlords, or foreign occupiers.

Thus the ferocity with which Mao frequently treated his enemies within China was not arbitrary cruelty. It was his response to the world as he saw it, a world in which the greatest sin was weakness of purpose. He once commented on *The History of China's Warring States*, one of the classic Chinese texts, 'It is a delight to read. But when it moves to the peaceful times I hate it . . . because a time of peace is not good for the development of the people. It is unbearable.' In speaking of the ruthlessness with which China's revolution had to be conducted Mao compared his own position and that of the Qin Shihuang, the emperor who in the third century BC had created China as a nation. Qin had employed the most extreme methods to achieve political unification. Mao regarded this as exemplary. Great rulers are realists who know that troubled times necessitate violent means. This attitude was perfectly captured by Li Rui, who had been one of Mao's personal secretaries at Zhongnanhai, when he summed up Mao's rule as 'Marx plus Emperor Qin'.[3]

For Mao, life was a constant and violent battle between opposites. He concluded that strength of will, expressed in a readiness to take whatever steps were necessary to overcome opposition, was the prerequisite for those who, like himself, wished to change the world. Mao one remarked to Dr Li, 'I graduated from the University of Outlaws.'[4] Li viewed Mao's hardness and callousness as a product of his bitter experiences as a revolutionary that left him inured against human suffering. Such interpretations of his behaviour go some way towards making sense of his refusal to be deterred from polices such as the Great Leap Forward and the Cultural Revolution, even when he knew that millions of his countrymen were dying because of them.

The vital and ironic point is that Mao's ruthlessness was deployed in pursuit of an inspiring cause – the salvation of China and its people. His outstanding characteristic was his intense nationalism. He wanted the restoration of China's greatness after a century of foreign occupation and internal corruption. He had rejoiced in the collapse of the Qing dynasty not merely because he hated the hierarchical structure of imperial China, but because the Qing had presided helplessly over the decline of the nation. He had resisted the Guomindang not simply because they were bourgeois oppressors, but because they had proved no more capable of saving the nation than had the Qing.

His adoption of Communism was also an expression of his longing to restore China to its original greatness. His saw in Marxism-Leninism, with its notion of dialectical struggle and its call for violent class warfare, a set of principles that he could turn into a practical programme for the deliverance of China from its internal and foreign oppressors. Mao never became a slave to Marxist theory; he interpreted the theory to suit his purposes for China. The persistent theme in his actions and his writings was that Chinese considerations always had primacy. That was why he refused during the Jiangxi and Yanan years to conform to the demands of the Comintern, continuing to pursue the goal of a rural, peasant revolution even when it was denounced by Stalin as Marxist heresy.

It was also the reason why he declined to join Stalin's Soviet successors in moving towards peaceful co-existence with the West; Mao felt that to do so on Khrushchev's or Brezhnev's terms would subordinate China's interests to those of the Soviet Union. Similarly when, towards the end of his life, he appeared to draw towards the United States, his primary aim was to leave the USSR diplomatically isolated. It is true that he used the language and rhetoric of revolution. His purpose, however, was not the pursuit of world revolution but the consolidation and protection of the Chinese People's Republic. The Sino-Soviet dispute showed how weak were the ties of international Communism and how strong the demands of great power status. It was as the leader of the Chinese people that Mao confronted his Soviet antagonists. He was not prepared to allow the cause of international Communism to weaken the China he had created. As André Malraux, the French philosopher and adviser to President Nixon, put it, 'the Chinese do not believe in any ideology. They believe primarily in China.'[5]

It was a similar concern for Chinese interests that led Mao towards the Cultural Revolution. He feared that unless China reasserted its unique character it would be absorbed into a creeping international mass culture. The nation had to purify itself from within. This involved a cultural cleansing. Culture in the sense that Mao understood it was synonymous with national identity. His reason for unleashing the Cultural Revolution was, therefore, to save China. His motives were essentially nationalist and were only incidentally to do with Communism. It was very much in the tradition of China's turning its face against foreign influences in order to emphasise its own distinctiveness. If that also meant turning away from modernity Mao considered it a price worth paying. The Cultural Revolution was a conservative exercise. It was another paradox: in order to preserve the achievements China had made under him since 1949, Mao was prepared to renounce further economic and social progress. He expressed his aim very simply: 'the poorer a people are, the more they want revolution.'[6]

The essence of Mao Zedong's thought, for which he became renowned during his lifetime, was its utility. The ubiquitous 'little red book', to be found in every home and workplace and in every soldiers' knapsack, contained a set of admonitions and exhortations that were intended to impinge directly on the reader's lives and shape their behaviour. To compare it with the bible, therefore, is not fanciful, but it is equally appropriate to see it as belonging to the Confucian tradition. The teachings of Confucius were a lesson in right behaviour; so, too, were the thoughts of Chairman Mao. When Chinese Communists spoke of 'Marxist-Leninist-Mao Zedong thought' this was not a simple lumping together of their heroes. The progression was a line of inheritance in which Mao was the final legatee. His thinking was the culmination of a process of enlightenment about the human condition. For the Chinese, what made Maoism so fitting was not the subtlety of its socialist analysis but the demonstrable wisdom of its instructions on how to live. In the end, for all his renunciation of Confucius and veneration of Marx, Mao stood much closer to the oriental sage than he did to the occidental revolutionary.

Mao must always be understood in his Chinese context. It is tempting to make easy comparisons between him and his contemporary revolutionaries, Lenin and Trotsky. They, however, were sophisticated cosmopolitans for whom the Bolshevik coup in Russia in 1917 was simply the first stage in an international revolution. Mao was a peasant who had travelled relatively little in his own country and had hardly any personal experience of other lands. He left China on only two occasions, and then not until the 1950s when he visited Moscow for short periods. It is true that his reading encompassed an impressive range of Western history; he studied the Reformation, the Enlightenment, and the industrial and political revolutions of the eighteenth and nineteenth centuries. Yet he necessarily understood things from a Chinese perspective; despite his desire to transform the world, his attitudes remained Sino-centric. China's needs were paramount. This was a critical factor in his disputes with the USSR and the USA, which did so much to determine the character of Chinese and international history during his time.

One key concept that Mao did share with a major contemporary Marxist was that of 'continuing revolution' which he define in these terms: 'Our revolutions come one after another. Our revolutions are like battles. After a victory, we must at once put forward a new task. In this way, cadres and the masses will forever be filled with revolutionary fervour.'[7] His notions in this regard tallied exactly with the views of Leon Trotsky, who, in his Kremlin power struggle with Stalin, had advanced the principle of 'permanent' revolution as being the essence of Marxism-Leninism. Mao shared with Trotsky the belief that revolution was not an event but an unfolding process that would not end until the final victory of the international proletariat was assured. Constant renewal of revolutionary activity and continual re-examination of revolutionary needs were absolute requirements. If the dedication and ardour of the comrades lessened, reaction would set in and the revolution would be lost. It was precisely such thinking that led Mao to launch the Cultural Revolution, his final act of Lear-like defiance against encroaching mortality.

One of the paradoxes in Mao as a revolutionary thinker is that despite the emphasis in his teaching on the need for realism, he was far happier dealing with abstractions, to which he could commit himself, than with the reality of the weakness and irresolution of individuals. He had the cast of mind of the revolutionary who is always more comfortable with abstract concepts, which require a grand design for their achievement, than with the reality of people as they ordinarily are. It has been a notable feature of many of the major figures in revolutionary history that they have admired 'the people' or the proletariat as a historical force but have been scathing and dismissive of individuals or groups who did not meet revolutionary expectations. The most fanatical of the French revolutionaries, Robespierre, was deeply depressed by the poor quality of the human material available for building the new world. Yet he was sustained by the belief that society was perfectible if its enemies were ruthlessly removed. Both Marx and Lenin rejected as worthless whole classes of people and whole cultures, but remained convinced that the will of the people made utopia not merely attainable but inevitable.

The absolutism of the belief in an ultimate goal enabled revolutionaries to come to terms with the invariably destructive consequences of their policies. Individual tragedy and disaster become acceptable. The grander the design in which they believed, the easier it was to regard people as merely the instruments for fashioning the design. It was essentially a process of depersonalising. People in a collective sense were a source of inspiration, but people as individuals, with all their weaknesses, were a cause of embarrassment. This attitude of mind often began with a detestation of injustice, moved to the view that the injustice was part of a structured system, and concluded that only by destroying the system could injustice be eradicated. Thus amelioration was not enough; reform could bring only temporary respite. Destruction was not an option but a necessity. There was a teleology attaching to it which appealed to the revolutionary mind. Because the goal was certain to be realised, come what may, the reverses and partial failures along the path, no matter how severe, were always bearable.

A critical aspect was the willingness to accept the suffering that the process might cause. The immiseration, even the death, of countless numbers of people might appear tragic at the time they occurred, but in the larger perspective all suffering would be redeemed when the goal of revolution was achieved. Those who suffer in the cause, friend and foe alike, were turned by fate into worthwhile sacrifices. Mao belonged to that tradition of thought. It makes his willingness to terrorise the Chinese people explicable, if not defensible.

NOTES

INTRODUCTION

1 See e.g., Kenneth Pomeranz, *The Great Divergence* (London, 1984) and Joanna Waley Cohen, *The Sextants of Beijing* (London, 1992). It has recently been claimed that Chinese navigators had reached America many decades before the European explorers: see Gavin Menzies, *1421: The Year China Discovered the World* (Bantam, 2002), pp. 38ff.
2 Jonathan Spence, *Mao* (London, 1999), p. xiii.
3 Sun Yatsen, 'The Revolution is the Path to the Regeneration of China', 1906, in Franz Schurmann and Orville Schell (eds), *China Readings 2, Republican China* (London, 1968), p. 9.
4 Sun Yatsen, *Memoirs of a Chinese Revolutionary* (London, 1918), p. 184.
5 E.g. Dennis Bloodworth, *The Messiah and the Mandarins* (London, 1982), Jonathan Spence, *Mao* (London, 1999) and Philip Short, *Mao: A Life* (London, 1999).

1 THE YOUNG MAO

1 William Lindesay, *Marching with Mao: A Biographical Journey* (London, 1993), p. 45.
2 Edgar Snow, *Red Star Over China* (London, 1972 revised edition), p. 155.
3 Stuart Schram, *Mao Tse-Tung* (London, 1967), p. 21.
4 Philip Short, *Mao: A Life* (London, 1999), p. 33.
5 'Essay on How Shang Yang Established Confidence by the Moving of the Pole', in Stuart Schram (ed.), *Mao's Road to Power 1912–1949, Revolutionary Writings* (Armonk, NY, 1989–97), vol. 1, p. 5.
6 Edgar Snow, *Red Star Over China* (London, 1972 revised edition), p. 158.
7 'The Orientation of the Youth Movement', 4 May 1939, *Selected Works of Mao Tse-tung* (Beijing, reprint, 1975), vol. II, p. 243.
8 Edgar Snow, *Red Star Over China* (London, 1972 revised edition), p. 166.
9 E.g. Jonathan Spence, *Mao* (London, 1999), p. 16.
10 Edgar Snow, *Red Star Over China* (London, 1972 revised edition), p. 168.
11 Ibid., p. 170.
12 'Classroom Notes', 1913, in Stuart Schram (ed.), *Mao's Road to Power 1912–1949, Revolutionary Writings*, vol. 1, pp. 13–49.
13 'Marginal Notes to: Friedrich Paulsen, A System of Ethics' (1917–18), ibid., vol. 1, p. 276.
14 Ibid., vol. 1, p. 66.
15 Mao to Xiao Zisheng, 18 July 1916, ibid., vol. 1, pp. 95–98.
16 Mao to Li Jinxi, November 1915, ibid., vol. 1, p. 85.
17 Philip Short, *Mao: A Life* (London, 1999), p. 33.

18 Harrison Salisbury, *The New Emperors Mao and Deng* (London, 1992), p. 52, quoting from Siao Yu, *Mao Tse-tung and I Were Beggars* (Syracuse, NY, 1959), pp. 190–91.

19 See below, p. 69.

20 Edgar Snow, *Red Star Over China* (London, 1972 revised edition), p. 172.

21 'A Study of Physical Education', 1917, in Stuart Schram (ed.), *Mao's Road to Power 1912–1949, Revolutionary Writings*, vol. 1, pp. 115, 120.

22 Mao to Xiao Zisheng, Summer 1917, in ibid., vol. 1, p. 129.

23 Mao to Li Jinxi, 23 August 1917, in ibid., vol. 1, p. 131.

24 'Marginal Notes to: Friedrich Paulsen, A System of Ethics' (1917–18) in ibid., vol. 1, p. 239.

25 Ibid., vol. 1, p. 306.

26 Mao to Li Jinxi, 23 August 1917, in ibid., vol. 1, p. 130.

27 Ibid., vol. 1, p. 131.

28 'The Great Union of the Popular Masses', July and August 1919 in ibid., vol. 1, pp. 387–89.

29 Edgar Snow, *Red Star Over China* (London, 1972 revised edition), p. 174.

30 *Manifesto on the Founding of the* Xiang River Review, 14 July, 1919, in Stuart Schram (ed.), *Mao's Road to Power 1912–1949, Revolutionary Writings*, vol. 1, p. 318.

31 Ibid., vol. 1, p. 319.

32 'Statutes of the Problem Study Society', September 1919, in ibid., vol. 1, pp. 407–13.

33 'Hunan is Burdened by China', 6–7 September 1920, in ibid., vol. 1, p. 553.

34 Ibid.

35 'The Fundamental Issue in the Problem of Hunanese Reconstruction', 3 September 1920, in ibid., vol. 1, p. 544.

36 'The Founding and Progress of the "Strengthen Learning Society"', 21 July 1919, in ibid., vol. 1, p. 372.

37 'Letter to Luo Xuezan', 26 November 1920, in ibid., vol. 1, p. 605.

2 MAO THE COMMUNIST AND NATIONALIST, 1921–30

1 In Lee Feigon, *Chen Duxiu: Founder of the Chinese Communist Party* (Princeton, NJ, 1983), p. 98.

2 'Letter to Cai Hesen', 1 December 1920, in Stuart Schram (ed.), *Mao's Road to Power 1912–1949, Revolutionary Writings* (Armonk, NY, 1989–97), vol. 2, p. 9.

3 'Letter to Cai Hesen', 21 January 1921, in ibid., vol. 2, p. 35.

4 'The Arrest and Rescue of Chen Duxiu', 14 July 1919, in ibid., vol. 1, p. 329.

5 'Letter to Cai Hesen', 1 December 1920, in ibid., vol. 2, p. 9.

6 'Letter to Peng Huang', 28 January 1921, in ibid, vol. 2, p. 38.

7 Hu Cheng (ed.), *A Concise History of the Communist Party of China* (Beijing, 1994), p. 34.

8 'My Hopes for the Labor Association', 21 November 1921, in Stuart Schram (ed.), *Mao's Road to Power 1912–1949, Revolutionary Writings*, vol. 2, p. 100.

9 'Telegram from Labor Groups to the Upper and Lower Houses of Parliament', 6 September 1922, in ibid, vol. 2, p. 120.

10 'Telegram from the All-Hunan Federation of Labour Organisations', in ibid., vol. 2, p. 148.

11 Tony Saitch, *The Rise to Power of the Chinese Communist Party, Documents and Analysis, 1919–1949* (Armonk, NY, 1995), p. 580.

12 'Resolution on the Peasant Question', June 1923, in Stuart Schram (ed.), *Mao's Road to Power 1912–1949, Revolutionary Writings*, vol. 2, p. 164.

13 'The Cigarette Tax', August 1923, in ibid., vol. 2, p. 189.

14 See S.A. Dalin, *Chinese Memoirs 1921–27* (Moscow, 1975), pp. 164–65.

15 V.I. Glunin, 'The Comintern and the Rise of the of the Communist Party in China (1920–1927)', in *The Comintern and the East* (Moscow, 1979), p. 314.

16 'The Struggle Against the Right Wing of the Guomindang', 21 July 1924, in Stuart Schram (ed.), *Mao's Road to Power 1912–1949, Revolutionary Writings*, vol. 2, p. 215.

17 E.g. Philip Short, *Mao: A Life* (London, 1999), p. 149.

18 Stuart Schram (ed.), *Mao's Road to Power 1912–1949, Revolutionary Writings*, vol. 2, p. 361.

19 'Reasons for the Breakaway of the Guomindang Right and its Implications for the Future of the Revolution', 10 January 1926, in ibid., vol. 2, p. 327.

20 'Report on Propaganda', 8 January 1926, in ibid., vol. 2, p. 319.

21 'Resolution Concerning the Peasant Movement', 19 January, 1926, in ibid., vol. 2, p. 358.

22 'The National Revolution and the Peasant Movement', 1 September 1926, in ibid., vol. 2, p. 389.

23 'Report on the Peasant Movement in Hunan', February 1927, in ibid., vol. 2, p. 435.

24 Ibid., vol. 2, p. 433.

25 'An Example of the Chinese Tenant-Peasant's Life', March 1927, in ibid., vol. 2, p. 478.

26 'Interview with the British Journalist James Bertram', October 1937, *Selected Works of Mao Zedong* (Beijing, 1975), vol. II, p. 54.

27 'Latest Directive of the All-China Peasant Association', 13 June 1927, in Stuart Schram (ed.), *Mao's Road to Power 1912–1949, Revolutionary Writings*, vol. 2, p. 516.

28 'Circular Telegram from Members of the Guomindang Central Committee Denouncing Chiang', 22 April 1927, in ibid., vol. 2, pp. 492–93.

29 Keiji Furuya, *Chiang Kai-shek. His Life and Times* (New York, 1981), p. 230.

30 'Comrade Peng Gongda's Report on the Autumn Harvest Rising', 8 October 1927, in *Revolutionary Base Areas in the Jinggang Mountains* (Beijing, 1987), vol. 1, p. 28.

31 'Views expressed at the First Meeting of the Hunan Provincial Committee of the Chinese Communist Party', 18 August 1927, in Stuart Schram (ed.), *Mao's Road to Power 1912–1949, Revolutionary Writings*, vol. 3, p. 35.

32 Hu Cheng (ed.), *A Concise History of the Communist Party of China* (Beijing, 1994), p. 106.

33 Philip Short, *Mao: A Life* (London, 1999), p. 200.

34 'The Xunwu Investigation', published in May 1930, in Stuart Schram (ed.), *Mao's Road to Power 1912–1949, Revolutionary Writings*, vol. 3, pp. 296–418.

35 'A letter from the Front Committee to the Central Committee', 5 April 1929, in ibid., vol. 3, p. 154.

36 Ibid.

3 TERROR AND SALVATION, 1930–35

1 See John Rue, *Mao Tse-tung in Opposition 1927–35* (Stanford, 1966), pp. 218–35.

2 See Stephen C. Averill, 'The Origins of the Futian Incident', in Tony Saitch and Hans Van de Ven (eds), *New Perspectives on the Chinese Communist Revolution* (Armonk, NY, 1995).

3 Party directive of February 1931, quoted in Hu Cheng (ed.), *A Concise History of the Communist Party of China* (Beijing, 1994), p. 139.

4 From unpublished documents in the CCP archives, quoted in Philip Short, *Mao: A Life* (London, 1999), p. 273.

5 Ibid., pp. 273–74.

6 See Lee Feigon, *Mao: A Reinterpretation* (Chicago, Ill., 2002), p. 53.

7 Edgar Snow, *Red Star Over China* (London, 1961), p. 206.

8 E.g. Hsiao Tso-liang, *Power Relations within the Chinese Communist Movement, 1930–1934* (Seattle, Wash., 1961), pp. 98–113.

9 'A Letter of Reply by the General Front Committee, December 1930', in Stuart Schram (ed.), *Mao's Road to Power 1912–1949, Revolutionary Writings* (Armonk, NY, 1989–97), vol. 3 p. 713.

10 Philip Short, *Mao: A Life* (London, 1999), pp. 265–84.

11 See above, p. 59.

12 'Eight Conditions for a Great Victory in the Second Major Campaign', March 1931, in Stuart Schram (ed.), *Mao's Road to Power 1912–1949, Revolutionary Writings*, vol. 4, pp. 45–51.

13 'Circular of the General Political Department on Investigating the Situation Regarding Land and Population', 2 April 1931, ibid., vol. 4, p. 155.

14 'A Letter to Our Brothers, the Soldiers of the White Army on the Forcible Occupation of Manchuria by Japanese Imperialism', 25 September 1931, ibid., vol. 4, pp. 154–56.

15 'Views Regarding the Political Appraisal, Military Strategy, and the Tasks of the Eastern and Western route Armies', 3 May 1932, ibid., vol. 4, p. 217.

16 'Proletariat and Oppressed Peoples of the World, Unite!', 30 August 1933, ibid., vol. 4, pp. 519 and 521.

17 'Letter to the Huangbai District Soviet in Ruijin Concerning the Land Investigation Movement', 13 July 1933; 'A Preliminary Summing Up of the Land Investigation Movement', August 1933, ibid., vol. 4, pp. 448 and 504.

18 'Closing Address at the Congress', 1 February 1934, ibid., vol. 4, p. 724.

19 Philip Short, *Mao: A Life* (London, 1999), p. 317.

20 Edgar Snow, *Red Star Over China* (London, 1961), p. 219.

21 'On the Tactics of Fighting Japanese Imperialism' 27 December 1935, in Anne Freemantle (ed.) *Mao Tse-tung: An Anthology of his Writings* (New York, 1962), p. xxxix.

22 Quoted in Dick Wilson, *The Long March 1935* (London, 1971), p. 68.

23 In Stuart Schram (ed.), *Mao's Road to Power 1912–1949, Revolutionary Writings*, vol. 4, p. xxix.

24 In Philip Short, *Mao: A Life* (London, 1999), p. 11, quoting Otto Braun, *A Comintern Agent in China: 1932–39* (London, 1982), pp. 94–108.

25 Comment of 1958, quoted in Stuart Schram (ed.), *Mao's Road to Power 1912–1949, Revolutionary Writings*, vol. 5, p. 8.

26 'Loushan Pass', 28 February 1935, in ibid, vol. 5, p. 8.

27 Edgar Snow, *Red Star Over China* (London, 1972 revised edition), p. 224.

28 Zhang Guotao, *The Rise of the Chinese Communist Party 1921–1927* (Lawrence, Kan., 1971), pp. 299ff.

29 'The Strategic Principle now that the First and Fourth Front Armies have Joined Forces', 28 June 1935, in *Selected Documents of the Central Committee of the CCP* (Beijing, 1991), vol. X, p. 516.

30 See Stuart Schram (ed.), *Mao's Road to Power 1912–1949, Revolutionary Writings*, vol. 5, p. xliv; Harrison Salisbury, *The Long March: The Untold Story* (New York, 1985), pp. 256–57.

31 'Supplementary Decision by the Politburo on General Strategic Policy at the Present Time', 20 August 1935, in Stuart Schram (ed.), *Mao's Road to Power 1912–1949, Revolutionary Writings*, vol. 5, p. 22.

32 Quoted in ibid., vol. 5, p. xlvii.

33 'For Comrade Peng Dehuai', 21 October 1935, in ibid., vol. 5, p. 37.

34 Quoted in ibid., vol. 5, p. 1.

4 MAO'S PATH TO POWER – THE YANAN YEARS, 1935–43

1 'Resolution of the Central Committee on Problems of Military Strategy', 23 December 1935, in Stuart Schram (ed.), *Mao's Road to Power 1912–1949, Revolutionary Writings* (Armonk, NY, 1989–97), vol. 5, p. 77.

2 'Interview with Edgar Snow on Foreign affairs', 15 July 1936, in ibid., vol. 5, p. 257.

3 'To Chiang Kaishek', 1 December 1936, in ibid., vol. 5, pp. 458–59.

4 *Autobiography of Chang Kuo-t'ao* (Lawrence, Kan., 1971) vol. 2, pp. 481–83).

5 There is no evidence that Japan was involved in the Xian Incident. Stalin's sensitivity at this juncture is explained by the fact that the USSR had been having secret talks with the GMD government with a view to enlisting Chiang Kai-shek as an ally to offset the threat represented by the Anti-Comintern Pact, signed by Germany, Italy, and Japan earlier in 1936. See John W. Garver, 'The Soviet Union and the Xiam Incident', *Australian Journal of Chinese Affairs*, no. 26, p. 153.

6 'A Statement on Chiang Kaishek's Proclamation of the 26th', 28 December 1936, pp. 569, 572, in Stuart Schram (ed.), *Mao's Road to Power 1912–1949, Revolutionary Writings*, vol. 5, p. 22.

7 Philip Short, *Mao: A Life* (London, 1999), p. 360.

8 *Selected Works of Mao Tse-tung* (Beijing, reprint, 1975), English edn, vol. I, p. 157.

9 In John W. Garver, *Chinese Soviet Relations 1937–1945* (Oxford, 1988), p. 78.

10 Cheng Yung-fa, 'The Blooming Poppy under the Red Sun: the Yan'an Way and the Opium Trade', in Tony Saitch and Hans Van de Ven (eds), *New Perspectives on the Chinese Revolution* (Armonk, NY, 1995), pp. 263–98.

11 Edgar Snow, *Red Star Over China* (London, 1972 revised edition), p. 255.

12 Anne Freemantle (ed.), *Mao Tse-tung: An Anthology of his Writings* (New York, 1962), p. xxiii.

13 Yves Chevrier, *Mao and the Chinese Revolution* (Florence, 1993), p. 65.

14 'Combat Liberalism', 7 September 1937, *Selected Works of Mao Tse-tung*, English edn, (Beijing, 1975), vol. II, pp. 32–33.

15 'The Struggle in the Jinggang Mountains', in ibid., vol. 1, p. 83.

16 'The Role of the Chinese Communist Party in the National War', October 1938, in ibid., vol. II, p. 205.

17 Agnes Smedley, *Battle Hymn of China* (London, 1944), p. 121.

18 E.g. 'On Contradiction', August 1937, *Selected Works of Mao Tse-tung*, Eng. edn, Beijing, reprint, 1975, vol. I, p. 311; 'On the Correct Handling of Contradictions among the People', February 1957, ibid., vol. V, p. 384.

19 'Reform Our Study', in ibid., vol. III, pp. 22–23.

20 'Problems of Strategy in Guerilla War', May 1938, ibid., vol. II, p. 79.

21 'Rectify the Party's Style of Work', February, 1942, ibid., vol. III, p. 42.
22 'On New Democracy', January 1940, in ibid., vol. II, p. 350.
23 'Problems of War and Strategy', 6 November 1938, in ibid., vol. II, p. 220.
24 'Stalin's Sixtieth Birthday', 21 December 1939, in Jerome Ch'en (ed.), *Mao Papers Anthology and Bibliography* (Oxford, 1970), p. 17.
25 Speech at the Yanan Forum on Literature and Art, May 1942, in Graham Hutchings, *Modern China* (London, 2001), p. 299.
26 Talks at the Yanan Forum on Literature and Art, 23 May 1942, in Anne Freemantle (ed.), *Mao Tse-tung: An Anthology of his Writings* (New York, 1962), p. 263.
27 'Mao Zedong's "Talks at the Yan'an Conference on Literature and Art"', 1942, quoted in Jonathan Spence, *The Search for Modern China* (New York, 1990), p. 473.
28 In Frederic C. Teiwes and Warren Sun, *The Formation of the Maoist Leadership* (London, 1994), p. 55.
29 Pyotr Vladimirov, in Georges Boudarel, *La Bureaucratie au Vietnam* (Paris, 1983), pp. 55–56, in Stephane Courtois *et al.* (eds), *The Black Book of Communism* (Cambridge, Mass., 1999), p. 474.
30 Frederic C. Teiwes and Warren Sun, *The Formation of the Maoist Leadership* (London, 1994), p. 55.
31 'Rectify the Party's Style of Work', 1 February 1942, *Selected Works of Mao Tse-tung*, English edn (Beijing, reprint, 1967), vol. III, pp. 43–47.

5 FROM PARTY LEADER TO LEADER OF THE NATION, 1943–50

1 'Our Study and the Current Situation', 12 April 1944, *Selected Works of Mao Tse-tung* (Beijing, reprint, 1975), vol. III, p. 163.
2 *The Liberation Daily*, 22 February 1943.
3 Harrison Salisbury, *The New Emperors Mao and Deng: A Biography* (London, 1992), pp. 20–21.
4 'On the Correct Handling of Contradictions among the People', 1957, *Selected Works of Mao Tse-tung* (Beijing. Reprint, 1975), vol. V, p. 405.
5 Eric Hobsbawm, *Interesting Times: A Twentieth-Century Life* (London, 2002), quoted in the *Sunday Telegraph*, 22 September 2002.
6 Theodore H. White (ed.), *The Stillwell Papers* (New York, 1948), p. 315.
7 David Barrett, *Dixie Mission: The United States Army Observer Group in Yenan, 1944* (Berkeley, Cal., 1970), p. 57.
8 Philip Short, *Mao: A Life* (London, 1999), p. 403.
9 Zhisui Li, *The Private Life of Chairman Mao* (London, 1994), pp. 108–9.
10 Shi Zhe, in Philip Short, *Mao: A Life* (London, 1999), p. 403.
11 'Talk with the American Correspondent Anna Louise Strong', August 1946, in Anne Freemantle (ed.), *Mao Tse-tung: An Anthology of his Writings* (New York, 1962), p. 179.
12 'Smash Chiang Kaishek's Offensive by a War of Self-Defence', 20 July 1946, *Selected Works of Mao Zedong* (Beijing, 1975), vol. IV, p. 89.

13 Ibid.
14 Ibid, vol. IV, pp. 89–90.
15 'The Present Situation and Our Tasks', 25 December 1947, ibid, vol. IV, p. 169.
16 Mao to Shi Zhe, March 1947, in Philip Short, *Mao: A Life* (London, 1999), p. 407.
17 Sidney Rittenberg, *The Man Who Stayed Behind* (London, 1993), pp. 118–19.
18 Associated Press Report, Shanghai, 24 July 1947.
19 Mao Zedong to Stalin, 13 January 1949, *Archive of the President of the Russian Federation*, pp. 110–13, Cold War International History Project (CWIHP), http//cwihp.is.edu/cwihplib.nsf.
20 Mao speaking in 1957, as quoted in the *People's Daily*, 2 Jan 1979, in Harrison Salisbury, *The New Emperors Mao and Deng: A Biography* (London, 1992), p. 15.
21 'Opening Speech of the First Plenary Session of the CPPCC', 21 September 1949, in Michael Y.M. Kau and John K. Leung, *The Writings of Mao Zedong 1949–1976* (Armonk, NY, 1886), vol. 1, p. 5.
22 'Proclamation of the Central People's Government of the PRC', 1 October 1949, in ibid., vol. 1 p. 11.
23 'Speech at the Tenth Plenum', 24 September 1962, in Stuart Schram (ed.), *Mao Tse-tung Unrehearsed* (London, 1974), p. 191.
24 Dimitri Volkogonov, *Stalin: Triumph and Tragedy* (London, 1991), p. 539.
25 Harrison Salisbury, *The New Emperors Mao and Deng: A Biography* (London, 1992), p. 97.
26 Conversations between Stalin and Mao in Moscow, 16 December 1949 and 22 January 1950, *Archive of the President of the Russian Federation*, pp. 9–17, 29–38–13, CWIHP, http//cwihp.is.edu/cwihplib.nsf.
27 26 February 1950, in Michael Y.M. Kau and John K. Leung, *The Writings of Mao Zedong 1949–1976* (Armonk, NY, 1986), vol. 1, p. 63.
28 Strobe Talbot (ed.), *Khrushchev Remembers* (Boston, Mass., 1974), vol. 2, p. 27.

6 MAO THE NEW EMPEROR, 1950–62

1 The accepted analysis is now Sergei N. Goncharov, John W. Lewis and Xue Litai, *Uncertain Partners: Stalin, Mao and the Korean War* (Stanford, CA, 1993).
2 Mao's telegram to Stalin, 2 October 1950, in ibid., p. 275.
3 Ibid., p. 161.
4 Quan Yanchi, *Mao Zedong: Man, Not God* (Beijing, 1992), p. 171.
5 Ibid, p. 172.
6 Philip Short, *Mao: A Life* (London, 1999), p. 434.
7 'On the Struggle Against the "Three Evils" and the "Five Evils", 26 January 1952, *Selected Works of Mao Tse-tung* (Beijing, 1977), vol. V, pp. 65–66.

8 'On the "Three-Antis" and "Five Antis" Struggle', 5 March 1952, 26 February 1950, in Michael Y.M. Kau and John K. Leung, *The Writings of Mao Zedong 1949–1976* (Armonk, NY, 1986), vol. 1, pp. 237–38.

9 John King Fairbank, *China: A New History* (Cambridge, Mass., 1994), p. 365.

10 Quoted in Philip Short, *Mao: A Life* (London, 1999), p. 446.

11 *Selected Works of Mao Tse-tung* (Beijing, reprint, 1975), vol. V, pp. 367.

12 Hu Sheng (ed.), *A Concise History of the Communist Party of China* (Beijing, 1994), p. 468. Mao had first stated the formula during the rectification campaign at Yanan in his article, 'Rectify the Party's Style of Work', 3 February 1942, *Selected Works of Mao Tse-tung* (Beijing, reprint, 1967), vol. III, p. 50.

13 Li Zhisui, *The Private Life of Chairman Mao* (London, 1994), p. 150.

14 *Selected Works of Mao Tse-tung* (Beijing. Reprint, 1977), vol. 5, pp. 121–22.

15 Estimates of the number of victims of the *sufan* vary between 80,000 and half a million. See Jean-Louis Margolin, 'China: A Long March into Night', in Stephane Courtois *et al.* (eds), *The Black Book of Communism* (Cambridge, Mass., 1997) p. 485.

16 'Talk at Enlarged Meeting of the Politburo', April 1956, in Michael Y.M. Kau and John K. Leung, *The Writings of Mao Zedong 1949–1976* (Armonk, NY, 1986), vol. 2, p. 69.

17 'On Correctly Handling Contradictions Among the People', 27 February 1957, in Michael Y.M. Kau and John K. Leung, vol. 2, p. 330.

18 Ibid., vol. 2, p. 332.

19 Ibid., vol. 2, p. 320.

20 Roderick MacFarquhar, *The Hundred Flowers Campaign and the Intellectuals* (New York, 1960), p. 108.

21 Li Zhisui, *The Private Life of Chairman Mao* (London, 1994), p. 201.

22 'What Is This For?', 8 June 1957, in Michael Y.M. Kau and John K. Leung, *The Writings of Mao Zedong 1949–1976* (Armonk, NY, 1986), vol. 2, pp. 566–67.

23 'Organize Our Forces to Counter the Reckless Attacks of the Rightists', 8 June 1957, in ibid., vol. 2, pp. 563.

24 See Jean-Luc Domenach, *The Origins of the Great Leap Forward* (Boulder, Col., 1995), p. 154.

25 Speech at the Third Plenum, 9 October 1957, in Michael Y.M. Kau and John K. Leung, *The Writings of Mao Zedong 1949–1976* (Armonk, NY, 1986), vol. 2, p. 720.

26 Ibid., p. 721.

27 'On learning from Each Other and Overcoming Complacency and Conceit', 13 December 1963, in Jerome Ch'en, *Mao Papers* (London, 1970), p. 91.

28 Speech at the Congress of Communist Parties in Communist Countries, 18 November 1957, in Michael Y.M. Kau and John K. Leung, *The Writings of Mao Zedong 1949–1976* (Armonk, NY, 1986), vol. 2, p. 788.

29 Strobe Talbot, (ed.), *Khrushchev Remembers* (Boston, Mass., 1974), p. 255.

30 Talk at an Enlarged Central Work Conference, 30 January 1962, in Stuart Schram (ed.), *Mao Tse-tung Unrehearsed* (London, 1974), p. 178.

31 Speech at the Third Plenum, 9 October 1657, in Michael Y.M. Kau and John K. Leung, *The Writings of Mao Zedong 1949–1976* (Armonk, NY, 1986), vol. 2, p. 720.

32 See Uta Saoshiro and Curtis Runyan 'Chairman Mao's War on Nature', *World Watch*, November–Dececember 2002, vol. 15.

33 Jonathan Spence and Annping Chin, *The Chinese Century* (London, 1996), p. 179.

34 Roderick MacFarquar, *Origins of the Cultural Revolution* (Oxford, 1974), vol. 2, p. 115.

35 Mao in conversation with his doctor, in Li Zhisui, *The Private Life of Chairman Mao* (London, 1994), p. 201.

36 From a speech of Mao's in 1959, in Roderick MacFarquar, Timothy Cheek and Eugene Wu, *The Secret Speeches of Chairman Mao* (Cambridge, Mass., 1989).

37 See Zhores Medvedev, *The Rise and Fall of T.D. Lysenko* (New York, 1969).

38 Li Zhisui, *The Private Life of Chairman Mao* (London, 1994), p. 148.

39 How these figures are arrived at is detailed in Jasper Becker, *Hungry Ghosts: China's Secret Famine* (London, 1996), pp. 266–75. See also the evidence in Judith Bannister, *China's Changing Population* (Berkeley, CA, 1987) and Wen Yu, *Disasters of Leftism in China* (Jiaohua, 1993).

40 See Jasper Becker, *Hungry Ghosts: China's Secret Famine* (London, 1996) and Jamphel Gyatso, *The Great Master Panchen* (Beijing, 1989).

41 'Decision Approving Comrade Mao Zedong's Proposal to Step Down', 10 December 1958, in Pei-kai Cheng and Michael Lestz with Jonathan Spence (eds), *The Search for Modern China: A Documentary Collection* (New York, 1999).

42 Li Rui, *A True Account of the Lushan Meeting* (Henan, 1995).

43 Harry Wu, a leading Chinese dissident who spent nearly twenty years in a range of PRC prisons, described the *laogai* as 'the biggest concentration camp system in history' (public lecture at London University School of Oriental and African Studies, November 1996).

44 Li Zhisui, *The Private Life of Chairman Mao* (London, 1994), p. 125. The inglorious role of the West should not be overlooked. One of the sub-themes of Jasper Becker's provocative study is the reluctance of the Western nations to acknowledge that a terrible famine was taking place. This gives irony to the title of his book, *Hungry Ghosts: China's Secret Famine* (London, 1996). See also the letter to the *Sunday Times*, 16 June 1996 by Sir Alfred Sherman (a contributor to *The People's Communes in China*, Survey and Library of International Studies) in which he asserts that the famine 'was deliberately ignored by the majority of the British media'.

45 Strobe Talbot (ed.), *Khrushchev Remembers* (Boston, Mass., 1974).

46 *Selected Works of Deng Xiaoping* (Beijing, 1975–82), pp. 278–79.

7 THE CULT OF MAO AND THE CULTURAL REVOLUTION, 1962–76

1 Publication of the *Selected Works of Mao Tse-tung* (Beijing reprints, 1967–77) began in the early 1950s and continued up to a year after Mao's death. They were described by the editors as the 'immortal monuments of Marxism-Leninism'.
2 *Quotations from Chairman Mao Tse-tung* (Beijing, 1966), p. 100.
3 Ibid., p. 99.
4 See Richard Baum and Frederick C. Teiwes, *The Socialist Education Movement of 1962–66* (Berkeley, Cal., 1968).
5 See Jonathan Spence, *The Search for Modern China* (New York, 1990), p. 598.
6 Zhisui Li, *The Private Life of Chairman Mao* (London, 1994), pp. 386–7.
7 Hu Sheng (ed.), *A Concise History of the Communist Party of China* (Beijing, 1994), p. 633.
8 In Stuart Schram, 'Mao Tse-Tung's Thought from 1949–76', in Merle Goldman and Leo Ou-Fan Lee (eds), *An Intellectual History of Modern China* (Cambridge, 2002), p. 476.
9 Zhisui Li, *The Private Life of Chairman Mao* (London, 1994), pp. 386–7.
10 *Beijing Review*, 11 August 1967, in Pei-kai Cheng, *et al.*, *The Search for Modern China* (New York, 1999), p. 426.
11 Stuart Schram, 'Mao Tse-tung's Thought from 1949–76', in Merle Goldman and Leo Ou-Fan Lee (eds), *An Intellectual History of Modern China* (Cambridge, 2002), p. 301.
12 *RN: The Memoirs of Richard M. Nixon* (New York, 1978), p. 570.
13 From the transcript of 'The Cultural Revolution', a BBC World Service programme, July 1996.
14 Ibid.
15 Harry Wu, *Troublemaker: One Man's Crusade against China's Cruelty* (London, 1996), p. 23.
16 Zhisui Li, *The Private Life of Chairman Mao* (London, 1994), pp. 386–87.
17 Roderick MacFarqhuar, *The Origins of the Cultural Revolution* (New York, 1983).
18 Henry Kissinger, *Years of Renewal* (London, 1999), p. 152.
19 Philip Short, *Mao: A Life* (London, 1999), p. 595.
20 Kuo, *Classified Chinese Documents*, p. 180, quoted in Philip Short, *Mao: A Life* (London, 1999), p. 594.
21 Zhisui Li, *The Private Life of Chairman Mao* (London, 1994), p. 534.
22 Harrison Salisbury, *The New Emperors Mao and Deng: A Biography* (London, 1992), p. 300–02.
23 Pei-kai Cheng, *et al.*, *The Search for Modern China* (New York, 1999), p. 433.
24 Michael Y.M. Kau, *The Lin Piao Affair: Power Politics and Military Coup* (New York, 1975), pp. 76–77.

25 See Barry Naughton, 'The Third Line: Defense Industrialisation in the Chinese Interior', *China Quarterly*, 115, September 1988.
26 Henry Kissinger, *The White House Years* (London, 1979), p. 747.
27 Ibid., p. 749.
28 Henry Kissinger, *Years of Renewal* (London, 1999), p. 144.
29 *RN: The Memoirs of Richard M. Nixon* (New York, 1978), p. 580.
30 Zhisui Li, *The Private Life of Chairman Mao* (London, 1994), p. 121.
31 Henry Kissinger, *Years of Renewal* (London, 1999), p. 142.
32 Ibid., p. 152.

8 MAO AND WOMEN

1 Edgar Snow, *Red Star Over China* (London, 1972 revised edition), p. 154.
2 Stuart Schram (ed.), *Mao's Road to Power 1912–49, Revolutionary Writings* (Armonk, NY, 1989–97), vol. 1, p. 419.
3 'Marginal Notes to: Friedrich Paulsen, A System of Ethics', 1917–18, in ibid., vol. 1, pp. 263–64.
4 'The Marriage Question – An Admonition to Young Men and Women', 19 November 1919, in ibid., vol. 1, p. 425.
5 'The Question of Love – Young People and Old People', 25 November 1919, in ibid., vol. 1, p. 439.
6 Mao to Luo Xuezan, 26 November 1920, in ibid., vol. 1, p. 608.
7 Mao to Tao Yi, 19 February 1920, in ibid., vol. 1, p492.
8 'New Directive of the All-China Peasant Association to the Peasant Movement', 7 June 1927, in ibid., vol. 2, p. 512.
9 'Draft Resolution of the Ninth Congress of the Chinese Communist Party', December 1929, in ibid., vol. 3, p. 217.
10 'The Greatest Defects of the Draft Provincial Constitution', 25 April 1921, in ibid., vol. 2, p. 40.
11 'Xunwu Investigation', May 1930, in ibid., vol. 3, 416.
12 'The Women's Revolutionary Army', 14 July 1919, in ibid., vol 1, p. 353.
13 'Hunan under the Provincial Constitution', 1 July 1923, in ibid., vol. 2, p. 171. The tight binding of women's feet to prevent them from growing was a centuries-old custom in imperial China. Small feet were regarded as highly erotic. Since the binding severely restricted women's ability to move, it also served as an effective form of social control. The practice was formally condemned by the Qing in 1905, although, as Mao recorded, it continued well into the twentieth century.
14 'Xunwu Investigation', May 1930, in ibid., vol. 3, p. 344.
15 'On the Organization and Work of the Committee for Upholding Women's Rights', 20 June 1932, in ibid., vol. 4, p. 227.
16 See above p. 73 and Philip Short, *Mao: A Life* (London, 1999), p. 272.
17 See ibid., p. 385.
18 See Edgar Snow, *Red Star Over China* (London, 1972 revised edition), p. 181.

19 'Poem to the Tune of "Congratulate the Groom"', in Stuart Schram (ed.), *Mao's Road to Power 1912–1949, Revolutionary Writings*, vol. 2, p. 196.

20 See above p. 207.

21 In 2003, there were reports in China that Xiong Huashi, a sixty-eight-year-old woman from Yunnan province, claimed to be one of the abandoned daughters of Mao and He Zichen. See article by Richard Spencer in the *Daily Telegraph*, 1 November 2003.

22 Note 107 by Anne F. Thurston in Li Zhisui, *The Private life of Chairman Mao* (London, 1994), p. 642.

23 Edgar Snow, *Red Star Over China* (London, 1972 revised edition), p. 522.

24 Quan Yanchi, *Mao Zedong: Man Not God* (Beijing, 1992), p. 126.

25 Harrison Salisbury, *The New Emperors Mao and Deng: A Biography* (London, 1992) p. 279.

26 Li Zhisui, *The Private Life of Chairman Mao* (London, 1994), pp. 382–84.

27 Philip Short, *Mao: A Life* (London, 1999), p. 376.

28 Quan Yanchi, *Mao Zedong: Man Not God* (Beijing, 1992), p. 126.

29 Ibid., p. 131.

30 William Lindesay, *Marching with Mao: A Biographical Journey* (London, 1993), p. 183.

31 See Harrison Salisbury, *The New Emperors Mao and Deng: A Biography* (London, 1992), p. 62, and Li Zhisui, *The Private Life of Chairman Mao* (London, 1994), p. 586.

32 Philip Short, *Mao: A Life* (London, 1999), p. 521.

33 Henry Kissinger, *Years of Renewal* (London, 1999), p. 154.

34 Li Zhisui, *The Private life of Chairman Mao* (London, 1994), pp. 578–79.

35 Ibid.

CONCLUSION

1 Li Zhisui, *The Private life of Chairman Mao* (London, 1994), p. 592.

2 Ibid., p. 5.

3 Harrison Salisbury, *The New Emperors Mao and Deng: A Biography* (London, 1992), p. 145.

4 Ibid., p. 120.

5 André Malraux, quoted in Henry Kissinger, *The White House Years* (London, 1979), p. 1052.

6 In Stuart Schram, 'Mao Tse-Tung's Thought from 1949–76', in Merle Goldman and Leo Ou-Fan Lee (eds), *An Intellectual History of Modern China* (Cambridge, 2002), p. 497.

7 Ibid., p. 432.

FURTHER READING

The following is a very selective list of the thousands of books now available in English on Mao and his times.

SOURCES

Stuart Schram (ed.), *Mao's Road to Power 1912–49, Revolutionary Writings*, 5 vols (M.E. Sharpe, 1989–97). All those studying Mao's China owe a great debt to Stuart Schram and his team of researchers. Their meticulous collecting, translating and editing of Mao's writings has provided a multi-volume treasure house of detail about his life in the pre-PRC period. Schram also edited *Mao Tse-Tung Unrehearsed: Talks and Letters, 1956–71* (Penguin, 1974). The CCP's official publication, the *Selected Works of Mao Tsetung*, 8 vols (Pergamon, 1967–99) is still a useful source; however, it has to be handled with care since the editors cut and modified the text in keeping with their aim of providing a hagiography of Mao. *Quotations from Chairman Mao Tse-tung* (Foreign Languages Press, 1966), edited by Lin Biao, and known worldwide in its day as the 'Little Red Book', has become something of a collector's item. It is well worth reading, if only to gain some idea of why Lin was able to describe its contents as 'a spiritual atom bomb of infinite power'. Roderick MacFarquhar, Timothy Cheek and Eugene Wu, *The Secret Speeches of Chairman Mao: From the Hundred Flowers to the Great Leap Forward* (Harvard University Press, 1989) contains key extracts from Mao's letters and speeches, as does Jerome Chen (ed.), *Mao Papers* (Oxford University Press, 1970). *The Writings of Mao Zedong 1949–1976* (M.E. Sharpe, 1986–92), edited by Michael Y.M. Kau and John K. Leung, provides a painstakingly annotated collection, largely made up of personal letters and formal papers. An interesting set of documents covering Mao's career down to 1966 is to be found in Anne Freemantle (ed.), *Mao Tse-tung: An Anthology of his Writings* (Mentor, 1971). Frank Schurmann and Orville Schell, two American scholars, produced a very serviceable three-volume set of readings and documents: *Imperial China* (Penguin, 1968), *Republican China* (Penguin, 1974) and *Communist China* (Penguin, 1976). A key work is Pei-kai Cheng, Michael Lestz and Jonathan Spence, *The Search for Modern China: A Documentary Collection* (W.W. Norton, 1999). This is the documentary companion volume to Jonathan Spence's celebrated text-book of the same title. An important set of documents with accompanying commentary is Tony Saitch, *The Rise to Power of the Chinese Communist Party: Documents and Analysis, 1919–1949* (M.E. Sharpe, 1995).

GENERAL HISTORIES

The standard work of reference is *The Cambridge History of China* (Cambridge University Press, 1982–91). The relevant volumes for the twentieth century are numbers 11 to 15, edited by D. Twitchett, Roderick MacFarquhar, Albert Feuerwerker and John K. Fairbank. Although the text is sometimes demanding, it repays the effort since the list of contributors includes many of the chief authorities on modern Chinese history. Anything by the outstanding sinologist, Jonathan Spence, is worth reading. His most accessible major study is *The Search for Modern China* (W.W. Norton, 1990). This covers a wide canvas and has many illuminating things to say about Mao and his times. Among other important works by this prolific British scholar are *The Gate of Heavenly Peace: The Chinese and their Revolution 1895–1980* (Faber & Faber, 1982) and *The Chinese Century: A Photographic History* (HarperCollins, 1996), in which he collaborated with Annping Chin, a colleague at Yale, to produce a masterly survey accompanied by superb illustrations. Other acknowledged authorities are John King Fairbank, whose *China: A New History* (Belknap Press, 1992) is recognised as a major contribution to Western understanding of Mao's world, and Immanuel C.Y. Hsü, whose *The Rise of Modern China* (Oxford University Press, 6th edition, 2000) has an eminently clear narrative and an up-to-date bibliography which lists key Chinese and English works. A very useful guide to some of the more recent Western reappraisals of modern China is Jeffrey Wasserstrom (ed.), *Twentieth Century China: New Approaches* (Routledge, 2003). Among student-orientated books which aim to provide an introduction to Mao and his times are P.J. Bailey, *China in the Twentieth Century* (Basil Blackwell, 2001), Michael Lynch, *China: From Empire to People's Republic 1900–49* (Hodder & Stoughton, 1996) and *The People's Republic of China since 1949* (Hodder & Stoughton, 1998). Graham Hutchings, *Modern China: A Companion to a Great Power* (Penguin, 2001) is an excellent reference book; arranged thematically and biographically, it is very convenient to use and maintains a pleasing balance between narrative and analysis. A similarly useful book, which concentrates on the political developments in Mao's time is Colin Mackerras, Donald McMillen and Andrew Watson, *Dictionary of the Politics of the People's Republic of China* (Routledge, 1998).

PARTICULAR THEMES

Edgar Snow's pioneering studies of Mao, of which the best known is *Red Star over China* (Penguin, revised edition, 1972), have long been superseded, but they remain a fascinating account of the Jiangxi and Yanan years by a sympathetic Western eyewitness. Snow's maturer but still sympathetic reflections on Mao's policies appear in *The Long Revolution* (Hutchinson, 1973). Harrison Salisbury has written a splendidly racy account of one of the great formative events in Chinese Communism, *The Long March* (Macmillan, 1985). In *New Perspectives on the Chinese Communist Revolution* (M.E. Sharpe, 1995), Tony Saitch has edited a series of articles by international scholars examining Mao's relations with the CCP in the Jiangxi and Yanan periods. The bitter CCP–GMD struggle is described in Suzanne Pepper, *Civil War in China: The Political Struggle, 1945–1949* (University of California Press, 1978). The details of Mao and China's involvement in the Korean war are illuminatingly explored in Sergei N. Goncharov, John W. Lewis and Xue Litai, *Uncertain Partners: Stalin, Mao and the Korean War* (Stanford University Press, 1993). China's greatest modern tragedy is analysed in Jasper Becker's *Hungry Ghosts: China's Secret Famine* (John Murray, 1996). The writer's detached approach to the state-organised famine of 1958–62 makes the story even more harrowing. A controversial work which has lengthy sections on China is Stephane Courtois *et al.* (eds), *The Black Book of Communism* (Harvard University Press, 1999). Compiled by a team of French scholars, this disturbing book portrays Mao's coercive policies as expressions of the organised terror that characterised all Marxist governments in the twentieth century. Arguably, the most enlightening analysis of the Cultural Revolution and the events that preceded it is still to be found in the works of Roderick MacFarquhar: *The Hundred Flowers Campaign and the Intellectuals* (Columbia University Press, 1960), *The Origins of the Cultural Revolution* (Columbia University Press 1983) and *From the Hundred Flowers to the Great Leap* (Harvard University Press, 1989). MacFarquhar also edited an important selection of articles from the *China Quarterly*, the leading journal on Chinese studies, in *China Under Mao: Politics Takes Command* (Massachusetts Institute of Technology Press, 1972). Other enlightening studies are Lynn White, *Politics of Chaos* (Princeton University Press, 1989), Anita Chan, *Children of Mao* (University of Washington Press, 1985) and Chihua Wen, *The Red Mirror* (Harper Row, 1996). Accounts by former Red Guards and those who suffered under them are to be found in Gao Yuan, *Born Red: A Chronicle of the Cultural Revolution* (Stanford University Press, 1987) and Nien Cheng, *Life and Death in Shanghai* (Grove, 1986). A fascinating perspective is supplied by Percy Craddock, British ambassador in China during the 1960s, in his *Experience of China* (John Murray, 1994). A powerful pictorial evocation of the Cultural Revolution is Li Zhensheng, *Red-Color News Soldier* (English language version edited by Robert Pledge, Phaidon Press, 2003), whose subtitle neatly conveys the book's contents: *A Chinese Photographer's Odyssey through the Cultural Revolution*. The politics of Mao's later years is ably disentangled in Japp van Ginneken, *The Rise and Fall of Lin Piao* (Penguin, 1974). There is now a plethora of books by victims of Mao's repression. Jung

Chang, *Wild Swans* (HarperCollins, 1991) is a moving account of how three generations of women in one family sought to cope with the horrors of their time. The female experience is also captured by Annping Chin in her *Four Sisters of Hofei* (Bloomsbury, 2003). The hell of the *laogai*, begun under Mao and still operating today, is chillingly detailed by Harry Wu, a leading Chinese dissident, in his *Bitter Winds: A Memoir of My Years in China's Gulag* (Wiley & Sons, 1994), and *Laogai: China's Gulag* (Chatto & Windus, 1993). Similar first-hand accounts are given by Zhang Xianliang in *Grass Soup* (Minerva, 1994) and *My Bhodi Tree* (Secker, 1996). The story of the PRC's genocide in Tibet is agonisingly described by Palden Gyatso in his *Fire Under the Snow* (Harvill, 1997). Gyatso is also a contributor to Kate Saunders (ed.), *Eighteen Layers of Hell: Stories from the Chinese Gulag* (Cassell, 1996). Two accessible studies of Mao's policies towards the USSR and the USA are Herbert J.Ellison (ed.), *The Sino-Soviet Conflict* (University of Washington Press, 1982) and Gordon H. Chang, *The United States, China and the Soviet Union, 1948–72* (Stanford University Press, 1990). The aims and consequences of Mao's economic policies are analysed in David J. Pyle, *China's Economy, 1949–94: From Revolution to Reform* (Macmillan, 1997), in which the writer takes a direct, no-nonsense approach to his theme. An understanding of the CCP's official line on Mao and his times is best gained from reading Hu Sheng (ed.), *A Concise History of the Communist Party of China* (Foreign Languages Press, 1994). Stuart Schram's latest thinking on Mao Zedong as a political theorist comes in the form of two long essays in Merle Goldman and Leo Ou-Fan Lee (eds), *An Intellectual History of Modern China* (Cambridge University Press, 2002). For those interested in tracing the fluctuations in Mao's reputation since his death, an absorbing analysis is provided by G.Barmé (ed.), *Shades of Mao: The Posthumous Cult of the Great Leader* (M.E. Sharpe, 1996). Mao's reputation as a Chinese poet is examined in Willis Barnstone (ed.), *The Poems of Mao Tse-Tung* (W.W. Norton, 1972).

BIOGRAPHIES

Philip Short's *Mao: A Life* (Hodder & Stoughton, 1999) is a very detailed and readable text. Notwithstanding its infuriatingly imprecise endnotes, which seem designed to make it as difficult as possible for the reader to check references, this book has quickly established itself as an indispensable introduction to Mao's life and times. It is complemented though not surpassed by Ross Terrill, *Mao: A Biography* (Stanford University Press, 2000). A fascinating set of reflections were set down by Xiao Yu, a close companion of Mao in his pre-Communist years, as *Mao and I were Beggars* (Syracuse University, 1959). This can be supplemented by the account of Mao's early years by Li Rui, *The Early Revolutionary Activities of Comrade Mao*

Tse-tung (M. E. Sharpe, 1979). Stuart Schram provided the first authoritative biography of Mao to appear in English, *Mao Tse-Tung* (Penguin, 1966). An analysis which is both lively and scholarly is provided by C.P. Fitzgerald, *Mao Tsetung and China* (Penguin, 1976). Jonathan Spence's succinct biography, *Mao* (Weidenfeld & Nicolson, 1999) is a must, even though its brevity denies the author the space for footnotes and an index. An even briefer study is Delia Davin's *Mao Zedong* (Sutton, 1997), but it is a little gem since the author has the gift of being able to say a great deal in a very short space. Her lively approach contrasts sharply with the worthy but plodding style of Sean Breslin's *Mao* (Longman, 1998), which is strong on politics but conveys little sense of Mao as a person. This could not be said of Harrison Salisbury's *The New Emperors Mao and Deng: A Biography* (HarperCollins, 1992). Arranged in short, punchy chapters, this work offers fascinating insights into the careers of its subjects. A distinctive feature, some might say a weakness, of Salisbury's work is that it relies heavily on personal interviews which the author subsequently had with many of the players in the drama. Since these were largely pro-Deng Xiaoping and anti-Mao in their sentiments, it leaves the work open to the charge of distortion. Similar suggestions of bias have been directed against *The Private Life of Chairman Mao* (Chatto & Windus, 1994), which is in effect the memoirs of Li Zhisui, Mao's doctor, who became disillusioned by his patient's brutalities. Nevertheless this remains a remarkable account by an insider of Mao's years as leader of the PRC after 1949. Another intimate portrait of Mao during the same period is to be found in Quan Yanchi, *Mao Zedong: Man, Not God* (Foreign Language Press, 1992), which contains the reflections of Mao's personal bodyguard, Li Yinqiao. A provocative revisionist study is provided by Lee Feigon, *Mao: A Reinterpretation* (Ivan R. Dee, 2002), in which the author, while accepting that the Great Leap Forward and the Cultural Revolution caused 'horrific damage', argues that these movements created the conditions without which the modern Chinese economy could not have been built. Richard Evans, *Deng Xiaoping and the Making of Modern China* (Hamish Hamilton, 1991) offers an absorbing study one of Mao's most ambiguous supporters. The remarkable career of Mao's loyal lieutenant and China's greatest international statesman, Zhou Enlai, is enjoyably covered in Dick Wilson *Chou: The Life of Zhou Enlai, 1898–1976* (Hutchinson, 1983). Lee Feigon, *Chen Duxiu, the Founder of the CCP* (Princeton University Press, 1983) is an informed treatment of one of the Chinese intellectuals who influenced Mao as a young man. Mao's extraordinary wife, Jiang Qing, is given a very lively treatment in Ross Terrill, *The White-Boned Demon: A Biography of Madame Mao Zedong* (Heinemann, 1984). Different perspectives of Mao may be obtained from biographies of his great antagonist, Chiang Kai-shek: among the most interesting of these are Keiji Furuya, *Chiang Kai-shek: His*

Life and Times (St John's University Press, 1981), Sean Dolan, *Chiang Kai-shek* (Chebea Howe, 1988), and Jonathan Fenby, *Generalissimo: Chiang Kai-shek and the China he Lost* (Free Press, 2003). Fenby's book has been swiftly acknowledged as an outstanding contribution to modern Chinese studies.

INDEX